Monetarism and the Methodology of Economics

Monetarism and the Methodology of Economics

Essays in Honour of Thomas Mayer

Edited by

Kevin D. Hoover
Associate Professor of Economics,
University of California, Davis

and

Steven M. Sheffrin
Professsor of Economics,
University of California, Davis

Edward Elgar

332.46
M7426

Published by
Edward Elgar Publishing Limited
Gower House
Croft Road
Aldershot
Hants GU11 3HR
England

Edward Elgar Publishing Company
Old Post Road
Brookfield
Vermont 05036
USA

British Library Cataloguing in Publication Data
Monetarism and the Methodology of
Economics: Essays in Honour of Thomas
Mayer
    I. Hoover, Kevin D. II. Sheffrin, Steven M.
332.401

Library of Congress Cataloguing in Publication Data
Monetarism and the methodology of economics : essays in honour of
   Thomas Mayer / edited by Kevin D. Hoover and Steven M. Sheffrin.
      p.   cm.
    "The economic works of Thomas Mayer : a bibliography": p.
    Includes bibliographical references and index.
    1. Monetary policy. I. Hoover, Kevin D., 1955– .
  II. Sheffrin, Steven M. III. Mayer, Thomas, 1927– .
  HG230.3.M832   1995
  332.4′8–dc20

95–5521
CIP

ISBN 1 85278 940 9

Printed and bound in Great Britain by
Hartnolls Limited, Bodmin, Cornwall

For Thomas Mayer,
economist, scholar, colleague, mentor, friend

Contents

Contributors

King Banaian, Pitzer College, Claremont Graduate School and St
  Cloud State University, USA
Mark Blaug, University of Exeter, UK
Martin Bronfenbrenner, Duke University, Durham, USA
Richard C.K. Burdekin, Claremont McKenna College and Claremont
  Graduate School, USA
Thomas F. Cargill, University of Nevada, USA
Milton Friedman, Hoover Institution, Stanford University, USA
C.A.E. Goodhart, London School of Economics and Political Science,
  UK
D. Wade Hands, University of Puget Sound, USA
Abraham Hirsch, Brooklyn College and Graduate Center of the City
  University of New York, USA
Kevin D. Hoover, University of California, Davis, USA
David Laidler, University of Western Ontario, Canada
James L. Pierce, University of California, Berkeley, USA
Steven M. Sheffrin, University of California, Davis, USA
Richard J. Sweeney, Georgetown University, USA
Thomas D. Willett, Claremont Graduate School and Claremont
  McKenna College, USA
Wing Thye Woo, University of California, Davis, USA

Acknowledgements

The editors would like to thank a number of people who have contributed to the production of this volume. The secretarial staff of the Economics Department of the University of California, Davis helped with typing, xeroxing and mailing. We note particularly the help of Marlene Baccala and Donna Raymond, who in addition provided expert assistance in preparing some of the graphics. Both were models of good cheer. Charles Haase and Jamie Woods completed, checked and organized the bibliography of Thomas Mayer's economic writings. We thank Edward Elgar, our publisher, for his extremely cooperative and receptive attitude toward this project and for his patience with the pace of its maturation. Our greatest thanks goes to Catherine Whitney Hoover, who produced this volume – handling the copy-editing, much of the graphics, indexing, and preparation of the final text in camera-ready copy – with exemplary care and dedication to quality.

PART I

Reflections

1. Thomas Mayer: An Appreciation

Kevin D. Hoover and Steven M. Sheffrin

"Yes," said Harriet, thoughtfully. "I can't see you burking a fact to support a thesis."

Dorothy Sayers, *Gaudy Night*

Tom Mayer's decision to retire came as a surprise. He had for many years declared his intention of retiring in the end of the 1995 academic year. But the University of California offered attractive incentives for early retirement as its principal response to the state budget crisis initiated by the recession of 1990. Rational economic Tom could not refuse. Tom announced his retirement in the middle of October 1992. We worked fast. On 1 December 1992 a dinner was held in Tom's honor, and he was presented with the table of contents of the current volume. Commitment is short; execution is long. Over 2 years later the volume is finally published. What we learned in putting the volume together is that affection and admiration for Tom is so great that, had we had no constraint on page extent, we could have published a volume with three times the number of articles.

Affection and admiration are the operative words. The volume is entitled *Monetarism and the Methodology of Economics* because Tom is most famous for advocacy of monetarism and much of his recent work, including the recently published *Truth versus Precision in Economics* (1993), concerns methodological issues. But it is not the substance of Tom's work – as important as that is – that accounts for the readiness with which his students, colleagues, friends and acquaintances chose to honor him; rather it is the personal characteristics that we all value so highly – his integrity, his intellectual honesty, his tolerance and his indefatigable generosity in spending time helping other scholars.

In many ways, Tom Mayer is a classic example of the great scholar. Unlike many economists today, he checks facts, reviews data and looks for anomalies in his work and the work of others. Probably only Tom would have discovered that the regression that underwrote Peter

Temin's (1976) claim that an unexplained shock to consumption caused the Great Depression was sensitive to the exclusion of a single observation. When that observation was removed from the regression, consumption behavior in 1930 was no longer anomalous. To those who know Tom's style, this is precisely the sort of discovery one expects from him.

The most scholarly of all Tom's work is probably his *Permanent Income, Wealth and Consumption.* Published in 1972, the book carefully reviewed all the studies of consumption and income and came to judicious conclusions about their relationships. Consumption is smoother than income and indeed resembles a centered moving average on income. There is little evidence for the proportionality hypothesis; the rich save more out of their permanent income than the poor.

In terms of influence, Tom's timing could not have been worse. The book was published at the onset of the rational expectations revolution. Robert Hall (1978) transformed the entire debate on consumption with his paper on rational expectations and consumption. Tom's book was neglected. After two decades of high-tech research on consumption, however, we are returning to the same issues that Tom raised. One cannot read Angus Deaton's recent book *Understanding Consumption* (1992) without realizing how little we learned about consumption from recent research. Tom's book still summarizes our knowledge better than any other single book on consumption.

Tom always advised his colleagues to keep publishing and let the profession decide what they believe to be significant. He was clearly disappointed by the reception of his permanent-income book, which he believed to be true, exhaustive science. But he was pleasantly surprised by the overwhelming reaction to his paper, "The Structure of Monetarism," published in two parts in *Kredit and Kapital* (not exactly *Econometrica*) in 1975. In this essay, later reprinted in a book of the same name, alongside commentaries from distinguished scholars on all sides of the monetarist debate, Tom captured the essence of an intellectual movement as he summarized the tenets of an emerging, dominant school of intellectual thought. With a clarity that many of his fellow monetarists lacked, Tom captured both the ideology and practice of an important force in macroeconomics. Although one may quarrel with the tenets of monetarism in the 1970s, no one can deny that Tom's succinct characterization provided intellectual cohesion for the movement. Indeed, the characteristics that Tom identified and that shaped the monetarist movement (e.g., monetarists prefer small models rather than large ones) were sometimes expressions of his own strong preferences.

Despite his fame as a monetarist, there is something not quite right in attaching any doctrinal label to Tom. Schools of thought require for their own cohesion at least a whiff of dogmatism. With Tom, dogmatism is in short supply. He is willing to try to see the other man's point of view, to charitably understand the strengths of the other man's argument and to humbly acknowledge the weaknesses of his own. As Tom tells it, he was let go from the Shadow Open Market Committee for left-wing deviationism. He had the nerve to suggest a more expansionary monetary policy than the stalwarts of monetarism thought wise. Thus, while to the profession at large, Tom personified monetarism, to the monetarists he was a closet Keynesian.

Tom's open-mindedness extends beyond doctrine to technique as well. Early on, Tom showed an unfashionable interest in the institutional background of monetary policy. He stressed the importance of institutional details such as the Federal Reserve's Regulation Q and the structure of deposit insurance for the conduct of monetary policy. And he was a pioneer in behavioral analysis of decision-making on the Federal Open Market Committee. When a shibboleth of serious economics was "surveys cannot be trusted," Tom was an advocate of the usefulness, in some circumstances, of survey data.

Monetarism died in the 1980s, a victim of financial innovation and shifting money demand. Tom did not try to pretend that the money demand curve had not shifted; as one of the pioneers in estimating money demand in work with Martin Bronfenbrenner in the early 1960s, he was too much the scientist to engage in any obfuscation. But the breakdown of the money demand function reinforced his own skepticism towards econometric relationships. This skepticism has manifested himself in many ways. His thesis students knew that Tom did not want to see just one regression but the whole panoply. He was one of the early writers about the pitfalls of data mining.

Yet, Tom did not let his skepticism about empirical work lead to pessimism. In fact, it is just the opposite. Tom always brought a cheerful optimism to his research and the work of his colleagues and students. He always admired good work and encouraged the highest standards of those around him. The flip-side of his admiration for good work was his impatience with laziness or shoddiness. The bureaucracy of the university was an object of particular scorn. Unfortunately his proposal for improving the administration of the economics department, that all faculty meetings be conducted while standing on one foot, was never tested.

Tom's reaction to the inefficiencies and absurdities of academic bureaucracy was to shirk. He never took on academic administration willingly or with a patient and cheerful heart. But in his dealings with other economists, colleagues and students, Tom was, and remains, patience and good cheer itself. Drafts of papers were always returned with single-spaced typed comments. On the days when Tom was home at Berkeley, he was always exactly one ring away on the telephone. In fact, it was much easier to talk to Tom when he was at Berkeley, because at Davis his office was always jammed with students. Tom spent long hours working with students who sometimes just did not seem to get it; he organized workshops to foster student research; and he took on extra duties, such as a course in research methods (stressing the mundane, but important, things often omitted in grander classes with similar titles – e.g., tricks for preserving the accuracy of data and how to deal with referee reports). The high quality of many of the completed dissertations – both those supervised by Tom and those he influenced less directly – testify to the success of his efforts.

We must end with a change of tense. For, truth be told, we have hardly noticed Tom's retirement. He continues to be remarkably productive. We still look forward to seeing him at lunch; we still find him one ring of the telephone away – hard at work at his desk in Berkeley. We rejoice in his freedom from faculty meetings. And we look forward to his friendship and collegiality for many years to come.

REFERENCES

Deaton, Angus (1992) *Understanding Consumption*, Clarendon Press, Oxford.
Hall, Robert E. (1978) "Stochastic Implications of the Life Cycle-Permanent Income Hypothesis: Theory and Evidence" *Journal of Political Economy*, 96, pp. 339–57.
Temin, Peter (1976) *Did Market Forces Cause the Great Depression?* Norton, New York, NY.

2. Getting Older, But Not Much Wiser

Thomas Mayer*

This essay is autobiographical. In it I describe some presuppositions that underlie my work as an economist, and show how these presuppositions bias me towards monetarism. But since these presuppositions did not arise out of thin air, I first discuss my background.

This may strike some readers as entirely inappropriate. Economics is a science, a domain of facts, reason and mathematics, and thus entirely independent of the background of the scientist. Hence, there is no reason to bother with the personal background of an economist and with his or her "presuppositions," whatever these are.[1] Are we not right to keep our personality so carefully out of our work that many consider it a *faux pas* even to use the first person singular in our papers?

Though many do claim to write with the disembodied Voice of Science, this claim is pretentious nonsense. As Don Patinkin (1972, p. 142) put it: "I will begin to believe in economics as a science when out of Yale there comes an empirical Ph.D. thesis demonstrating the supremacy of monetary policy in some historical episode and out of Chicago, one demonstrating the supremacy of fiscal policy." Since Patinkin wrote this, Yale may have become more willing to accept the importance of monetary policy, but the principle still holds. What theories we adhere to depends to a considerable extent on our pre-scientific (one might almost say metaphysical) presuppositions, which, in turn, depend in part on our personal experiences.

Karl Brunner and William Meckling (1977, pp. 71–3) have contrasted the economic perception of man as a "resourceful, evaluating, maximizing" entity with the sociological conception of man as a "conformist and conventional" creature, who is "not an evaluator, any more than ants, bees and termites are evaluators." One's view on many

* Editors' note: This essay first appeared in Thomas Mayer's *Monetarism and Macroeconomic Policy* (1990) published by Edward Elgar Publishing, Aldershot, Hants. It is reprinted here, with minor amendments, with the kind permission of the author and publisher.
[1] For criticisms of this position, see William Breit (1987).

issues in economics is likely to depend upon which of these perceptions of man one holds. But surely, one's choice between them is not determined so much by regression coefficients and t-statistics, as by one's preconceptions, and hence one's personal experience. Those who have found that their planning has paid off are more likely to accept the economic interpretation of man, and hence oppose government planning, than are those who have felt helpless in their personal lives.

In pointing to the influence of an economist's personal background I do not denigrate economics as a science or justify subjectivism. The progress of science is not nullified by scientists' preconceptions on which even the most austere physical sciences rely. In Lakatos' picture of scientific research programs there is a core (akin to ideology) that is usually treated as outside empirical testing, and a protective belt of testable hypotheses derived from this metaphysical core. It is in the protective belt that the scientific action takes place. What I have called preconceptions are part of the metaphysical core, and scientists as a group will adhere to or abandon this core depending upon what happens in the protective belt. The progress of science depends no more upon each scientist being rational and objective in choosing his or her metaphysical core, than the validity of neoclassical economics depends upon each economic agent being rational. If my preconceptions, regardless of why I uphold them, induce me to formulate hypotheses that survive the scientific competition of the protective belt, then these hypotheses are scientific, even though my adherence to the metaphysical core that generated them may be the result of my being dropped on my head as a child. All this should be quite obvious, but the adherents to the Voice-of-Science taboos act as though any personal references would cause economics to be stripped of its mantle of scientific validity.

Although a cataloging of the preconceptions that lurk behind a set of hypotheses obviously cannot determine the validity of these hypotheses, it is still useful because it can clarify them. Thus it can demonstrate a link that explains why a particular person accepts, or rejects, all of them. More generally, preconceptions function as hidden assumptions, and hence should be brought out into the open.

Consider, for example, Sir Roy Harrod's (1951) masterly analysis of the preconceptions of Keynesian policy recommendations, of what he called "the presuppositions of Harvey Road."[2] These induced Keynes to believe that governments, or at least British governments, are enlightened enough to be trusted with the tools of fiscal policy. By

---

[2] Harvey Road was the address of Keynes's parents.

bringing these preconceptions into the open, and by explaining what in Keynes's background induced him to adhere to them, Harrod enables us to understand Keynes's thinking more clearly. Moreover, he allows us to evaluate Keynes's views better because we can decide whether or not we agree with these presuppositions. Someone who is not aware of them may well feel uneasy about Keynesian policy, but not know why.

MY BACKGROUND

In Vienna, around the time I was born, in 1927, a popular joke was: "Things are so bad that it would be better not to have been born at all. But who has such luck? One in ten thousand." The economy had received a massive shock from the breakup of the Hapsburg empire after World War I, a shock that generated massive unemployment among white-collar workers in particular. Then came the Great Depression. One of my graphic childhood memories, dating from about 1936, is looking into the eyes of an unemployed man who tried to get passers-by to enter an exhibit made by unemployed people. Somehow it dawned on me that not only was he hungry today, but that he had been hungry the previous day, and expected to be hungry the next day too. The way in which the scourge of unemployment had marked the Viennese was brought home to me many years later in New York when I told my mother that I had decided to look for a better job. She replied: "It is almost sinful to look for a job when you already have one."

Soon the threat of Hitler added political danger to depressed conditions. In my parents' circle of middle-class Jews, the response to this threat was denial – "Oh the West would never allow Hitler to annex Austria." (After the Anschluss my father said that if it comes to war Germany will collapse like a house of cards.) But they knew they were whistling in the dark. In case they ever forgot, an illegal, but active, local Nazi party was there to remind them of it.

With no other job being available my father worked as a sales agent, conscientiously, but not successfully. He was deeply interested in languages and in science, particularly in natural history, lacked any interest in business, and was modest and shy. He was thus utterly miscast as a sales representative. My mother helped out by doing occasional work as a typist at home. She was a warm person with numerous friends. I was an only child, born late in my parents' life, and rather spoilt.

This early environment seems to have significantly affected my subsequent thinking. Although my father had never attended university he had great respect for education. My mother, in accordance with Viennese custom of her time, had only a limited formal education, but had absorbed quite a bit from her environment. On both sides of my family everyone traditionally published something, even if only cooking recipes. It is therefore not surprising that I became an academic. However, in my early years I was not a good student, except in those few subjects I was interested in, such as biology and Latin. At ten I barely passed the entrance exam for an academic high school (Gymnasium).

Another thing I absorbed from my parents, both social democrats, was concern for the welfare of the poor. I refrain from calling it a "social conscience," which mainly seems to be a fervent belief that *other* people should be made to help the poor. People like to buy their feeling of moral worth, as they do other things, in the cheapest market, and having the "right" political opinions allows one to bask in a feeling of moral worth at no cost. But concern about other people has not kept me on the left of the political spectrum because of a deep pessimism, which I will discuss later. I do not know all the origins of this, but some of it I probably absorbed in my childhood from the pessimism I saw around me.

A further attitude I absorbed as a child is a feeling that life is serious; that you get nothing for nothing. I was not brought up in the belief that seems so prevalent today, that one has a right to success and fortune as a natural reward for having allowed oneself to be born. And clearly, seeing around me economic misery and political crimes, such as the assassination of Chancellor Dollfuss by the Nazis, spurred an interest in economics and politics. Political decisions could, and did, affect one's life.

For some unknown reason I also developed as a child the attitude of a loner and outsider, someone who was reluctant to play with other children. This has stuck with me all my life, and has prevented me from joining wholeheartedly any school of economics.

In March 1938 Hitler marched into Austria. In September 1938 I marched out. It was clear to my parents that we would have to emigrate, but that was easier said than done. The problem was not so much being permitted to leave, which would not become a serious problem until much later, but being allowed to enter another country. Getting a visa became the focus of one's life. Britain had a provision for accepting refugee children, and hence I could get a visa for Britain. At the last moment a hitch developed. I could not get a transit visa to travel through Belgium – this was before flying became the normal way to travel. I left without it, and fortunately was not stopped at the Belgian frontier.

My parents could leave only later, and separately. In November my father was arrested. He was then given the choice of staying imprisoned or leaving the country within 48 hours. Under these conditions he too could get a visa to Britain, but my mother would have to stay behind. My father rightly chose to go to England without her since he could do more to get her a visa in England than he could in Vienna. And she did get one just a few days before war broke out. But the British consulate in Vienna having already packed up, my mother could not pick up her visa. In March 1938 my parents had applied for a visa to the United States, and in November 1941 their quota number came up. My mother left for New York on the last boat before Pearl Harbor closed that escape route. My father and I could not join her until April 1944.

In England I attended three schools. In the first, near Brighton, where I spent about 6 months, I was taught only English, of which I knew very little when I left Vienna. The teaching consisted of lectures on English grammar – in English – a catch-22 situation. But eventually I did learn English from the other children. Then, in 1939 I was sent to a very poor school in London in which I learned little.

Fortunately in 1942 my father, who had been interned as an "enemy alien," was released and was able to take care of me. (Prior to his internment he had no work permit. But now during the war this regulation was waived.) He sent me to an excellent school called Bunce-Court that had been evacuated from Germany to England in the 1930s and was located in Shropshire for the duration of the war. It was a remarkable place. It gave not only a first-rate classroom education but provided what so few schools do, a highly intellectual atmosphere. Students were interested in, and indeed excited about, what they were learning. Moreover, our intellectual interests were not confined to classroom learning, but encompassed politics, literature and art. Given the impact that political events had on our lives, it is hardly surprising that we were highly politicized. At least one other economist, Lucien Foldes of the LSE, emerged from this intellectual pressure cooker.

This school had an immense effect on me. What would have become of me had I not moved there? In the previous school, our normal activity had been on the level of playing with toy soldiers, and here it was discussing postwar reconstruction. I took to this atmosphere with great delight. I was in my element. Most of the students were socialist, and I developed a socialist ardor that outdid that of most others. My life centered on political arguments.

It was at that school that I encountered economics, though this subject was not taught. I realized that I would need to know some economics to substantiate my political opinions, so I read a short "Principles" text which I found unexciting. But I decided to read another and asked a friend who was going to the local library to bring me one. He brought the *General Theory*. I was hooked. Of course I understood none of it. But mystery makes for fascination. I decided to stay with economics until I understood that book. Eventually I did, but by that time it was too late; I was an economist.

It was fortunate that none of my teachers had much interest in economics, at least in technical economics. Thus, having nobody to steer me to the unchallenging, and hence mostly rather dull books that are appropriate for a beginner, I read widely, from Marx and Engels to Adam Smith, with a heavy dose of Fabian pamphlets. Trying to learn a subject such as economics entirely on one's own is in many ways inferior to formal training. But it can also be extremely beneficial. It allows one to explore the most interesting parts, and forces one to think for oneself. It therefore helps greatly in making the transition from being a reader of economics to being a "producer" of economics, a transition that many graduate students find so difficult when the time comes to write a dissertation. (It is a terrible indictment of our graduate training that so many students have to ask their teachers: "What should I write about?" In my ideal university students would not take any classes for the first semester. They would just be given a library card and told that at the end of the semester they will be examined in the subject or subdiscipline of their choice.)

In April 1944 my father and I left England to join my mother in New York. Although I have lived happily in the United States since then, I retain fond memories of England and usually spend a few days in London whenever a conference gives me an excuse to go to Europe.

I experienced culture shock in the United States. Here was a capitalist system that seemed radically different from the one I had known. It was dynamic and growth-oriented. The capitalist class was proud to welcome able recruits from the working class. My views slowly changed from socialist to liberal, and ultimately to fairly conservative. In part, this was probably the result of studying economics – a typical reaction, as George Stigler (1959) has shown. But learning economics can better explain my shift from socialism to liberalism than the subsequent shift to conservatism, since many of my teachers were liberals.

After working as a stock clerk for a few months, I enrolled at Queens College, one of the (then) free municipal colleges operated by the City of New York. After completing a semester, having reached 18, I entered the army. The war ended when I was still in basic training, and I spent the remainder of my short service working as a clerk in separation centers. In September 1946 I was back at Queens College, now with the benefit of the G.I. Bill which gave me a modest stipend for almost 3 years. By taking extra courses I was able to get my B.A. in 2 years plus the semester I had taken before entering the army, so that I had a year left on the G.I. bill for graduate work.

Queens College, which then was rather selective, provided a good education, because it was much more demanding than colleges are nowadays. We were expected to show our gratitude for receiving a free education by working hard. For example, in the senior year there were comprehensive exams covering material studied in the freshman and sophomore years, as well as a comprehensive exam in the major. The prevailing philosophy at Queens College stressed a rounded education, and we were loaded down with numerous required courses, some of them quite poor. Not being allowed to specialize "excessively," I felt that I had too little freedom of choice.

It is probably very different now, but at that time the economics department at Queens did not offer a good education, both because it was too easy-going and because of its anti-theoretical bent. No intermediate micro-theory course was offered. (The absence of an intermediate macro-theory course was standard at the time.) With the "Principles" course lasting just one semester students could get by with virtually no economic theory. To learn some theory I had to take a graduate course at the New School for Social Research. I did, however, have one fortunate experience in my undergraduate economics training. One of my professors, William Withers, invited me to write a paper with him on the optimal savings rate. He then went away for the semester break, leaving me on my own. I found Frank Ramsey's classic paper, which I could not understand, and that was that. But this invitation reinforced my convictions that economics can be written as well as read. All the same, I was eager to finish college and get to graduate school, where I thought the real action was.

I then entered Columbia University, expecting to get an MA, and then work for some time to accumulate the funds needed to go on to a PhD. At that time, 1948, graduate students faced a quite different situation than they do now. If I remember correctly, among the 200 or so graduate economics students at Columbia there was only one teaching assistant; about half a dozen students taught an evening course (which paid a salary just equal to the tuition); about three held fellowships that provided a stipend in excess of tuition; and a handful had tuition scholarships. I was lucky to get a fellowship for the second year, as well as a job teaching an evening course, so I was able to complete all my class work and reach the all-but-dissertation stage in 1950.

The teachers who influenced me the most were Albert Hart and George Stigler, particularly the former. They provided a sense of excitement about and commitment to economics that was lacking in some of my other classes. I remember in particular Hart's course on stabilization policy. He would come into class and talk about a book or paper he had just read, then he would wait for a student to raise some issue and respond to that. Hardly a well-prepared performance that would win plaudits from the educational establishment, but extraordinarily exciting and helpful for students who could learn the basics of the subject on their own. James W. Angell was just the opposite, a rather stodgy but extremely methodical teacher, whose lectures could be understood at various levels of sophistication, depending on the students' preparation.

I wrote my MA thesis with William Vickrey, a delightful person as well as a first-rate economist, whom I could not appreciate enough because of my lack of mathematics. The thesis, which dealt with the effect of a wage cut on employment, was subsequently published in the *Economic Journal* (1951).

After my second year, having completed everything except the dissertation, it was time to take a job. This was then standard practice in economics. Finding a job turned out to be difficult. The postwar enrollment boom had come to an end, leaving many schools with larger faculties than they desired. The outbreak of the Korean war, with the resulting resumption of the draft, did not help. And, unlike now, economics was then not a good field for academic jobs. In addition, the academic job market was badly organized. Jobs were not advertised; when they had vacancies, department chairs would notify a few graduate schools as well as their friends. If your professors were not plugged into this network, did not want to play this game, or did not push you, that was that. Eventually, however, through the good offices of Albert Hart, I got a job at the tax research division of the Treasury.

Although this was a good job in one of the more prestigious government agencies, I did not like it, nor did I perform well. It emphasized persuasive writing, since much of the work involved trying to influence congressional decisions on taxes. Not only did I write badly, but being still a callow youth, I was more oriented to making obscure theoretical points than to setting out the more pedestrian arguments that actually persuade people. Moreover, like most jobs that give you the potential for influencing policy, you also had to let policy influence you. In many cases you knew what conclusions your memos were supposed to reach. This I did not like. However, I did have the good fortune to work some of the time for Joseph Pechman, from whom I learned much. He invited me to coauthor a paper (*Review of Economics and Statistics*, 1952) criticizing Colin Clark's hypothesis that taxes cannot in the long run exceed 25 percent of income.

After about 15 months I switched to the Office of Price Stabilization. That turned out to be a bad move. In the Division of Research and Statistics, where I was located, there was little work to do. Since it would not have been appropriate to leave right away, I stuck it out for a few months until Congress had enough sense to abolish price controls. I then went to work on the input-output project, mainly on deriving lead times for investment in various industries. This experience was the impetus behind my subsequent work on the lag of monetary policy. The input-output project was divided among various government agencies, my part being located in the Bureau of Mines. This was the only one of my three government jobs that I enjoyed. There was useful work to be done, the research was entirely objective and, unlike the Treasury job, it did not stress writing.

All in all, I was at that time not cut out for a government job. I do not derive any enjoyment from one of the great benefits of government work, the feeling of having influence. I have never hankered after power, probably because I lack sufficient conviction that I am right. And I do not readily adjust my views to conform with those of my superiors. I am much happier in academia where I can say what I want. If it has no effect on anything, that does not really bother me.

In any case, I had never intended to stay in Washington permanently, planning to leave as soon as I finished my dissertation, when I hoped to be more marketable in academia. (At that time many academics lacked a PhD, so having one gave you a competitive edge.) I had worked on my dissertation nights and weekends, and in 1953 finally had it done. That was just in time, because in that year the input-output project was wound up, and I had to look for another job. Having the degree made a big difference in the job market, though the dissertation was a failure. It dealt with the demographic aspects of the stagnation thesis, a topic that had lost all relevance by 1953, so it was never published.

I found a 1-year visiting assistant professorship at West Virginia

University. I loved it. It was so wonderful being back in academic life that I did not even mind exchanging the cultural opportunities of Washington for those of Morgantown, West Virginia. The next year, 1954, I moved to the finance department at Notre Dame University. Although I enjoyed many things about it, I felt uncomfortable being not in the economics department but in the finance department, where there were few courses I could teach. Nor was there much contact between the two departments. Moreover, at that time the finance department did not offer graduate work, so there was little emphasis on research, and teaching loads were high. When I hear some of my young colleagues complain about their teaching loads I tell them that I wrote the major part of my most labor-intensive, and perhaps best, paper (on the lag of monetary policy) while teaching 12 hours per week.

I was therefore happy when, in 1956, I was offered an assistant professorship at Michigan State University. It was a remarkable place. At that time, at least in economics, the US academic landscape was very different from what it is now. A handful of research universities accounted for most of the papers published in the better journals, and most other schools had little use for research. I suspect that having publications on one's CV helped a candidate for an assistant professorship in one-quarter of the schools, hurt in another quarter, and made no difference in the rest. Unlike now, there did not exist a substantial number of economics departments trying get into the big time.

Michigan State was one of the first to attempt this transition. Since most schools did not compete for researchers, and since Michigan State paid higher salaries than most others, it was able to gather a remarkably hardworking and ambitious group of young economists. At that time the journals did not carry papers that rated schools, so to raise morale, I once had my research assistant rank departments by their contributions to major journals. Helped by being an unusually large department, Michigan State came in among the very top, ahead of both Berkeley and Stanford. It was a extraordinarily exciting atmosphere where one could get much stimulus and help from numerous colleagues. I benefited particularly from Paul Strassmann's assistance. As mentioned previously, my writing was very bad. I had not had any difficulty in English classes, when I wrote on topics that did not matter to me. But when writing economics and presenting my own ideas I froze up, qualifying everything into an unqualified mess. Paul forced me to drop this awful habit and to improve my writing.[3]

---

[3] There now exists an excellent book for anyone suffering from such problems, Becker (1986).

I loved the hardworking, striving atmosphere of Michigan State, but there were three drawbacks. One was that, despite our high productivity, economists in the better universities still looked down their noses at us. The second was that there was a great deal of turmoil and animosity, perhaps in part the result of having so many ambitious people in the department. The third, and the one I felt the most, was that East Lansing, where Michigan State is located, was not a pleasant environment, particularly for a bachelor. I felt that it was a great place for working, but not for anything else. (I have never liked small towns that are not near large cities.)

Accordingly, when I was invited to spend the 1960–61 academic year at Berkeley I jumped at the opportunity. But, alas, Hyman Minsky, whom I was replacing for the year, came back. Despite its stimulating professional atmosphere, I could not face returning to Michigan State. Fortunately I was offered a professorship (I had since been promoted to professor at Michigan State) at the Davis campus of the University of California. This campus, located about 60 miles from Berkeley, was in the process of expanding from a specialized agricultural school into a general campus. I accepted, even though it meant moving to a department with only four other economists, one that was just about to start MA courses, and would not have a PhD program for some time. But that seemed minor compared to the fact that when I had audited a philosophy of science course given by Karl Popper, I had met a young lady who was to become my wife. In any case, it was clear that the Davis economics department would expand greatly, both in size and in quality, as it in fact did. However, I continue to live in Berkeley, in part because I cannot stand the hot weather of the Sacramento Valley, and in part because Davis, like East Lansing, is a small town. The commute is a nuisance, though a manageable one, but I do miss the opportunity of seeing more of my colleagues. During what has been a long teaching career, my first main field was macroeconomics, followed by a drift into monetary economics. I also taught a course on research in which I tried to give graduate students practical hints on doing research and on generating ideas.

Although I have written a few papers on microeconomic topics, such as on the distribution of ability and earnings (1960), and on financial institutions, such as on a proposal to set FDIC insurance premiums on the basis of risk (1965), most of my work has been in applied macroeconomics and monetary economics. My first substantial paper (1958) in this area was an early attempt to measure the lag of monetary policy. The most elaborate one was a book on the permanent income theory and life-cycle hypothesis (*Permanent Income, Wealth and Consumption,* 1972), in which I tried to synthesize the existing empirical evidence on these theories, as well as present new tests. With great bad luck, this appeared just before Robert Hall's fundamental reformulation of consumption-function theory. Besides, to reconcile all the existing evidence I had to use a theory with imprecisely defined parameters, something that offended the growing taste for precision. But perhaps the book's criticism of the proportionality hypothesis (i.e., the hypothesis that the savings ratio is independent of the level of permanent income) did contribute to the modern deemphasis of that part of the original permanent income theory. In recent years I have worked mainly on monetary policy. I have also developed an interest in the more down-to-earth aspects of methodology, and have published a monograph arguing that much of what masquerades as rigor in economics is actually only a pseudo-rigor that inhibits progress (*Truth versus Precision in Economics,* 1993). In a subsequent book of essays, *Doing Economic Research: Essays on the Applied Methodology of Economics,* I try to bridge the gap between the technical work of methodologists and the issues that concern applied economists.

Like most economists of my generation, I did not receive as a student the mathematical training that is now standard. But unlike many I never made a serious effort to remedy this deficiency, for two reasons. First, I lack mathematical aptitude, and second I believe in division of labor. When everyone else is using a shovel you do very well indeed if you have a bulldozer. But if everyone else if using a bulldozer, you can do quite well with a shovel.

In December 1992 my university responded to a serious budgetary problem by offering a generous incentive to retirement, and since I was already 65 I decided to retire a few years earlier than I had planned. But I am continuing research, and the main difference I notice between being retired and being on a sabbatical is that now I finish reading *The Wall Street Journal* at breakfast.

PRECONCEPTIONS, BIASES AND BELIEFS

One preconception that conditions my thinking both on economic theory and policy is a pervasive pessimism (which, fortunately, I do not carry forward into my personal life). At least partly as a result of this pessimism I do not hanker after The Truth. I do not deny that it is out there somewhere, but I doubt that we can grasp it at this stage in the development of economics. Hence, I prefer theories that present little truths to those that claim to have solved the whole grand maximization problem in one elegant formulation. Moreover, even when we think that we have grasped a little truth, such as the correct theory of the consumption function, we should be skeptical and remember how often what seems obviously true to one generation is shown to be an error by the next.

My pessimism also makes me skeptical of many liberal prescriptions. I agree that a private enterprise economy suffers from excessive unemployment and inflation, and from misallocations resulting from consumer ignorance, externalities and monopoly power. Many economists seem to jump from this to the conclusion that government intervention is desirable. But that seems to me a leap of faith, based at least in part on an unwarranted "can-do" spirit, and on a belief that somehow human misery can be reduced if we just apply enough goodwill and common sense. I cannot make this leap of faith. There is something to Senator Moynihan's dictum: "No good deed goes unpunished." This does not mean that we should eschew all government intervention, but it does mean that the mere recognition that a situation is bad does not imply that we should try to eliminate it. That is an obvious point, but one that is often ignored in the urge to demonstrate one's goodness and also one's ability to overcome a popular, but often naively rationalized, anti-government attitude.

My methodological prejudices are, to a considerable extent, those of a logical empiricist. I too have read and enjoyed Kuhn, and realize that logical empiricism is no longer a feasible position. But I do wish it were. In a field like economics, where the observable facts provide so little discipline, the attitude that anything goes, as long as the relevant scientists accept it, is a dangerous prescription. Apart from this I greatly prefer research that explains puzzling observations to research that polishes and makes more rigorous some previously-known result. Didn't someone (Einstein?) once say: "Elegance is for tailors"? If I believe that a certain hypothesis has a 99 percent probability of being true, I am not all that interested in a paper that raises this probability to 99.99 percent. Time is short; there are too many other hypotheses to think about, and besides, I am impatient. This impatience also makes me dissatisfied with the high degree of roundaboutness in the structure of production of economics. I am less interested in papers that teach me something about an economic model than in those that teach me something about the economy per se.

In addition, I hold the Marshallian view that economics comprises "the study of mankind in the ordinary business of life" (Marshall, 1920, p. 1) rather than the Robbinsian view that it is the application of the tools for maximizing utility. Hence, we should pay attention to how the government makes economic decisions, even if these decisions cannot be explained entirely, or even largely, by the tools of economic analysis. In doing so one usually cannot achieve the degree of precision that is obtainable in dealing with problems to which the tools of economic analysis are more applicable. But a vague analysis is preferable to what is so often done when giving policy advice: ignoring a relevant aspect of the problem entirely, or else resorting to mere assertion.

Finally, as already mentioned, I am an outsider. Even if I agree with a certain school on many issues, I do not feel any great urge to agree with it on all issues or to be a loyal member of it.

As I will discuss shortly, given these characteristics it is not surprising that eventually I became attracted to monetarism. But as a graduate student, like nearly all my colleagues, I was strongly Keynesian. The *General Theory* was the text to be read and reread. When assigned some book in a macroeconomics course, I would first look at the index to see how often Keynes was cited. That told me how seriously to take it. Yet I was also skeptical of Keynesian orthodoxy. For example, at that time Keynesians made a great fuss about speculative liquidity preference. Unlike others I was bothered by the lack of data on the proportion of the money supply that was held in speculative balances. Perhaps it was trivial. Arguments by assertion and group-think seemed to play too large a role in the then prevailing Keynesian orthodoxy.

When Milton Friedman's *Studies in the Quantity Theory of Money* appeared in 1956, I was excited by it and assigned it as a text in a graduate course that summer. (Only to have one student complain that I should have used a more up-to-date textbook!) Here was a new approach, or at least new to anyone who, like me, had not been privy to the Chicago oral tradition. It might be wrong, but was certainly worth exploring. Some major developments of Keynesian economics, such as the life-cycle hypothesis, were still to come, but its main structure was already well established, and offered little opportunity for new work. By contrast, the research program of the quantity theory offered dazzling prospects to both potential supporters and critics. My first publication on it (DePrano and Mayer, 1956) was mainly critical. But as Chicago economists piled up more and more evidence on the importance of money, and as they (and Brunner and Meltzer) provided impressive evidence on the damage that Fed policy had done, I moved closer to monetarism. Yet I never came close enough for monetarists to consider me one of their own. I did serve for some time on the Shadow Open Market Committee, set up by Brunner and Meltzer to pressure the Fed into adopting monetarist policies. But I continually argued for a more moderate policy than the Committee wanted, so it is not surprising that after some time I was purged for left-wing deviationism.

I do call myself a moderate monetarist, but that is an arbitrary label, which I adopt in part because monetarists are in a minority. If it were the dominant school I would probably call myself a moderate Keynesian.

It was surely not just the objective evidence, but also my preconceptions and biases and my background that drew me to monetarism. I would have found it more difficult to break with the Keynesian tradition had I done my graduate work at Keynesian Harvard and come under the personal influence of Alvin Hansen, rather than at more middle-of-the-road Columbia, where I was influenced by the partially-Chicagoan Albert Hart. Similarly, had I taught at the Keynesian University of Michigan instead of at more intellectually diversified Michigan State, peer pressure would have made it harder for me to break with Keynesian theory. Not impossible perhaps, since I am by inclination an outsider, but certainly harder. Being an outsider, as well as being skeptical of any claims to have discovered The Truth, also made it easier for me to abandon the dominant tradition.

Perhaps more important is that I share many of the methodological presuppositions of Friedman, and hence felt strongly sympathetic to his work, not only on money, but also on other topics. I was unaware of this source of attraction until reading, a few months ago, Abraham Hirsch's and Neil De Marchi's (1990) superb book on Friedman's methodology. They show that Friedman focuses on hypotheses that throw light on specific problems rather than seeking grand over-arching generalizations, and that he relies on an interplay of theory and empirical tests. These are characteristics I have always found strongly appealing. Friedman's pragmatism and insistence on economics as a discipline that addressed practical issues also appealed to me, particularly in the late 1950s and the 1960s when so much of Keynesian analysis consisted of proliferating growth models. In addition, Friedman's work is imbued with a Marshallian spirit, and this too I like. These characteristics are also found in the work of Brunner and Meltzer, and if I have focused on

Friedman's methodology it is because of the availability of Hirsch's and De Marchi's work on that subject.[4]

The monetarists' doubts about the efficacy of stabilization policy appeals to me both because of my sense of pessimism and my doubts about how much we really know about the economy. This may seem strange because the monetarists' pessimism about the ability to pursue stabilizing policy is matched by their optimism about the inherent stability of a market economy. But monetarists spend much more time expounding why stabilization policy will not work than in documenting that the private sector is stable. Hence, in reading their work one gets the impression of pessimism. I do not, however, believe that they have demonstrated the superiority of rules over discretion. I am too much of a skeptic to think that this issue is settled. But I do value their work as a counter to Keynesian smugness and self-congratulation.

While I share some of the monetarists' doubts about government intervention as an effective tool to improve the economy, I am not as eager as most of them are to cut government expenditure. The government is not efficient enough to cut out unnecessary items while leaving necessary ones. And I am more favorably disposed to moderate income redistribution than are some monetarists: I do like Friedman's idea for a negative income tax.

From what I have said so far it should come as no surprise that while I am suspended uneasily between monetarism and Keynesianism, I have a strong negative reaction to new classical theory. It seems to me that the new classicals are using a cannon to shoot at a sparrow – and missing. What bothers me even more is that new classical theory radiates an aura of the True Believer. New classicals *know* that a certain type of micro-theory *must* be right, and all that needs to be done is to hammer what we observe into conformity with the theory. While I agree that the assumption of rational maximizing behavior can explain much, I do not believe that it can explain everything. After all, it surely does not hold precisely. New classicals seem to ignore that the trick in economics is to deduce valid propositions from assumptions that are only partly valid. Yet, having said that I must admit that my disdain for new classical theory might also be due to my inability to work in that mode and to the fact that its validity would negate much of what I have done.

---

[4] The best-known characteristics of Friedman's methodology, his rejection of tests by assumptions, always struck me as a somewhat too radical statement of what is a sound heuristic position.

REFERENCES

Becker, Howard (1986) *Better Writing for Social Scientists*, University of Chicago Press, Chicago, IL.

Breit, William (1987) "Biography and the Making of Economic Worlds" *Southern Economic Journal*, 53, April, pp. 823–33.

Brunner, Karl and Meckling, William (1977) "The Perception of Man and the Conception of Government" *Journal of Money, Credit and Banking*, vol. 9, pt 1, February, pp. 70–85.

DePrano, Michael and Mayer, Thomas (1965) "Tests of the Relative Importance of Autonomous Expenditures and Money" *American Economic Review*, 59, September, pp. 729–52.

Harrod, Sir Roy (1951) The Life of John Maynard Keynes, Macmillan, London.

Hirsch, Abraham and De Marchi, Neil (1990) *Milton Friedman: Economics in Theory and Practice*, Cambridge University Press, New York, NY.

Marshall, Alfred (1920) *Principles of Economics*, 8th edn, p. 1, Macmillan, London.

Patinkin, Don (1972) "Keynesian Monetary Theory and the Cambridge School" *Banca Nazionale del Lavoro, Quarterly Review*, June, pp. 138–58.

Stigler, George (1959) "The Politics of Political Economists" *Quarterly Journal of Economics*, 73, November, pp. 522–32.

PART II

Monetarism

3. Monetarism: The Good, the Bad and the Ugly

James L. Pierce*

During a long and productive career, Thomas Mayer described and promoted the principles of monetarism. This paper looks back to see what was good with monetarism, what was bad with it, and what was just plain ugly in the struggle of monetarists with their Keynesian arch rivals. This is an exercise in the history of economic thought: hard-core monetarism has largely disappeared; its useful elements have been integrated into modern macroeconomics, while the rest has been discarded. The same fate has befallen hard-core Keynesianism. Monetarism has become an historical curiosity because the high correlation between "money" and nominal GNP, which had served as monetarism's practical rationale for many years, has disappeared.

For an approach that occupied so much attention in macroeconomics from the mid-1950s until well into the 1980s, monetarism is difficult to define or even to characterize with any degree of precision. The term meant different things to different people – both proponents and critics – just as Keynesianism did. Thomas Mayer (1975a,b) described the essence of monetarism when he put forth 12 propositions that identified monetarists and allowed them to be clearly distinguished from Keynesians. Although some monetarists quibbled about individual elements in the list, there was consensus that Mayer had captured monetarism with his 12 propositions. My paper uses Mayer's list to discuss monetarism's contributions to macroeconomics.

It is important to bear in mind that the path-breaking work on the "new macroeconomics" by Lucas, Sargent, Prescott and others had not appeared in print when Mayer published his paper and was probably not

* I am grateful to Steven Sheffrin for encouraging me to write on this topic and for many valuable comments on an earlier draft.

available to him.[1] The paper was subsequently reproduced in Mayer (1978), which contained comments and observations by eight economists ranging from hard-core monetarists – Karl Brunner and Allan Meltzer – to unrepentant Keynesians – Benjamin Friedman. Several of the monetarist commentaries, including those of Brunner and Meltzer, claimed that the new macroeconomics embodied what monetarism had in mind all along. I shall not deal with such revisionist monetarism, preferring to discuss the monetarism that was extant when Mayer originally published his paper. His 12 propositions will be the vehicle for assessing monetarism's lasting contributions to macroeconomics. While I shall try to "play fair" and assess monetarism by the standards of the 1970s, there is no avoiding the fact that my (and virtually everyone else's) perspective has been affected by the tremendous advances that have been made in macroeconomics since the publication of Mayer's paper.

MAYER'S LIST

According to Mayer, a monetarist adhered to the following principles:

1. Accept the quantity theory of money, in the sense of the pre-dominance of the impact of monetary factors on nominal income.
2. Use the monetarist model of the transmission process.
3. Believe in the inherent stability of the private sector.
4. Accept the irrelevance of allocative detail for the explanation of short-run changes in money income, and believe in a fluid capital market.
5. Focus on the price level as a whole rather than on individual prices.
6. Rely on small rather than large econometric models.
7. Use the reserve base or similar measure as the indicator of monetary policy.
8. Use the money stock as the proper target of monetary policy.
9. Accept a monetary growth rule.
10. Reject an unemployment-inflation trade-off in favor of the natural unemployment rate.
11. Have a greater concern about inflation than unemployment.
12. Dislike government intervention.

---

[1] Lucas (1972) did not achieve the influence it deserved until more accessible accounts became available later in the 1970s.

Some general comments are in order before discussing each of the monetarist principles in detail. Mayer's list may appear to be longer than necessary to describe the essence of monetarism. Karl Brunner, who coined the term, claimed that the core of monetarism could be described by three propositions:

> First, monetary impulses are a major factor accounting for variations in output, employment and prices. Second, movements in the money stock are the most reliable measure of the thrust of monetary impulses. Third, the behavior of the monetary authorities dominates movements in the money stock over business cycles. (Brunner, 1968, p. 9)

Milton Friedman put the issues in even simpler terms:

> I regard the description of our position as 'money is all that matters for changes in *nominal* income and *short-run* changes in real income' as an exaggeration but one that gives the right flavor of our conclusions. (Friedman, 1974, p. 27)

But Mayer's list is not too long because it describes issues that are central either to the monetarist–Keynesian debate or to identifying who a monetarist was. Much of monetarist writing was devoted to debunking Keynesianism, the dominant paradigm in macroeconomics at the time. Mainstream textbooks presented the standard Keynesian model as if it were the final word. There was little discussion of the price level or inflation; fiscal policy was presented as the method for stabilizing the economy; and monetary factors were included but from the perspective of an economy in which monetary policy was weak.

Although a Keynesian could not be precisely identified as one who failed to subscribe to Mayer's 12 principles, it was almost possible to do so. This helps explain why so many of the principles are negative in the sense that they involve rejection of propositions that were considered fundamental to Keynesianism, such as the desirability of government intervention in macroeconomic affairs. The strongly negative aspect of monetarism, while perhaps understandable, was unfortunate because it made monetarism appear to have less legitimacy of its own. Much of monetarists' time and effort was expended on attacking Keynesian orthodoxy rather than on developing an alternative paradigm. The problem was most evident when monetarists presented issues as if they involved theoretical principles, when, in fact, they involved practical policy issues. For example, there was nothing in monetarist theory that implied the optimality of a constant money-growth rule; its appeal lay in practical considerations. Monetarists spent too much time trying to justify their distaste for government interference in the economy and not enough time on developing theoretical reasons for rejecting the conventional Keynesian proposition that an aggressive fiscal policy was necessary and sufficient to stabilize the economy and eliminate the business cycle. Monetarists did champion the "crowding out" hypothesis, which holds that an expansionary fiscal policy unaccompanied by monetary expansion would be ineffective.[2] But their distaste for government intervention prevented them from considering the use of monetary policy, or a combination of monetary and fiscal policy, to stabilize the economy.[3]

Monetarist–Keynesian debates were often acrimonious because they involved ideology rather than scholarly disagreements about theory or even about testable propositions. It would certainly be wrong to blame all of the acrimony on the monetarists – Keynesians share the blame. There was a singular unwillingness for the proponents on either side to listen to the positions of the other.[4] This was the ugly aspect of the debate.

From the perspective of modern macroeconomics, Mayer's 12 propositions seem almost quaint. Monetarism reached its peak about the time that Mayer's paper was published. This was before the revolution in macroeconomics that swept away much of the old order, both monetarist and Keynesian. This was a time before rational expectations, observational equivalence, the "Lucas critique" or asymmetric information. Attention had not been focused on the "real" side of the economy and the possibility of real business cycles. The burden of proof had not yet been shifted to those who assert the importance of monetary and financial factors in affecting real economic activity, or who contended that certain markets do not always clear. A consensus (that prolonged inflation is necessarily a monetary phenomenon) had not yet formed. Much that had been debated by monetarists and Keynesians, such as the extent of an economy's stability in the absence of counter-cyclical policy, or the relative abilities of monetary and fiscal policies to affect real activity, had not yet been modeled in ways conducive to resolving the issues. It is remarkable that, given the inadequacies of their approaches, both monetarist and Keynesian economists had stronger and more confident views than do their modern counterparts.

With these observations in mind, we now turn to review Mayer's list of monetarist principles to determine which elements have survived as lasting contributions to macroeconomics and which have not.

---

[2] See commentaries in Mayer (1978) and Stein (1976).
[3] Milton Friedman argued that long and variable lags precluded effective counter-cyclical monetary policy.
[4] A small amount of progress was temporarily visible in Stein (1976).

1–2: The Quantity Theory and the Monetarist Model

This is not the place to discuss the nuances of the quantity theory of money. It suffices to say that the quantity theory, with its prediction that the price level is proportionate to the quantity of money, was the center point of monetarism. The monetarist model of the transmission mechanism was an attempt to add some structure to the quantity theory by explaining how changes in the quantity of money affected aggregate demand and the price level.[5]

The basic tenet of monetarism was that money matters most for determining fluctuations in aggregate nominal income. Monetarists made little of the decomposition of changes in nominal income into changes in the price level and changes in real output. They assumed a neoclassical, market-clearing world in which the economy tends to produce at potential. Fluctuations in real output were viewed as primarily involving equilibrium fluctuations in the desire to supply labor services and other inputs. Involuntary unemployment was viewed as transitory at most.[6]

The monetarist transmission mechanism attempted to describe how changes in the quantity of money increased aggregate demand and aggregate nominal income. Perhaps the easiest way to motivate the monetarist approach is to compare it with a simple Keynesian textbook model in vogue at the time. In the simple Keynesian model, money is a substitute for bonds.[7] An increase in the quantity of money produces an excess supply of money and an excess demand for bonds. The interest rate for bonds is the "price" equating money demand and supply, and bond demand and supply. Thus, the interest rate is the "price" of money. Changes in this price affected investment spending and aggregate economic activity.

Monetarists objected strenuously to the simple Keynesian model that made money a substitute only for bonds. Monetarists insisted on the quantity theory's "general equilibrium" approach, in which money substitutes for goods and assets generally.[8] To a monetarist, the price level is the price of money, not the interest rate on bonds.

Monetarists viewed their approach as more general than the simple

---

[5] This structural approach was most evident in the work of Brunner and Meltzer (1972, 1976) which provided detailed structural models of the transmission mechanism.

[6] See Allan Meltzer (1978).

[7] This simple textbook model should not be confused with the rich portfolio approach used by James Tobin and his followers.

[8] See Brunner and Meltzer (1972, 1976). It was never clear why monetarists failed to discuss Tobin's general equilibrium approach.

Keynesian model because it imposed fewer restrictions *a priori*. Changes in the quantity of money could not only affect demands for assets generally (not just bonds), but also demands for goods and services. While the "general equilibrium approach" of the monetarist transmission mechanism was without empirical content at the level at which it was advanced, it was used to justify why monetarists thought money was more important than Keynesians did.

Monetarists placed great emphasis on the stability of money demand as the justification for their assertion of money's importance. This was always an unsatisfactory argument. The demand for peanuts may be stable but it does not follow that "peanuts matter most," as might be argued by a "peanutist."

Monetarists were never able to explain on theoretical grounds why money, among all assets in the economy, deserves the attention they lavished on it. Monetarists dealt with models in which there were no close substitutes for money and in which money was required to conduct transactions. But they were never able to explain why there are no close substitutes for money or why money should even arise endogenously in the well-functioning, neoclassical world with optimizing agents that monetarists assumed. This is not surprising; theorists are still trying to find a convincing role for money in general equilibrium models. But it always seemed strange that monetarists were so convinced of the singular importance of money even though there was no definitive theoretical demonstration of its importance.

Although they appealed to theory when possible, monetarists ultimately fell back on the empirical record to justify the importance of money. They could show that in country after country, money and aggregate nominal income were highly correlated, and rapid inflation accompanied rapid money growth. While aware that correlation does not imply causation, monetarists claimed that this was strong evidence of the validity of the quantity theory. We shall return to empirical issues later.

3: Inherent Stability of the Private Sector

Mayer correctly identifies "belief" in the inherent stability of the private sector as an important element of monetarists' dogma. Although Mayer is not precise about what he means by "stability," the term apparently entails the absence of substantial, erratic shocks.[9] Monetarists viewed the private sector to be stable because they believed that the demand for

[9] See Bronfenbrenner (1978).

money is not subject to such shocks. By this interpretation, fluctuations in nominal income must be the consequence of the monetary authorities who produce an unstable money supply. Thus, misguided monetary policy produces instability.

It probably goes without saying that many Keynesians believed the private sector could be unstable. Investment demand was viewed as particularly subject to large, erratic shocks, but consumption demand was not immune. For a Keynesian, the government sector, through fiscal policy, was a force for good, offsetting fluctuations in aggregate output produced by an unstable private sector.

Neither monetarists nor Keynesians could prove their point concerning the stability or instability of the private sector, or even construct tests that might reveal truth. Both sides appealed to casual empiricism. Monetarists pointed to prolonged periods of stability when governments were weak. They claimed that the Great Depression would not have been nearly so severe had it not been for ill-advised government policies, such as passage of the Smoot-Halley Act, and a Federal Reserve System that failed to prevent a collapse of bank reserves. Keynesians looked at the same data and saw evidence of instability. They interpreted the (apparent) relative stability of the post-World War II period as evidence that government intervention stabilizes the economy.

Such widely different interpretations of the same events are evidence that the differences were more a matter of dogma than economics. Monetarists basically disliked government intervention (Mayer's point 12) so they were inclined to look for evidence that intervention was unnecessary and potentially counterproductive. Keynesians approved of government intervention and looked for evidence that it worked. It is encouraging that modern macroeconomics is less prone to engage in such unproductive debates. More emphasis is put on analytical proofs and on carefully constructed empirical tests. Perhaps the profession had to go through the embarrassing process of engaging in what was largely a religious debate before it could go on with serious efforts to analyze and test the issues.

4: Irrelevance of Allocative Detail for Explaining Short-Run Changes in Money Income and Belief in the Fluidity of Capital Markets

The quantity theory allowed a monetarist to take a "top-down" approach in which changes in the quantity of money produce changes in nominal income. According to the quantity theory, it makes no substantive difference where or how money is injected into the system; the rise in nominal income is roughly the same. With the quantity theory, sectoral detail is just that; it adds little or nothing to predicting changes in nominal income.

It was argued by many monetarists that their neoclassical transmission mechanism is too complex and too fluid for detailed, structural specification.[10] According to monetarists, only the quantity of money is important for determining money income. Other financial variables are of little interest because of the assumed perfection of money and capital markets. To a monetarist, the amounts and kinds of other financial assets or credit depend upon the circumstances of the time, but capital markets are so fluid and perfect that these financial variables make no material difference for nominal income.

In the smoothly functioning world assumed by monetarists, it was considered better to treat the transmission mechanism as a "black box" than to attempt specification of what is essentially a general equilibrium system. Thus, monetarists used the complexity of general equilibrium systems to justify their black-box approach of predicting changes in nominal income from changes in the quantity of money, without specifying how or why these changes occurred.

Keynesians by contrast, thrived on sectoral detail. In their model, sectoral demands differed in important ways that could be specified *a priori* and that could, in principle, be estimated. Keynesians sought to specify, sector by sector, the channels through which monetary or fiscal factors operate. In the Keynesian approach, credit markets were assumed neither to be completely fluid nor to operate perfectly at all times. It was argued that credit rationing and other imperfections made it important to know several financial and credit magnitudes, not just the quantity of money.

Keynesians rejected the monetarists' neoclassical approach, with its assumed perfectly competitive and complete markets conducting frictionless adjustments to various disturbances, as a useful model for studying economic fluctuations. They asserted that prices often do not clear labor markets and capital markets, so that quantities must adjust. It was essential to their approach that adjustments in specific sectors and markets be specified. Thus to Keynesians, sectors were not a mere detail but essential elements of a whole.

Whether sectoral detail improves the ability to predict changes in nominal income is largely an empirical issue and is discussed below.

[10] Brunner and Meltzer were the exceptions; their models did allow for sectoral differences.

5: Focus on the Price Level Rather Than on Individual Prices

Monetarists viewed price-level determination to be a purely macro-economic process in which aggregate demand is brought into balance with (exogenous) aggregate output. It is a top-down process in which changes in the quantity of money produce changes in aggregate demand and the price level. The behavior of individual prices is a matter of sectoral detail and is not considered to be of interest in a macro setting. Individual prices depend upon relative demands and supplies, but these demands and supplies must adjust until they are consistent with aggregate demand, aggregate output and the price level.

According to Mayer, Keynesians did not view the price level as a macroeconomic variable equating aggregate demand with aggregate supply. Rather, they pursued a "bottom-up" approach in which the price level was computed as a weighted sum of individual prices. These prices in turn were determined by the interactions of demands and supplies in individual sectors. According to Mayer, these sectoral demands and supplies were affected by, but they were not constrained by, aggregate demand and supply.

In defending his assertion, Mayer refers to Eckstein and Fromm (1959) as an example of how at least some Keynesian economists tended to view price-level determination as involving the summation of prices in separate individual industries and sectors. But as discussed in more detail later, by the 1970s Keynesian economists had adopted econometric models using a "Phillips curve" approach in which aggregate wage and price changes vary directly with unemployment and/or capacity utilization.[11] They used a top-down approach just as the monetarists did, but it was a different one.

Monetarists conceded that changes in the quantity of money could affect both real output and the price level in the short run.[12] But they seemed uninterested in the decomposition of nominal income into real output and the price level. By all appearances, they were interested only in changes in the price level. In focusing on the price level, monetarists were implicitly assuming that the behavior of individual prices provides no useful information about the mix of nominal output changes between real output and price level changes following a monetary shock, i.e., individual price movements give no useful clues as to how quickly the

[11] For a number of such models see Eckstein (1972).
[12] In the longer run, of course, the effects are totally on the price level. The distinction between unanticipated and anticipated changes in money had not yet found its way into monetarist literature.

price level will adjust. This might be the case but it has nothing to do with monetarism.

6: Reliance on Small Models Rather Than Large Econometric Models

Monetarists contended that their approach yielded closer predictions of nominal income than did the Keynesian model. The gauntlet was first thrown down by Milton Friedman and David Meiselman (1963) in a paper that compared performance of a simple money-income relation to an equally simple Keynesian autonomous expenditure model. They claimed that the monetarist model won hands-down. There were many criticisms of the Friedman–Meiselman paper and many attempts to put the tests on more equal footing; all succumbed to the temptation of "keeping it simple" when testing Keynesian models.[13] As might be expected, the paper generated a furious response by Keynesians who argued among other things that Friedman and Meiselman misrepresented the Keynesian model and that high correlation between money and nominal income does not imply causality.

Furthermore, Keynesians asserted that the issue was not money versus autonomous spending, but rather the relative sizes and predictability of various policies, including monetary and fiscal policy. By the mid-1960s, few, if any, Keynesians of note denied the importance of monetary factors and monetary policy. They argued, however, that money did not explain everything and that there was an important role for financial variables other than money, and for fiscal policy. Keynesians objected to the monetarists' "black-box" approach because it failed to explain why money was so important and why non-monetary influences were so unimportant for predicting nominal aggregate income. Keynesians did not want a model that simply predicted nominal GNP; they wanted a model that explained how the macroeconomy worked.

The work of Friedman and Meiselman shifted the burden of proof to the Keynesians, who had to provide empirical support for their approach. But it soon became clear that to specify the linkages of monetary and fiscal policy and embed them in a general Keynesian econometric model was a major undertaking. Although advances in computer technology made such projects feasible, they were formidable. Efforts to specify and estimate their structural models were to occupy

[13] See Hester (1964), Ando and Modigliani (1965), DePrano and Mayer (1965) – yes the same Thomas Mayer – and Friedman and Meiselman (1965).

the attention of Keynesian economists for many years.[14]

While Keynesian modeling efforts were underway, monetarists were not idle. A particularly influential effort occurred at the Federal Reserve Bank of St Louis – a bastion of monetarism within the Federal Reserve System.[15] The St Louis model was slightly more complex than the monetarist model used by Friedman and Meiselman but it was simplicity itself compared to Keynesian models under construction, which ran to hundreds of equations and thousands of coefficients.

The "reduced form" model of the St Louis Fed regressed changes in nominal GNP on current and lagged changes in the quantity of money and on current and lagged measures of fiscal policy.[16] Most of the variance of changes in GNP could be "explained" by changes in the quantity of money, and only a small amount of the variance was accounted for by changes in fiscal policy. Furthermore, the model's estimated coefficients were consistent with the monetarist "crowding-out" hypothesis that changes in fiscal policy unaccommodated by changes in the quantity of money have no lasting effect. The St Louis model indicated that velocity only rises temporarily when there is an expansionary fiscal policy with no change in the quantity of money; in effect, the interest elasticity of money demand is zero in the longer run.[17]

The St Louis "reduced-form" model was difficult to interpret because it is not possible to determine what structure, if any, generated it. Furthermore, like other monetarist approaches, it confused correlation and causation; there was little to support the proposition that the quantity of money was exogenously determined. Despite these problems, the St Louis model was highly influential.

Keynesians responded with results from their "structural" models.[18] These models, as exemplified by the Federal Reserve-MIT-Penn (FMP) model, were large and complex. They specified real consumption and investment demands to a considerable level of disaggregation; they had detailed international sectors; they sought to describe the labor market in considerable detail, including determination of unemployment; they determined the price level through a Phillips curve and individual prices through sectoral demand and supplies; and they had detailed specification of monetary, financial and fiscal sectors, including

[14] The two most ambitious efforts were the Brookings model (see Fromm and Taubman, 1968) and the FRB-MIT-Penn (FMP) model (see Ando and Modigliani, 1969).

[15] Andersen and Jordan (1968).

[16] Fiscal policy was measured by the high-employment deficit or surplus.

[17] For an excellent discussion see Gordon (1971).

[18] Ando and Modigliani (1969), Gramlich (1971) and Modigliani and Ando (1976).

specification of the channels through which these sectors affected real activity and the price level. The models were highly complex, nonlinear, dynamic systems whose dynamic simulations (solutions) were sensitive to initial conditions and to minor changes in coefficient values. Despite their problems and complexities, the Keynesian models produced predictions for nominal GNP at least as good as those generated by the St Louis model and they appeared to be able to explain how monetary and fiscal policy affect the economy.

Keynesian econometric models indicated that changes in fiscal policy affected nominal GNP even if the quantity of money remained constant. But the models did indicate that changes in fiscal policy accompanied by sympathetic changes in the quantity of money had a much larger effect on nominal GNP than did fiscal policies with a constant quantity of money.

Because the econometric models used by monetarists were small and those used by Keynesian were large, the monetarist–Keynesian debate seemed to be over small versus large econometric models. Mayer argued that the issue of small versus large models was something that divided monetarists from Keynesians. Model size, however, had nothing to do with monetarism versus Keynesianism. Milton Friedman did argue that economists should "keep it simple" because we do not know enough to specify an elaborate structure for the macroeconomy,[19] but that point is independent of monetarism and was not accepted by many monetarists. For example, the analytical monetarist models of Brunner and Meltzer were at least the equal of analytical Keynesian models in size and complexity.

It is true that monetarists seemed interested only in estimating the relationship between money and nominal GNP. Other issues, such as the mix between real output and the price level, or various other questions of interest to macroeconomists generally, were not of empirical interest to monetarists. They were a highly focused group.

To their credit, Keynesians were interested in much more than the determination of nominal GNP. They wanted to specify and estimate real output determination and they wanted to know how real output responded over time to shocks – not just monetary shocks, but fiscal and other types of shocks as well. They wanted to understand how monetary and financial variables affected both nominal and real quantities in the economy. In short, they were interested in expanding economic knowledge.

Keynesians were interested in explaining "behavioral" relationships, which involved estimating "structural" parameters. There were no

---

[19] See Mayer (1978, p. 24)

analytical solutions to the multi-equation, nonlinear, dynamic systems specified by the Keynesians, but advances in computer power allowed the models to be solved numerically, given the values of the "exogenous" variables and given initial conditions. Thus, it was believed that computer simulations provided reliable estimates of how the economy responds to changes in the quantity of money, or in fiscal policy, or in any other "exogenous" policy variable.

Keynesian econometric model builders were overly ambitious and overly optimistic about their ability to answer the questions they posed, but this had nothing to do with the size of Keynesian econometric models *per se*. The efforts of *both* monetarist and Keynesian econometric model builders have proved largely fruitless because of fundamental problems that had nothing to do with model size. Simulations of the response of the economy to changes in the quantity of money or any other policy variables were questionable because, as Lucas demonstrated, the coefficients of the system change when policies change.[20] Neither monetarist nor Keynesian models could be used reliably to estimate the response of the economy to policy changes. If this were not enough, the models also suffered from observational equivalence problems that were "solved" for Keynesian models by imposing incredible and indefensible identifying restrictions.[21]

Both monetarist and Keynesian economists were trying to do too much with their models. Vector autoregressions have replaced the "reduced form" and "structural" estimation attempted by monetarists and Keynesians. Results from the VARs indicate that the economy is not the simple place that the monetarists seemed to believe.

7–9: Use the Reserve Base as the Indicator of Monetary Policy; Use the Money Stock as the Target of Monetary Policy; and Accept a Money-Growth Rule

Because principles 7 through 9 relate to monetary policy, it is convenient to discuss them together. From the point of view of monetarist doctrine, the three principles seemed obvious. Behavior of the monetary base (or similar reserve measure) is, according to monetarist doctrine, an "indicator" of monetary policy, because "where the monetary base leads, money will follow." The quantity of money is the appropriate "target" of monetary policy because "where money

[20] Lucas (1976).
[21] Sargent (1976) and Lucas and Sargent (1978).

leads, income will follow." And money growth should be at a constant rate consistent with real output growth and any trend in velocity. Thus, the monetary authority should set the monetary base so as to achieve constant growth in the quantity of money.

Despite the superficial appeal of the three monetarist policy principles, it was well known, as Mayer indicated in his paper, that the principles had scant analytical justification. It had been shown that it is inefficient to go from instrument to intermediate target to ultimate target.[22] Intermediate targets such as the quantity of money are an inefficient fifth wheel. Monetary policy should set its instruments (open market operations) to achieve ultimate targets (e.g., nominal GNP). In determining the appropriate setting of policy instruments, the central bank should "look at everything" including previous misses of the targets. Furthermore, even if the inefficient intermediate-target approach is used, the three monetarist principles still do not necessarily hold. There are circumstances under which the quantity of money can be controlled more closely by using a short-term interest rate rather than the monetary base as the "instrument."[23] Similarly, under certain circumstances the objectives for nominal income can be achieved more closely by aiming at an interest rate rather than at the quantity of money.[24] Finally, constant growth of nominal income may be achieved more closely by pursuing an active feedback policy than constant money growth.[25]

Even as suboptimal policy actions, the appropriateness of the monetarist principles versus other approaches depended on the relative sizes of shocks and on a host of parameters. Whether it was desirable to adhere to the three policy principles involved empirical issues, not questions of doctrine. Of course it was shown subsequently that if agents have rational expectations, elaborate feedback rules lose their attractiveness; constant money growth might be a superior policy rule. But this was not the argument set forth by monetarists.

Although realizing that the three policy principles were not fundamental to their cause in a technical sense, monetarists clung to the principles as fundamental to monetary policy in a practical sense. The reason is that the principles were code for other issues.

Monetarists asserted, quite properly, that sustained inflation is a monetary phenomenon; a consequence of sustained, excessive money

[22] Kareken, Muench and Wallace (1973).
[23] Pierce and Thomson (1972).
[24] Poole (1970).
[25] Kareken, Muench and Wallace (1973) and Craine (1979).

growth. Their paramount objective was to propose a monetary policy that was non-inflationary. The policy strategy contained in the three principles might not be optimal in some abstract sense but it had the singular virtue of avoiding inflationary monetary policy. A monetarist might be willing to concede certain matters in the abstract: the quantity of money might be better controlled by using a short-term interest rate rather than the reserve base as the instrument; or the quantity of money might not be the best target to pursue; or constant money growth might not be the best policy. But a monetarist would never concede that actual policy be conducted in a manner inconsistent with the three policy principles. The purpose of the policy principles was to tie the hands of government so that it could not pursue economically inappropriate but politically attractive policies. The three policy principles can be viewed as practical attempts to avoid destabilizing policies in the short run while achieving monetary policy credibility in the longer run.

10: Reject the Phillips Curve

Monetarists, along with many other economists, flatly rejected the claim of some Keynesians that there was an exploitable trade-off between unemployment and inflation in the long run. To monetarists (and many others) attempts to exploit a long-run trade-off was potentially highly inflationary. Monetarists conceded that involuntary unemployment accompanies short-run reductions in real output, but this was viewed as a relatively unimportant phenomenon. They seemed to fear that attempts to exploit a short-run trade-off between inflation and unemployment could lead to inflationary policies in the longer run.

In discussing the Keynesians' treatment of the price level, it is important to distinguish between their analytical models and their econometric models. Keynesian analytical models typically assumed the price level to be constant. This practice drove monetarists crazy. Although Keynesians did deal with the price level and with relative prices in their econometric models, monetarists did not approve of the way that the price level was determined. In the Keynesian approach, the quantity of money determines nominal interest rates, which in turn affect spending. The price level is determined by a Phillips-curve relation between inflation and unemployment. In early versions of the models, estimated coefficients implied a permanent trade-off between inflation and real output. In later versions, the Phillips curve became progressively steep and finally vertical.

While the properties of individual Keynesian econometric models differed, the role of the Phillips-curve trade-off in those models was typically overstated by monetarists.[26] Again let us look at the FMP model. When used for policy, coefficients in the wage-price sector were adjusted so that there was no long-run trade-off implied by the Phillips curve – a natural unemployment rate was imposed on the model as a long-run property.[27] In the short run, the price level and unemployment moved inversely, just as they did implicitly in the monetarists' St Louis model, but in the long run, stimulative monetary policy affected the price level, not output. Furthermore, the model had the property that a fiscal stimulus unaccompanied by monetary expansion was far less expansionary and/or inflationary than one accompanied by an increase in the quantity of money. And because unemployment could not be driven below the natural rate in the long run, stimulative fiscal policy could not permanently raise real output. In total, the FMP model had long-run properties not seriously at odds with monetarist (neoclassical) doctrine.

One area of apparent disagreement lay in the treatment of supply-side shocks. Keynesian models such as FMP, with appropriate adjustments, predicted that the huge increases in the price of oil that occurred in 1973 and 1979 would temporarily raise the inflation rate substantially while producing major recession.[28] Eventually, inflation would go away if not supported by monetary expansion, but the effects would be long lasting. These predictions were roughly accurate. Substantial ingenuity was required to adapt the aggregate-demand-oriented Keynesian models to study the effects of supply-side shocks. Problems encountered in using them for this purpose indicated that monetarist criticism to the contrary, the models were not detailed enough; they needed more fully developed supply sides. More generally, one cannot properly question the extent of detail in a model without first knowing the kinds of questions that the model will address.

Monetarist models were totally unable to deal with supply-side shocks. Neither their analytical nor their econometric models allowed for any effects of the supply side on inflation and aggregate nominal income. Apparently, monetarists thought that an unexpected, four-fold increase in the price of oil would smoothly work its way through the economy's general equilibrium system. With the developments of the 1970s, monetarism had to confront the unwelcome realities that at least

[26] All of the major models are described in Eckstein (1972).
[27] See Pierce (1974) for a description of how the model was used for monetary policy.
[28] Pierce and Enzler (1974).

some shocks are not monetary, and that a rise in a single price can affect the price level if the item is sufficiently important and if the increase is large enough. Their quantity theory approach was unable to deal with such issues.

11: Monetarists Care More About Inflation Than Unemployment

There was a division of labor between monetarists and Keynesians: the former worried about inflation while the latter worried about unemployment. Monetarists were relatively unconcerned about unemployment because they viewed the world in neoclassical terms. They believed that the economy naturally tended to produce at potential; increases in measured unemployment were temporary and often voluntary. Furthermore, monetarists believed that pursuit of constant money growth would not only prevent inflation, it would provide the economic stability consistent with production at potential. Thus, low inflation and low unemployment were perfectly consistent. Keynesians viewed much of the swings in employment to be involuntary and relatively long-lived. They tended to support stimulative policies designed to reduce this involuntary unemployment.

12: Monetarist Dislike of Government Intervention

There can be little doubt that most if not all monetarists had a fundamental dislike of government intervention into the private market system. Although personal political beliefs and preferences played a part, presumably more was involved. Monetarists believed that economists did not know enough to be able to design stabilization policies that were more likely to do good than harm, and even if such policies became available, politicians could not be trusted to pursue them. Better to stick to a simple, anti-inflationary macroeconomic policy. Subsequent theoretical work indicates that monetarists had good policy instincts. It is difficult to design activist policies that are credible and effective.

It is ironic that monetarists abandoned their anti-interventionist approach when it came to money. They believed money too important to be left in private hands. Money should be "nationalized" not only to assure its quantity but also its safety – both currency and bank-account money. Monetarists actively supported policies to achieve tight control over money, e.g. uniform reserve requirements, and they were highly critical of the central bank when it failed to control the quantity of money. Although monetarists were unstintingly critical of policies designed to fine-tune the economy, they were highly supportive of policies to fine-tune the quantity of money. Somehow, they never saw the contradiction.

THE CONTRIBUTIONS OF MONETARISM

On a superficial level, monetarism's contributions to macroeconomics are obvious. There is a near consensus in the profession that inflation is a monetary phenomenon caused by excessive growth of money and credit. Textbooks now deal extensively with aggregate supply, inflation and monetary policy, and fiscal policy receives much less attention. Virtually every model of nominal aggregate demand gives "money" a central role.

It appears that monetarists won their war with Keynesians, but such a conclusion may not be justified. We do not want to confuse correlation with causality when it comes to monetarism's contributions. Just because monetarists espoused certain principles that became part of modern macroeconomics does not imply that monetarists "caused" these principles to be adopted. One cannot help but wonder what would have been the development of macroeconomics had there been no monetarists. Would the Keynesians have stubbornly clung to models in which monetary factors and inflation played little role, or would they have adapted their models to the reality of rising inflation in the 1960s and 1970s? Would they have retained models in which fiscal policy was dominant, or would they have modified their models to account for the mounting evidence that monetary policy matters a great deal? Would they have clung to a Phillips curve with a permanent trade-off between unemployment and inflation, or would mounting theoretical results and empirical evidence have led them to accept a "natural" unemployment rate? Would Keynesians have stuck with models in which adaptive expectations were imposed, or would have begun to use models with rational expectations?

We will never know the answers to questions like these, but it can be argued from one perspective that modern macroeconomics would have developed much as it did even if there had been no monetarists. Probably the two most influential "Keynesian" macroeconomists during the height of monetarism were James Tobin and Franco Modigliani.

Both of these economists have great interest in monetary economics and made highly significant contributions to the field. They were not trying to show that monetary factors are unimportant, far from it. Furthermore, each made fundamental contributions to macroeconomics using models that assumed optimizing, representative agents. For example, Tobin's path-breaking paper on liquidity preference (Tobin, 1958) was the first derivation of a rational expectations equilibrium (although he did not call it that), and Modigliani had the life-cycle hypothesis in Modigliani and Brumberg (1954). Thus, the theoretical work of Tobin and Modigliani (not to mention Samuelson, Solow and other Keynesian notables) provided the foundation upon which Lucas, Sargent, Prescott and others built their revolution of macroeconomics. It is conceivable that an even greater foundation would have been built if these Keynesian theorists and their scores of followers had not squandered so much time and effort in endless bickering with monetarists.

While there are elements of truth in the above argument, it does not recognize the large, positive role monetarism played. It is true that monetarism was more a set of principles than a fully developed model and not, therefore, the stuff of which a new paradigm is built.[29] But it greatly influenced that paradigm. Perhaps the most important contribution of the monetarists was to hold the neoclassical fort until reinforcements could arrive in the form of Lucas et al. The contribution was not in formal modeling but in insisting that agents anticipate inflation and other relevant economic variables, and that there is a long run in which real factors dominate. Monetarists constantly carped that "main-stream" macroeconomists were paying insufficient attention to such basic neoclassical propositions as the long-run neutrality of money, the ability of agents eventually to "get it right" in terms of expectations, and the dominance of the supply side in the long run. Perhaps economists would have turned to these issues in any event, but pressuring by monetarists almost certainly helped to put the burden of proof on those who posited non-optimizing behavior. Interestingly, this had nothing to do with money or monetarism *per se*, but rather with the neoclassical orientation that characterized monetarists.

Another huge contribution of monetarists in general and of Milton Friedman in particular was in stressing how uncertainty can limit the ability of government to conduct activist stabilization policy. One of the major uncertainties is the state of agents' expectations. Monetarists laid

---

[29] Monetarists never reached consensus on "the" monetarist model despite the attempts of Brunner, Meltzer and others to develop it.

the groundwork for later demonstrations that simple policy rules are preferable to complex ones and that we do not know enough to fine-tune the economy. Monetarists and the rational-expectations theorists who followed were able to show that the dominance of simple policy rules over complex ones is not a matter of tastes or political persuasion, it involves economic principles. Any doubt that Milton Friedman's brand of monetarism influenced Lucas, Sargent and others evaporates upon checking their citations, where Friedman figures as prominently as Muth and Debreu.

Deregulation of market interest rates in the 1980s, and the proliferation of money substitutes that high technology allowed, conspired to eliminate the high correlation between various measures of money and nominal income. Although there is now near-universal agreement that inflation is a monetary phenomenon and that central banks must have credible policies to limit money growth, we no longer have a reliable measure of monetary ease or tightness. With velocity acting like a random variable, central banks have been forced back to setting interest rates. They have learned the lesson taught by monetarists but are forced of necessity to set policy as if they were old-fashioned Keynesians. There is a major difference, however. Central banks are much more aware of the potential inflationary consequences of their actions and are prepared to control inflation. The most fundamental lesson of monetarism has been learned.

REFERENCES

Andersen, Leonall C. and Jordan, Jerry L. (1968) "Monetary and Fiscal Actions. A Test of their Relative Importance in Economic Stabilization" *Review*, Federal Reserve Bank of St Louis, vol. 50, no. 11, November, pp. 11–24.

Ando, Albert and Modigliani, Franco (1965) "Relative Stability of Monetary Velocity and Investment Multiplier" *American Economic Review*, vol. 55, no. 4, September, pp. 693–728.

Ando, Albert and Modigliani, Franco (1969) "Econometric Analysis of Stabilization Policies" *American Economic Review*, vol. 59, no. 2, May, pp. 296–314.

Bronfenbrenner, Martin (1978) "Thomas Mayer on Monetarism" in Mayer, Thomas (ed.), *The Structure of Monetarism*, W.W. Norton, New York, NY.

Brunner, Karl (1968) "The Role of Money and Monetary Policy" *Review*, Federal Reserve Bank of St Louis, vol. 50, no. 7, July, pp. 5–24.

Brunner, Karl and Meltzer, Allan (1972) "Money, Debt and Economic Activity" *Journal of Political Economy*, vol. 50, no. 5, September/October, pp. 951–77.

Brunner, Karl and Meltzer, Allan H. (1976) "An Aggregative Theory for a Closed Economy" in Stein, Jerome (ed.), *Monetarism*, North-Holland, New York, NY.

Craine, Roger (1979) "Optimal Monetary Policy with Uncertainty" *Journal of*

Economic Dynamics and Control, I, pp. 59–83.

DePrano, Michael and Mayer, Thomas (1965) "Tests of the Relative Importance of Autonomous Expenditures and Money" *American Economic Review,* vol. 55, no. 4, September, pp. 729–52.

Eckstein, Otto (ed.) (1972) *The Econometrics of Price Determination,* Board of Governors of the Federal Reserve System, Washington, DC.

Eckstein, Otto and Fromm, Gary (1959) "Steel and the Postwar Inflation" Study Paper No. 2, US Congress, Joint Economic Committee, 86th Congress.

Friedman, Milton (1974) "A Theoretical Framework for Monetary Analysis" in Gordon, Robert (ed.), *Milton Friedman's Monetary Framework,* University of Chicago Press, Chicago, IL.

Friedman, Milton and Meiselman, David (1963) "The Relative Stability of Monetary Velocity and the Investment Multiplier in the United States 1897–1958" in *Stabilization Policies,* Commission on Money and Credit, Prentice-Hall, Inc., Inglewood Cliffs, NJ.

Friedman, Milton and Meiselman, David (1965) "Reply to Ando and Modigliani and to DePrano and Mayer" *American Economic Review,* vol. 55, no. 4, September, pp. 753–85.

Fromm, Gary and Taubman, Paul (1968) *Policy Simulations with an Econometric Model,* Brookings Institution, Washington, DC.

Gordon, Robert J. (1971) "Notes on Money, Income, and Gramlich: A Comment" *Journal of Money, Credit and Banking,* vol. III, no. 2, pt 2, May, pp. 533–45.

Gramlich, Edward M. (1971) "The Usefulness of Monetary and Fiscal Policy as Discretionary Stabilization Tool" *Journal of Money, Credit and Banking,* vol. III, no. 2, pt 2, May, pp. 506–32.

Hester, Donald (1964) "Keynes and the Quantity Theory of Money: Comment on Friedman and Meiselman CMC Paper" *Review of Economic and Statistics,* vol. 46, no. 4, November, pp. 364–68.

Kareken, John, Muench, Thomas and Wallace, Neil (1973) "Optimal Open Market Strategy: the Use of Information Variables" *American Economic Review,* vol. 58, no. 1, March, pp. 156–172.

Lucas, Robert E. (1972) "Expectations and the Neutrality of Money" *Journal of Economic Theory,* April, pp. 102–23.

Lucas, Robert E. (1976) "Econometric Policy Evaluation: A Critique" in Brunner, Karl and Meltzer, Allan (eds), *The Phillips Curve and Labor Markets,* Carnegie-Rochester Conference Series on Public Policy, pp. 19–46.

Lucas, Robert E. and Sargent, Thomas (1978) "After Keynesian Economics" in *After the Phillips Curve,* Federal Reserve Bank of Boston, Conference Series No. 19.

Mayer, Thomas (1975a) "The Structure of Monetarism (I)" *Kredit und Kapital,* 8, pp. 191–218.

Mayer, Thomas (1975b) "The Structure of Monetarism (II)" *Kredit und Kapital,* 8, pp. 293–316.

Mayer, Thomas (1978) *The Structure of Monetarism,* W.W. Norton, New York, NY.

Meltzer, Allan (1978) "Monetarist, Keynesian and Quantity Theories" in Thomas Mayer, *The Structure of Monetarism,* W.W. Norton, New York, NY.

Modigliani, Franco and Ando, Albert (1976) "Impacts of Fiscal Actions on Aggregate Income and the Monetarist Controversy: Theory and Evidence" in Stein, Jerome (ed.), *Monetarism,* North-Holland, New York, NY.

Modigliani, Franco and Brumberg, Robert (1954) "Utility Analysis and the Consumption Function: An Interpretation of Cross-Section Data" in Kurihara,

Kenneth (ed.), *Post-Keynesian Economics,* Rutgers University Press, New Brunswick, NJ.

Pierce, James L. (1974) "Quantitative Analysis at the Federal Reserve" *Annals of Economic and Social Measurement, Special Issue on Stochastic Control,* National Bureau of Economic Research, January, pp. 11–19.

Pierce, James L. and Enzler, Jared J. (1974) "The Effects of External Inflationary Shocks" Brookings Papers on Economic Activity: 1.

Pierce, James and Thomson, L. Thomas (1972) "Some Issues in Controlling the Stock of Money" in *Controlling Monetary Aggregates II: The Implementation,* Federal Reserve Bank of Boston, Boston, MA.

Poole, William (1970) "Optimal Choice of Policy Instruments in a Simple Stochastic Macro Model" *Quarterly Journal of Economics,* vol. 84, no. 2, May, pp. 197–216.

Sargent, Thomas (1976) "The Observational Equivalence of the Natural and Unnatural Rate Theories of Macroeconomics" *Journal of Political Economy,* vol. 84, no. 3, June, pp. 631–40.

Stein, Jerome L. (ed.) (1976) *Monetarism,* North-Holland, New York, NY.

Tobin, James (1958) "Liquidity Preference as Behavior Toward Risk" *Review of Economic Studies,* vol. 25, no. 67, February, pp. 65–86.

4. Is the Quantity Theory of Money True?

Mark Blaug

My paper is prompted by another, David Laidler's 'The Quantity Theory is Always and Everywhere Controversial – Why?' (1991a), but my answer to the question posed by that title is different from his. Laidler believes that the controversy has continued because of the technical difficulty of sorting out the direction of causation between money and prices and, on a deeper level, because ideological issues about the functioning of markets are at stake in the controversy. My answer is that the theory manifests a common difficulty shared by most economic theories, namely, that they are expressed in logical time and not in real time; hence we are rarely provided with 'correspondence rules' to tell us how to distinguish the so-called short-run and long-run consequences of the theory. This opens the door to endless arguments about what observations are to count as confirmations or refutations of the theory.

Since this problem is not unique to the quantity theory of money (QTM), we ought to direct our attention to the limitations of current econometric techniques rather than to the QTM. But there are special features of the QTM that make it an ideal candidate for a discussion of the classic problem of testing economic theories. For one thing, this is one of the oldest of reputable economic doctrines, going back to a remarkably complete statement of the theory by David Hume in 1752, and one which survived the marginal revolution of the 1870s without being affected in any of its essentials to emerge in modern times as 'the monetarist counterrevolution' to Keynes.[1] For another, it was one of the first economic theories to have been extensively 'tested', or at least

---

[1] As Milton Friedman (1968, p. 433) has said: 'The contemporary economist can still read David Hume's essay "Of Money" (1752) with pleasure and profit and find few if any errors of commission'. Thomas Mayer (1990) noted the striking similarity of Hume's writings on the QTM to those of Friedman on monetarism: of the twelve propositions that he identified as characteristic of modern monetarism, five are explicit in Hume's works.

massively confronted, by economic data in Thomas Tooke's famous
History of Prices (1838–57); since then it has been tested again and
again by historical, statistical and econometric methods. If we still
cannot agree whether and in what sense this theory is true or false, we
might as well write off the truth-value of all economics. Finally, it turns
out that, despite two centuries of debate, the theory remains imprecisely
expressed – this in a subject that prides itself on analytical rigour.
Precisely what is meant by the QTM? Does it apply to any
commodity–money regime or only to irredeemable fiat money? Is it
essentially a long-run equilibrium theory about the relationship between
the quantity of money and the level of prices, or is it rather a short-run
theory about the transmission mechanism relating money and prices?
Does money cause prices to change or can prices also cause money to
change, in which case what is left of 'the quantity of money theory of
the purchasing power of money'? We can learn a great deal about what
are called 'theories' in economics by studying the history of the QTM.
Perhaps that is sufficient justification to go once more down this well-
worn road.

DEFINING THE QTM

There is absolutely no doubt that the QTM is, and always has been, a
theory of the behaviour of the general price level, which treats the price
level as the variable to be explained and the quantity of money as the
key factor causing it to change (Humphrey, 1986, ch. 1).[2] Likewise,
there has been, since at least Henry Thornton's 1803 treatise on *The
Paper Credit of Great Britain*, broad agreement that the transmission
mechanism between money and prices is made up of 'direct' and
'indirect' elements. When there is an exogenous increase in the supply
of nominal money, it must flow into the pockets of at least some
economic agents, who, being satisfied with their existing holdings of
cash, will spend the extra money on goods and services; the resulting
pressure on scarce resources will cause prices to rise. This is the 'direct'
or 'real balance' effect of an increased quantity of money. In addition,

---

[2] It is worth stating this emphatically since it was explicitly denied in Milton Friedman's
opening salvo in the monetarist counterrevolution: 'The quantity theory is in the first
instance a theory of the *demand* for money. It is not a theory of output, or of money income,
or of the price level' (Friedman, 1969, p. 52). Patinkin (1981) showed conclusively that this
was historically inaccurate, and Friedman's reply to Patinkin touched on every issue in
Patinkin's critique (Friedman, 1970, pp. 158–68) but not on his characterization of the QTM.

the new money will typically be injected into the economy via the banking system. Banks will either receive new deposits or have their reserves enhanced; in either case, they are liable to increase their lending operations. If we started out with the bank loan rate equal to the real rate of return on physical capital, including a margin for the riskiness of physical investment, the new lower loan rate will encourage borrowing for productive investment (alternatively, technical progress may lift the real rate of return above an unchanged loan rate with similar results). Via this 'indirect' mechanism, prices will rise independently of more direct consumption spending. The sum of these two effects constitutes the reason that quantity theorists believe that an increase in the stock of money will cause prices to rise.

It is obvious from all this that the QTM really consists of three interrelated propositions: (1) the causal arrow runs from money to prices, and not from prices to money, which is to say that changes in the quantity of money are exogenous; (2) there is a stable demand for nominal money-balances-to-hold, sometimes known as the velocity of circulation of money, meaning that the demand for money changes slowly if at all, and in particular, that it changes independently of changes in the money supply; and (3) the volume of transactions or the volume of output (depending on whether we use a Fisherine transactions-approach or a Cambridge income-approach to the QTM) is determined by real variables such as endowments, preferences and technology – independently of the quantity of money or the level of prices. All three propositions are highly controversial and by no means truisms. Having been brought up on the idea that the Equation of Exchange, $MV \equiv PT$ or $M \equiv kPY$, is an identity, we are faced with the problem of so defining the QTM that all quantity theorists would accept the definition. In fact, it is surprising how often the QTM is defined by some authorities as if the theory were adequately captured by the Equation of Exchange.[3] But whatever definition is used, the direct and

---

[3] For instance, Lawrence Boland (1991, p. 97) remarks:

There are some statements which are of the form that economists call tautologies, yet that can also appear to be confirmed. The most obvious example is the 'quantity theory of money'. This 'theory' is represented by the equation $MV=PT$. On close examination it turns out that the two sides of this equation are merely what is obtained by reversing the order of summation between i and j for the double summation $\Sigma\Sigma \, p_{ij} \, q_{ij}$. Confirming a statement which cannot conceivably be false cannot really contribute anything positive to economic science.

(continued on p. 52)

indirect transmission mechanism is the very heart of the theory, and nothing in the Equation of Exchange tells us that the theory can deal only with exogenous changes in M or that V and T are assumed to change independently of each other.

The object of the QTM, from its very outset in Hume's formulation, was to demonstrate that the absolute size of the money stock was of no real significance in an economy: the price level *would eventually adjust* via the direct and indirect transmission mechanism to equate the real value of the nominal money stock M, that is, M/P, to the real demand for it, the fraction $1/V$ of the real volume of transactions T that the public wished to hold in the form of real cash balances. Written as $M/P=T/V$, the QTM stands exposed immediately as a particular species of demand-and-supply explanations of economic phenomena.

'Would eventually adjust!' This is the notorious Proportionality Theorem, the idea that money and absolute prices will in the long run vary proportionately, such that a doubling of M will double P, no more, no less, leaving relative prices, including the rate of interest, and hence the level of real output, unaffected. This theorem came to be known in the 1930s as 'neutrality of money' (Patinkin, 1987) but it was a familiar quantity-theory proposition all through the nineteenth century, long before a memorable name for it had been invented. Alongside this long-run theorem about neutral money ran the notion that money in the short run was almost certainly nonneutral; here too, the inspiration was Hume (and possibly Richard Cantillon), who had argued not only that the level of output in an economy is invariant to the level of the money supply but also that it can be raised by a positive rate of change of the money supply (Hume, 1955, pp. lxiii–xvi; Duke, 1991). What was called 'neutral' money in the interwar period has come to be known more recently as the vertical long-run Phillips curve or the 'policy ineffectiveness' proposition of the new classical macroeconomics. Hume

Similarly, Joseph Schumpeter (1954, p. 703) defines the QTM to mean four propositions: (1) that M varies independently of P and T; (2) that V is an institutional datum that varies slowly and independently of P and T; (3) that T or output is unrelated to M; and (4) that variations in M 'unless they are absorbed by variations in output in the same direction, act *mechanically* on all prices, irrespective of how an increase in the quantity of money is used and on what sectors of the economy it first impinges [my italics]'. This definition does not mention either the direct or indirect transmission mechanism, although elsewhere in the book Schumpeter (1954, pp. 720–4) does of course recognize them; likewise, the suggestion that money according to the QTM is 'neutral' even in the short run (see text below) is belied later in the book (1954, pp. 724–5, 1115–16n). Samuel Hollander (1987, p. 265) quotes this definition of the QTM by Schumpeter uncritically, after which he has no difficulty, or rather less difficulty, clearing Ricardo of the charge of being a crude quantity theorist (which of course he was).

apparently did not believe in the neutrality of money with respect to a sustained rate of change of the money supply. Had he expressed himself in modern language, he would have repudiated Friedman's notion of a natural rate of unemployment and insisted on the existence of a trade-off between output and inflation even in the long run (see Blaug, 1985, pp. 20–1). Be that as it may, the QTM is still relevant and discernible in modern macroeconomic arguments.

THE CLASSICAL ECONOMISTS AND THE QTM

The QTM received its greatest fillip with the suspension of specie payments in 1797, which introduced an entire generation of monetary thinkers to the notion of inconvertible fiat paper money and floating exchange rates, a monetary regime in which the money supply is exogenous as it had never been before. When David Hume and Richard Cantillon wrote about the effects of an increase in the money supply, Britain was an open economy on a fixed-exchange-rate gold standard, in which case the price level and the money supply are simultaneously and endogenously determined by the workings of the balance of payments and the international flow of specie. It is true that Hume had introduced the idea of a mental experiment involving an exogenous increase of the money supply – 'suppose that all the money of Great Britain were multiplied fivefold in one night' as he expressed it – but that was not the typical way in which classical economists thought about the effects of a given stock of nominal money in an economy. Believing as they did in cost-of-production theories of value, they applied their value theories as much to the money metal as to any other commodity and argued that absolute prices are determined by comparative costs in the production of gold and of goods in general. This was perhaps the reason that Adam Smith never mentioned Hume's specie-flow mechanism and more or less rejected the QTM, endorsing as he did the 'real bills doctrine': if banks confined their lending to self-liquidating commercial transactions (i.e., issued only real bills) bank credit would never exceed the 'needs of trade', in which case even the volume of fiat money, not to mention the volume of bank credit, would be endogenously determined (Humphrey, 1986, pp. 80–9, 180–7; Perlman, 1991).

In any case, 1797 created a new era in which the supply of money was determined either by the Bank of England if David Ricardo was to be believed or by grain imports and war remittances if Henry Thornton was to be believed: for the first time, causality ran clearly and unambiguously from money to prices and not the other way round.

But Ricardo continued to expound a labour theory of value of the monetary metal while at the same time espousing a hard-line version of the QTM. He might have reconciled the two by reserving the QTM for short-run problems and for inconvertible paper, while maintaining the cost-of-production theory for the long run and for specie money and convertible paper only. In fact, however, he left the two doctrines standing in an unresolved relationship to each other (Blaug, 1985, pp. 130, 198–9).[4] When convertibility of paper money was restored in 1821, the members of what soon came to be known as the Currency School argued as if the QTM was relevant even for commodity money, while the members of the Banking School echoed the truly classical, pre-Ricardian cost-of-production theory.

The irony of the great Currency–Banking controversy that divided the early Victorians on the questions of monetary policy was that the quantity-theorists, Lord Overstone, George Norman and Robert Torrens, upheld *the* currency principle, namely, that a mixed gold-convertible-paper currency should so be regulated that it would vary in the same way as a purely metallic currency, thereby responding automatically to any inflow or outflow of gold. But if this could have been achieved, which it never was, it would have tied the currency to the movement of the foreign exchanges and thus re-established the endogeneity of the money supply that ruled in the eighteenth century. In other words, the currency school employed the QTM to advocate a form of statutory control of the currency that would have made the QTM irrelevant.

Be that as it may, it is evident that all the monetary controversies that led up to the Bank Charter Act of 1844 and attended the many amendments of the Act in the 1850s and 1860s turned almost exclusively on short-run issues. The 'neutrality of money in the long run' was a convenient stick with which to beat the Birmingham paper-credit inflationists (like Thomas Attwood), but apart from such special uses, not much was heard of the notorious Proportionality Theorem and certainly little emphasis was placed on it. As for the short run, every

---

[4] The tension between them was never resolved in the classical tradition, and even John Stuart Mill and Karl Marx discussed the QTM and the labour theory of value applied to money as if the two had little to do with each other (see Lavoie, 1991). Nassau Senior (1992) went so far in his *Three Lectures on the Value of Money* (1840) to attack Mill for suggesting that relative prices are determined by costs of production, while the value of money is determined by a completely different theory, the QTM. On all this, see Niehans (1978, pp. 145–8).

classical economist regarded money as nonneutral in the short run, and since the label 'classical economist' is frequently misused, we may as well say that we refer to such writers as Hume, Malthus, Ricardo, Thornton, Jeremy Bentham, John Ramsay McCulloch, James Mill, John Stuart Mill and Robert Torrens (O'Brien, 1975, pp. 162–5; Humphrey, 1994, ch. 2).[5] Short-run nonneutrality was explained by a variety of phenomena: sticky prices, sticky nominal wages, sticky nominal interest rates, fixed nominal charges such as rents and taxes, fixed nominal incomes of wage earners and rentiers even under conditions of full employment ('forced saving'), fixed inventory–sales ratios, absolute-price–relative-price confusions à la Lucas, market size encouragements to specialization, and lastly, deliberate efforts on the part of organized groups to maintain real incomes (O'Brien, 1975, pp. 162–5; Humphrey, 1994, ch. 2, pp. 8–10). It is true that Ricardo and especially James Mill only grudgingly admitted nonneutrality in the short run but admit it they did (Ahiakpor, 1985). And while they asserted long-run neutrality of money, it was of course fiat money that they had in mind.

I wish these were original thoughts but, in fact, this has become almost a standard interpretation of classical monetary economics in recent years. 'The central message', says Humphrey (1994, p. 4), 'is that the notion of at least some nonneutrality is part of an enduring classical monetary tradition and that theories stressing neutrality are always a departure from that tradition'.[6] Likewise, Niehans (1987, p. 413) remarks that the Proportionality Theorem, widely regarded as the centrepiece of classical monetary theory, 'is only a secondary offshoot of somewhat suspect legitimacy ... The controversies were all about the short-term adjustments'.

Having robbed the classical QTM of much of its punch, some commentators have taken historical revisionism one step further, going so far as to argue that classical monetary theory has been misunderstood by just about everybody. We noted earlier that the QTM applies fully only to exogenously determined fiat money and that its application to a convertible paper currency as obtained in Britain after 1821 was

---

[5] Thus, when Don Patinkin (1981, ch. 5) published his famous 1954 paper on 'The Indeterminacy of Absolute Prices in Classical Economic Theory', he meant 'in neoclassical economic theory' because his argument was all about Walras, Pareto and general equilibrium theory. A whole series of papers then appeared on the dichotomization of pricing in neoclassical economics, the watertight separation of value theory and monetary theory, all under the heading of 'classical economic theory'. Eventually, Samuelson and Patinkin (1981, ch. 6) switched labels to 'the neo-classical dichotomy'.

[6] Having cited Humphrey once again, it must be said that he is to monetary economics what Jacob Viner was to international trade, the undisputed master of its history.

controversial: it depended on whether the monetary authorities had any real control of 'money' produced by the banking system. Now the Banking School denied that the Bank of England had such effective control; they used the real bills doctrine and the 'law of reflux' to argue that the money supply was demand-driven and endogenously determined by the 'needs of trade', any tendency of banks to overissue bank notes being corrected in the process of interbank note-clearing by rival competitive banks and external drains via the specie flow mechanism. The recent revival of the theory of free banking has drawn attention to a classical-period literature in favour of competitive, unregulated banking driven underground by the Bank Charter Act of 1844, which complimented the arguments of the Banking School (White, 1984, ch. 3). In any case, the new thesis is that the victorious Currency School applied the QTM to a monetary regime for which it was, strictly speaking, inappropriate: 'many classical theorists sometimes confused their theories by introducing quantity-theoretic propositions into arguments in which the quantity theory was not applicable. Such misplaced propositions have fostered the misconception that the quantity theory was the essential classical monetary theory' (Glasner, 1991a, p. 226).

If this is a misconception, however, it was one widely shared by the classical writers themselves: Glasner concedes that Hume and Ricardo and to some extent John Stuart Mill had it wrong with only Thornton and Nassau Senior getting it right (Glasner, 1991a, pp. 226–8, 232). Much of this reinterpretation therefore depends for its force on the trick of confining the label 'classical monetary theory' to those who either denied the exogeneity of the money supply, like the members of the Banking School, or who confined their arguments essentially to inconvertible paper-money, like Ricardo and Thornton.[7] In the final analysis, the issue of the relevance of the QTM in that or any other period depends on the exogeneity or endogeneity of the money supply, which is in every case a matter of fact and not a question of textual exegesis. This is an issue to which we will return.

---

[7] Glasner (1991a, p. 226) himself wonders whether 'I have exaggerated the difference between what I call the classical theory and the quantity theory'. He then proceeds to redefine the classical theory: 'Those that I have called the classical theorists [Smith, Thornton, Ricardo, J.S. Mill, Tooke and Fullarton] excluded the convertible money created by the banking system from the quantity of money that could be said to have an independent effect on prices. From their point of view, the quantity of money produced by the banking system behaved passively' (1991b, p. 282). It is difficult to imagine how this statement can be made to fit Thornton, Ricardo and even J.S. Mill.

THE NEOCLASSICAL ECONOMISTS AND THE QTM

As mentioned earlier, so far as the QTM is concerned, the Marginal Revolution of the 1870s might just as well never have happened. The short-run nonneutrality of money that characterized the classical versions of the QTM also appeared in the writings of such major neoclassical quantity theorists as Marshall, Pigou, Walras, Cassel, Fisher, Wicksell, Hawtrey and Lavington (Patinkin, 1981, pp. 3–24). They devoted even more attention to the short run than had the classical authors and in some cases did not even mention the idea that money was supposed to be neutral in the long run. The denial of 'superneutrality' in the sense of conceding that output would react to a change in the rate of growth of the money supply, which had been argued by Hume over a century earlier, reappeared in the writings of Fisher and Wicksell and provided still more reasons (forced saving, falling real rates of interest, wages lagging behind prices, etc.) for doubting the Proportionality Theorem (Patinkin, 1987, pp. 640–3).[8]

It is true that Marshall, Walras, Wicksell and Pigou drew a 'demand curve' for money, distinguished from other demand curves, by being a rectangular hyperbola asymptotic to the two axes, $1/P$ and M, thus suggesting that the elasticity of demand for money is always equal to unity – the Proportionality Theorem. We have learned from Hegeland (1951, pp. 135, 170–3) and Patinkin (1956, pp. 169–73, 187, 605–10) that this is a simple confusion between an individual money demand curve and a market-equilibrium money demand curve; the market-equilibrium demand curve will exhibit unitary elasticity because it is a locus cutting through a family of individual demand curves for each of which the price level is adjusted to the money supply in accordance with market-clearing requirements, thus defining the precise sense in which money is said to be neutral in the long run. Despite such diagrams and frequent references in the literature on monetary economics to the alleged unitary elasticity of the demand curve for money, the emphasis in monetary economics throughout the last quarter of the nineteenth and first quarter of the twentieth century was on the question of an appropriate monetary policy to stabilize prices in the wider interest of

---

[8] It is noteworthy that Keynes in *The General Theory* took exactly the same position in 1936 that Fisher and Wicksell took in 1911 and 1903, namely that long-term neutrality of money implied by what Keynes (1973, pp. 289–91) called 'the crude quantity theory of money' was qualified 'practically' because of adverse expectations and falling real interest rates in a credit boom.

ironing out the fluctuations of the business cycle; in other words, the short run was just as much in the forefront for neoclassical economists as it had been for classical economists (Schumpeter, 1954, pp. 1095–1122).[9] In consequence, the old long-run cost-of-production theory of the value of the monetary commodity was abandoned, it now being accepted that, even if it were true, the gold stock was so large relative to the annual output of gold mines that the cost of producing gold could only have a negligible effect on its exchange value (Laidler, 1991b, pp. 83, 120–3).

Was this The Golden Age of the Quantity Theory, to cite the title of a recent study by David Laidler (1991b)? 'No', say some, because the 'golden age' (1870–1914) was also the era *par excellence* of the international gold standard in which the nominal stock of money in small, open economies like that of Great Britain was adjusted to the level of prices via the balance of payments, so that the QTM was simply irrelevant. 'The mainstream of the classical and neoclassical tradition focussed on commodity money', says Niehans (1987, p. 412), 'to which the quantity theory does not apply. The quantity theory is, so to say, the illegitimate sideline of the classical tradition, the classical theory for unclassical fiat money'. If that were all there was to it, we should be surprised, not that the long-run neutrality of money is mentioned so rarely by neoclassical monetary writers, but that it is acknowledged at all. What could monetary theorists have been thinking of when they referred to the special case of the unitary elasticity of demand for monetary gold?

REVERSE CAUSATION

We have seen that there are and always have been good arguments for believing that the quantity of money is endogenously determined under a fixed-exchange rate gold-standard regime, in which case it might be more appropriate to speak of a 'contraquantity theory of money'. The great exponents of the contraquantity theory in the nineteenth century were Thomas Tooke (Arnon, 1990, ch. 7) and Laurence Laughlin (Girton and Roper, 1978). Although neither Tooke nor Laughlin made the best of their case, the fact remains that even convinced quantity-theorists have always conceded that the money supply is almost never

---

[9] But perhaps Milton Friedman (1968, p. 433) goes too far when he denies that anyone ever held the Proportionality Theorem, 'although statements capable of being so interpreted have often been made in the heat of argument or for expository simplicity'.

entirely exogenous and that, even so, reverse causation from prices to money is always possible.

Causation in economics does not necessarily imply that the cause must temporally precede the effect; agents may forecast the variable constituting the cause and act in anticipation of it. Thus, John Elliot Cairnes, writing on the Californian and Australian gold discoveries in the 1850s – an exogenous increase in the money supply if there ever was one – argued that the new gold acted on British prices even before British exporters to the colonies had been paid in gold. Similarly, according to the indirect transmission mechanism of money on prices, if the rate of profit on capital rises above the loan rate of interest, say, because of a burst of technical innovations, money creation will occur endogenously, leading to rising prices. As Irving Fisher always argued, nominal interest rates are sticky and therefore real rates of interest always tend to fall during periods of inflation. In consequence, there is a further rise in the demand for productive loans, which leads to still further price rises. Under these circumstances, if monetary policy is not accommodating, or if for any other reason bank loan rates are not raised, we have a situation in which the money supply is increasing because prices are rising, not because the QTM is false but because it is true. Finally, if cost-push factors are causing prices to rise, quantity theorists have typically argued that, whatever is the monetary regime, prices would never have risen unless the cost-push had been accommodated by an increase in the money supply; nevertheless, on the face of it, such circumstances will look like a contraquantity-theory scenario.

These and other examples of possible reverse causation between money and prices prompted David Laidler (1991a, p. 299) to comment: 'the test of the quantity theory position, at least as set out by its exponents, lay not in evidence on the timing of data, but in the outcome of a counter-factual experiment: what would happen if the time path of the money supply were different'. Summing up with particular reference to the US monetary accommodation of the oil price shock in the early 1970s, he concluded: 'it is precisely the impossibility of bringing empirical evidence directly and unambiguously to bear on questions concerning the feasibility of non-accommodating policy and, if feasible, upon its consequences for prices, which lie at the heart of continuing controversy about the quantity theory' (Laidler, 1991a, p. 299).

But, surely, we must bring to bear the whole weight of evidence of past episodes, of fiat paper and commodity money regimes, of relatively open and relatively closed regimes? And as we shall see, we have ample

empirical evidence of both the direct and indirect transmission
mechanism to provide us with evidence of the effects of this or that policy
shock. In the meanwhile, note that even Milton Friedman and Anna
Schwartz in their magisterial study of the history of money in the United
States do not deny that there is reverse causation of prices on money even
if, on balance, the causal chain runs fundamentally from money to prices.

> While the influence running from money to economic activity has been
> predominant, there have also been influences running the other way. Mutual
> interaction, but with money clearly the senior partner in long-run movements and
> in major cyclical movements, and more nearly an equal partner with money
> income and prices in the shorter run and milder movements – this is the
> generalization suggested by our evidence. (Friedman and Schwartz, 1963, p. 695)

THE EXOGENOUS–ENDOGENOUS ISSUE

Again and again throughout its long history, the exogeneity or
endogeneity of money has been at the back of every controversy
surrounding the QTM. We have repeatedly touched on the issue but we
have not so far confronted it directly. We must now ask: How does one
decide whether a change in the supply of money is exogenous, meaning
that it is not itself explained by our economic model, or whether it is
endogenous, meaning that it is set off by forces that are part of the
phenomena we are explaining with the aid of our model? I choose my
language carefully because it is always conceivable that what is
exogenous in, say, orthodox economics might be endogenous in some
unorthodox, wide-ranging, socio-politico-economic theory; at the same
time, it is worth noting that many variables are exogenous even in
general equilibrium theory, Marxism, radical economics, structural-
functional theory, or just about any theory in social science that I can
think of: there is no such thing as a theory that explains everything.

In the QTM, the standard interpretation of the basic assumption that
the money supply is exogenous is that it is capable of being varied
without any prior change in the demand for money, the demand for
goods and services, the supply of goods and services, and hence the
level of prices; in the language of the equation of exchange, M may vary
without any prior change in V, T or P. There are essentially two ways in
which this can happen: (1) under an international gold standard, if there
is a discovery of new gold mines or if there are cost-reducing
innovations in gold production anywhere in the world; and (2) the
monetary authorities alter the volume of 'high-powered money', of coins

and currency held by the public and the cash reserves of banks, which they may do even under a gold standard even though it violates the gold-standard 'rules of the game'. The second case is particularly troublesome because it is always a matter of degree, not a matter of kind. The question really is: Even if the monetary authorities control the monetary base, how much control do they actually have over the total money supply?

Under a fully 'loaned up' fractional-reserve banking system, the monetary authorities control the quantity of 'outside money' (such as fiat money, the quantity of gold and foreign exchange reserves), the reserve–deposit ratio and the currency–demand deposit ratio, but the volume of demand deposits and that of bank credit is endogenously determined. When the banks are not fully loaned up, there is only loose control of 'high-powered money'. It is evident, therefore, that the total money supply is almost never entirely exogenously determined even under classic gold-standard conditions, and in any case control of the money supply is always a matter of degree.

An analogy may be helpful. Does the government control the crime rate? Yes and no. In the short run, there is no doubt that additional policing is capable of reducing the crime rate. But in the long run, the crime rate depends on a host of sociological, psychological and economic variables such as standards of law and order, moral attitudes inculcated at home and in schools, and levels of employment and living standards; in the long run, the authorities as such have virtually no control over the crime rate. Analogously, we may say that the money supply is always more exogenous in the short run than in the long run. In other words, the QTM is always a better explanation of the price level in the short run than in the long run. But how long is the run relevant to the determination of something like the level of prices?

Friedman and Schwartz (1991, pp. 41–2) deny that exogeneity or endogeneity ever is a characteristic of the money supply as such; it all depends, they say, on the purpose of the analysis in question. Thus, even under a gold standard, the monetary authorities do have considerable control over domestic monetary policy over short periods, but for a run of 'more than a few years', the stock of money in each country is determined by the requirement that international prices must be such as to preserve equilibrium in the balance of payments. So presumably, the QTM was of little use in explaining secular changes in absolute prices in the period before World War I, when both the purpose of the analysis and the monetary regime in question indicated that the money supply was endogenously determined. However, in accounting for the role of the Federal Reserve System in contracting the money supply in 1929–33, in effect producing the Great Depression of the 1930s, Friedman and Schwartz (1963, ch. 7; Bordo, 1986, pp. 353–63) clearly treat the money supply as exogenous.

In other words, there is no hard and fast answer to the question whether the money supply is exogenous and hence whether it is legitimate to employ the QTM. In part, the answer depends on the purpose at hand and, for the rest, it depends on the prevailing monetary regime. We are fairly safe in doubting the exogeneity of the money supply since 1971, when the entire world adopted a regime of irredeemable fiat paper without any anchor in commodity money; the deregulation of financial markets in the late 1970s and the spread of offshore banking in the 1970s and 1980s further reduced the degree of control exerted by governments over the money supply. Nevertheless, even under today's entirely fiduciary standard, there are profound disagreements among monetary experts over the extent to which governments can vary the monetary base and control various monetary aggregates. Thus, in *The New Palgrave Dictionary of Economics* we find Charles Goodhart (1987, p. 501) denying that the money supply is an exogenously determined variable and Karl Brunner (1987, pp. 527–9) asserting that it is. The most famous proponents of the endogenous money thesis in modern times are Nicholas Kaldor (1978) and James Tobin (1970), but that is not to say that they would insist on the endogeneity of money and hence the contraquantity theory of money for all past monetary regimes (see Humphrey, 1994, ch. 7). Similarly, post-Keynesian economists (see Lavoie, 1992, ch. 4) have made the endogeneity of money one of their major themes but without necessarily coupling it to an attack on the QTM as such. The exogeneity–endogeneity of money issue is of course intimately connected with the famous difficulty of defining precisely what is 'money'. It is noteworthy that, with the passage of time, the set of assets referred to as 'money', whose quantity is supposed by the QTM to determine the price level, has systematically broadened from gold and silver coin in Hume to coins and bank notes in the Currency School to coins, notes and bank deposits, time deposits, bank reserves and the liabilities of financial intermediaries in modern monetarism (Laidler, 1991a, p. 295). The boundaries of a nation's money supply have become surrounded by an ever fuzzier penumbra which have further bedevilled the issue of whether money is or is not exogenous.

THE DEMAND FOR MONEY

Exogeneity of money is, as we have said, the first of three critical propositions that define the QTM. The second, to which we now turn, is the notion that there is a stable demand for money-to-hold. There have always been two traditions within the QTM: the 'motion theory of money', captured by Fisher's transactions approach and the quantity equation $MV=PT$, and the 'rest theory of money', enshrined in the Cambridge income approach and the equation $M=kPY$. Both approaches assumed that people will want to hold, for transactions and possibly precautionary motives, a constant quantity of real cash balances at the economy's full-capacity level of output and that this demand function is stable in the sense that it is not subject to erratic shifts; it varies, when it does vary, slowly and independently of both the size of the money stock and the level of prices. But the better-known transactions approach made the velocity of money a function of payment habits, the spread of banking institutions, and advances in the means of transportation and communication, i.e., non-price variables. The rate of interest as the opportunity cost of holding cash did not appear explicitly in the equation of exchange, and although Fisher was of course perfectly aware of the Thornton-Wicksell doctrine of the 'two rates', the fact is that the indirect transmission mechanism of money on prices almost disappeared from view in the transactions approach to the QTM (Patinkin, 1956, pp. 165–9).

It was the income approach in Marshall, Pigou and Lavington that bequeathed the idea of the interest-elasticity of the demand for money to the generation of which Keynes was a prominent member. What in Keynes appeared as 'motives' for liquidity-preference were nothing more than the renaming of ideas found repeatedly in the writings of Cambridge monetary economists. However, Keynes entirely rejected the notion that there was a stable demand for money and indeed his principal criticism of the QTM was the assertion that V or k was unstable and unpredictable.

Somehow Keynes and Keynesians planted the idea that the old quantity theorists had believed in the virtual constancy of V or k, but nothing could be further from the truth: the doctrine of the two rates required an inverse relationship between V and the money rate of interest, not to mention V and the rate of inflation (as the result of a falling real rate of interest), and the usual list of the determinants of velocity suggested that V would rise over time as a consequence of improvements in communication and monetization.[10] Such vulgarizations of the QTM may have been encouraged by the statistical work of Carl Snyder and Holbrook Working in the 1920s, purporting to demonstrate that procyclical fluctuations in V were always neutralized by contracyclical fluctuations of T, producing a rigidly constant T/V ratio, the Proportionality Theorem or long-run neutrality of money (Humphrey, 1994, ch. 29).

Notwithstanding these distortions of the evidence, stability of the money demand function remains a vital element in the QTM and in modern statements of monetarism. It is a principal bone of contention in Friedman and Schwartz's study of *Monetary Trends in the United States and United Kingdom* (Hendry and Ericsson, 1991, pp. 13, 16; Friedman and Schwartz, 1991, p. 47; also Mayer, 1982, pp. 1532–5) and has been the subject of a book-length survey by Laidler (1985). The question is given added piquancy because it is generally agreed that, no matter how money is defined, the income-velocity of money on both sides of the Atlantic became extremely unstable in the early 1980s, leading to the abandonment of money supply targets in the United Kingdom and a marked decline in the popular appeal of monetarism in the United States (Mayer, 1990, pp. 70–6). Nevertheless, despite the instability of the demand for money function in the 1980s, the weight of the empirical evidence surveyed by Laidler (1985, pp. 124, 135, 143) supports the idea that there is a stable negative relationship between the demand for nominal money and the rate of interest, and a stable proportional relationship between the demand for nominal money and the general price level (see also Goldfeld and Sichel, 1990, pp. 302–7, 349–50).

THE NEUTRALITY OF MONEY

The QTM depends, as we have said, on three propositions: (1) the exogeneity of the money supply; (2) the stability of the demand for money function; and (3) the real determinants of the level of output or transactions. The notion that physical output is a function only of real variables and is therefore determined independently of both M and P is of course implied by the doctrine of the long-run neutrality of money. This is often said to be a key proposition of the QTM, and it is now time that we ask what reasons we have for believing that prices indeed vary

---

[10] Actually, V has displayed a V-shaped pattern over the past century in a large number of advanced countries, declining from about 1890 to 1945 and then rising secularly to the 1980s (Bordo, 1986, pp. 350–2).

equiproportionately with money. Whatever are these reasons, they are empirical, not analytical. Of course, we can set up a correct general equilibrium model à la Patinkin in which every individual's utility function includes cash balances held as a good, in which every exogenous increase in the money supply is distributed equiproportionately to the initial money endowments of individuals, and in which the 'real balance effect' will ensure that absolute prices will rise in the same proportion as the money stock, but we can hardly expect the real world perfectly to mimic this theoretical scenario. All the great economists of the past, as we have seen, had no difficulty in conjecturing why money might fail to be neutral in the long run and very few laid much emphasis on the alleged long-run neutrality of money. So the question remains: What evidence is there that money and prices vary proportionately?

No one disputes the remarkably close correlation between money and nominal income over the medium and long run in most industrialized countries for which we have historical data. But nominal income is PY and the split of PY into P and Y is very much in dispute. The QTM consists of the assertion that any increase of M will begin by affecting PY but will eventually affect only P. Here is a distinction so often encountered in economics, between effects in the short run and effects in the long run, the actual length of the run being left unspecified. Although this is fair comment in respect of the long history of the QTM, it is actually belied by the pronouncements of the most recent prominent advocate of the QTM, Milton Friedman. Milton Friedman has always been most explicit about the length of the short run and long run during which the effects of an increase in the money supply work themselves out.

> For most Western countries, a change in the rate of monetary growth produces a change in the rate of growth of nominal income about six to nine months later ... The effect on prices, like that on income and output ... comes some twelve to eighteen months later, so that the total delay between a change in monetary growth and a change in the rate of inflation averages something like two years ... In the short run, which may be as long as three to ten years, monetary changes affect primarily output. Over decades, on the other hand, the rate of monetary growth affects primarily prices. (Friedman, 1992, p. 478; also 1987, pp. 16–17; 1991, p. 16) [11]

[11] Carefully worded statements such as these have to be set next to more dramatic claims in Friedman's writings, such as 'There is perhaps no empirical regularity among economic phenomena that is based on so much evidence for so wide a range of circumstances as the connection between substantial changes in the quantity of money and in the level of prices' (Friedman, 1987, p. 15) and 'For the United Kingdom ... a simple quantity theory that regards price change as determined primarily by monetary change and output by independent other factors fits the evidence for the period as a whole [1871–1985] (excluding wars)'. (Friedman and Schwartz, 1982, p. 463)

So, money is certainly nonneutral in the short run and the 'short run' is typically 2 years but may be as long as 3–10 years; long-run neutrality will only be observed after a decade and will only amount in any case to *near*-proportionality between money and prices. If 'neutrality' and 'super-neutrality' are standardly defined so that they imply that the effects of either a once-and-for-all change in the stock of money or a change in the rate of growth of the stock of money are nil, then there is only lukewarm support for either concept in Friedman's writings. (On whether these definitions are 'standard' see Patinkin, 1987, pp. 641–3.) Superneutrality is the same thing as a vertical long-run expectations-augmented Phillips curve set at the so-called 'natural rate of unemployment', and of course this is one of Friedman's most famous contributions to modern macroeconomics. But its actual importance to Friedman's thinking about economic policy may have been exaggerated. Certainly, an effect that can take as long as 10 years to show itself is not a practical policy proposition. Nevertheless, it may take on importance as ideological ammunition against Keynesian fiscalism. In any case, it is interesting to note that the QTM, which began with Hume as a qualified argument in favour of creeping inflation, has come full circle in Friedman with the denial that there is any trade-off between output and inflation in the long run. At one point in the 1980s, the new classical macroeconomics even went so far as to deny that there was any negatively sloped Phillips curve even in the short run.

EMPIRICAL EVIDENCE

At the end of our story, one is struck by the open-endedness, almost looseness, of the QTM. Money can affect both output and prices in the short run and it may even affect output in the long run, depending on how and at what rate the extra money is injected into the economy. Do we really have the heavy artillery of the QTM to tell us this? No doubt, it is a wonderful framework for thinking about monetary questions and it certainly comes into its own during every hyperinflation. When irresponsible governments seek to finance fiscal deficits in periods of civil war or social unrest by printing unbacked paper notes, we get all the conditions required to make the QTM operative: exogenous money, a stable or slowly changing demand for money, and output unable to respond quickly to monetary expansion.[12] But in normal times, it is largely irrelevant except for the very long run and it is hopelessly indeterminate in the short run.

Nevertheless, painting with a broad brush, it is supported by an overwhelming body of empirical evidence. This is evidence that goes back to Thomas Tooke, whose data were admittedly anecdotal, but which were greatly extended and improved by Irving Fisher. We tend to forget that a quarter of the text and one-third of the appendices of *The Purchasing Power of Money* (1911) were devoted to the 'statistical verification' of the QTM (see Laidler, 1991b, pp. 79–82; Friedman, 1987, p. 5). The equation of exchange, as Humphrey (1994, pp. 288–9) has said, 'was the chief single-equation macroeconomic model in use up to the 1930s'. The historical studies of Friedman and Schwartz mark the next step in what has now become a major research industry (see Bordo, 1986).[13] In addition, there is a mountain of econometric evidence, partly summarized by Laidler (see also Schwartz, 1990; Blanchard, 1990). Laidler's conclusion at the close of his discussion of the quantity theory of money is so judiciously worded that it may serve as our own (1991a, p. 303): 'The overwhelming weight of evidence is ... consistent with the quantity theory and inconsistent with certain extreme criticisms of it. To the extent that one comes to this evidence with a prior belief that the quantity theory is a plausible doctrine, that belief is strengthened by it'.

The point is, and perhaps this is my main point, if we believe that the QTM is true, it is not because we find the theory underlying it so plausible and precisely expressed. It is facts and not analytical rigour that makes the QTM good economics. I venture to assert that this is so with most if not all economic theories.

---

[12] The great German inflation of 1922–23 is an awful reminder of what happens when the central bank and all the leading economists of a country have been brought up on the contraquantity theory of money (Barkai, 1989). The present Russian regime seems to be duplicating the German experience.

[13] That this historical method of inquiry, so much praised by Marxists, Radicals and Institutionalists should have been the principal research tool of that arch libertarian, Milton Friedman, is one of the great ironies of intellectual history.

REFERENCES

Ahiakpor, J.C.W. (1985) 'Ricardo on Money: The Operational Significance of the Non-neutrality of Money in the Short Run' *History of Political Economy*, vol. 17, no. 1, Spring, pp. 17–30, reprinted in Blaug, M. (ed.) (1991), *David Ricardo*, pp. 55–68, Edward Elgar Publishing, Aldershot, Hants.

Arnon, A. (1990) *Thomas Tooke: Pioneer of Monetary Theory,* Edward Elgar Publishing, Aldershot, Hants.

Barkai, H. (1989) 'The Old Historical School: Roscher on Money and Monetary Issues' *History of Political Economy*, vol. 21, no. 2, Summer, pp. 170–200.

Blanchard, O.J. (1990) 'Why Does Money Affect Output? A Survey' in Friedman, B.M. and Hahn, F.H. (eds), *Handbook of Monetary Economics*, vol. 2, pp. 942–63, North-Holland, Amsterdam.

Blaug, M. (1985) *Economic Theory in Retrospect*, 4th edn, Cambridge University Press, Cambridge.

Boland, L.A. (1991) 'Current Views on Economic Positivism' in Greenaway, D.A., Bleaney, M. and Stewart, I. (eds), *Companion to Economic Thought*, pp. 88–164, Routledge, London.

Bordo, M.D. (1986) 'Explorations in Monetary History: A Survey of the Literature' *Explorations in Economic History*, 23, pp. 339–415.

Brunner, K. (1987) 'Money Supply' in Eatwell, J., Milgate, M. and Newman, P. (eds), *The New Palgrave. A Dictionary of Economics*, vol. 3, pp. 527–29, Macmillan, London.

Duke, M.I. (1991) 'David Hume and Monetary Adjustment' *History of Political Economy*, Winter, 1979, reprinted in Blaug. M. (ed.), *David Hume and James Steuart*, Edward Elgar Publishing, Aldershot, Hants.

Friedman, M. (1968) 'Money, Quantity Theory' in Sills, D.L. (ed.), *International Encyclopedia of the Social Sciences*, vol. 10, pp. 433–7, Macmillan, New York, NY.

Friedman, M. (1969) 'The Quantity Theory of Money: A Restatement' in *Studies in the Quantity Theory of Money*, 1956, reprinted in *The Optimum Quantity of Money,* Aldine Publishing, Chicago, IL.

Friedman, M. (1970) 'Comments on the Critics' in Gordon, R.J. (ed.), *Milton Friedman's Monetary Framework. A Debate with his Critics*, pp. 132–77, University of Chicago Press, Chicago, IL.

Friedman, M. (1987) 'Quantity Theory of Money' in Eatwell, J., Milgate, M. and Newman, P. (eds), *The New Palgrave. A Dictionary of Economics*, vol. 4, pp. 3–19, Macmillan, London.

Friedman, M. (1991) *Monetarist Economics*, Basil Blackwell, Oxford.

Friedman, M. (1992) *Monetary Mischief. Episodes in Monetary History,* Harcourt Brace Jovanovich, New York, NY.

Friedman, M. and Schwartz, A.J. (1963) *A Monetary History of the United States, 1867–1960*, Princeton University Press, Princeton, NJ.

Friedman, M. and Schwartz, A.J. (1982) *Monetary Trends in the United States and the United Kingdom: Their Relation to Income Prices and Interest Rates, 1867–1975*, University of Chicago Press, Chicago, IL.

Friedman, M. and Schwartz, A.J. (1991) 'Alternative Approaches to Analyzing Economic Data' *American Economic Review*, vol. 81, no. 1, March, pp. 39–49.

Girton, L. and Roper, D.J. (1978) 'J. Lawrence Laughlin and the Quantity Theory of Money' *Journal of Political Economy*, vol. 86, no. 4, August, pp. 499–625.

Glasner, D. (1991a) 'A Reinterpretation of Classical Monetary Theory' *Southern Economic Journal*, July, 1985, reprinted in Blaug, M. (ed.), *George Scrope, Thomas Attwood, Edwin Chadwick, John Cairnes,* pp. 217–38, Edward Elgar Publishing, Aldershot, Hants.

Glasner, D. (1991b) 'On Some Classical Monetary Controversies' *History of Political Economy*, Summer, 1989, reprinted in Blaug, M. (ed.), *George Scrope, Thomas Attwood, Edwin Chadwick, John Cairnes,* pp. 257–86, Edward Elgar Publishing, Aldershot, Hants.

Goldfeld, S.M. and Sichel, D.E. (1990) 'The Demand for Money' in Friedman, B.M. and Hahn, F.H. (eds), *Handbook of Monetary Economics*, vol. 2, pp. 1012–47, North-Holland, Amsterdam.

Goodhart, C. (1987) 'Monetary Base' in Eatwell, J., Milgate, M. and Newman, P. (eds), *The New Palgrave. A Dictionary of Economics*, vol. 3, pp. 500–2, Macmillan, London.

Hegeland, H. (1951) *The Quantity Theory of Money*, Göteborg, reprinted 1969, Augustus Kelley, New York, NY.

Hendry, D.F. and Ericsson, N. (1991) 'An Econometric Analysis of U.K. Monetary Demand' *American Economic Review*, vol. 81, no. 1, pp. 8–38.

Hollander, S. (1987) *Classical Economics*, Basil Blackwell, Oxford.

Hume, D. (1955) *Writings on Economics,* Rotwein, E. (ed.), University of Wisconsin Press, Madison, WI.

Humphrey, M. (1986) *Essays on Inflation,* 5th edn, Federal Reserve Bank of Richmond, Richmond, VA.

Humphrey, M. (1994) *Fundamental Ideas in the History of Economic Thought,* Edward Elgar Publishing, Aldershot, Hants.

Kaldor, N. (1978) 'The New Monetarism' *Lloyd's Bank Review,* July 1970, reprinted in *Further Essays on Applied Economics,* pp. 3–27, Gerald Duckworth, London.

Keynes, J.M. (1973) *The General Theory of Employment, Interest and Money,* in *The Collected Writings of John Maynard Keynes*, Macmillan, London.

Laidler, D. (1985) *The Demand for Money. Theories, Evidence and Problems,* 3rd edn, Harper and Row, New York, NY.

Laidler, D. (1991a) 'The Quantity Theory is Always and Everywhere Controversial – Why?' *The Economic Record*, December, vol. 67, no. 199, pp. 289–306.

Laidler, D. (1991b) *The Golden Age of the Quantity Theory*, Philip Allan, New York, NY.

Lavoie, M. (1991) 'Marx, the Quantity Theory, and the Theory of Value' *History of Political Economy*, Spring, 1986, reprinted in Blaug, M. (ed.), *Karl Marx,* pp. 257–72, Edward Elgar Publishing, Aldershot, Hants.

Lavoie, M. (1992) *Foundations of Post-Keynesian Economic Analysis,* Edward Elgar Publishing, Aldershot, Hants.

Mayer, T. (1982) 'Monetary Trends in the United States and the United Kingdom: A Review Article' *Journal of Economic Literature*, vol. 20, no. 4, December, pp. 1528–39.

Mayer, T. (1990) *Monetarism and Macroeconomic Policy,* Edward Elgar Publishing, Aldershot, Hants.

Niehans, J. (1978) *The Theory of Money,* John Hopkins University Press, Baltimore, MD.

Niehans, J. (1987) 'Classical Monetary Theory, New and Old' *Journal of Money, Credit and Banking*, vol. 19, no. 4, November, pp. 409–24.

O'Brien, D.P. (1975) *The Classical Economist,* Clarendon Press, Oxford.

Patinkin, D. (1956) *Money, Interest and Prices*, Harper and Row, New York, NY.

Patinkin, D. (1981) 'The Chicago Tradition, the Quantity Theory, and Friedman' *Journal of Money, Credit and Banking,* February, 1969, reprinted with a postscript in *Essays On and In the Chicago Tradition,* Duke University Press, Durham, NC.

Patinkin, D. (1987) 'Neutrality of Money' in Eatwell, J., Milgate, M. and Newman, P. (eds), *The New Palgrave. A Dictionary of Economics,* vol. 3, pp. 639–45, Macmillan, London.

Perlman, M. (1991) 'Adam Smith and the Paternity of the Real Bills Doctrine' *History of Political Economy*, Spring, 1986, reprinted in Blaug, M. (ed.), *Adam Smith*, vol. 2, pp. 265–78, Edward Elgar Publishing, Aldershot, Hants.

Schumpeter, J. (1954) *A History of Economic Analysis*, Oxford University Press, Oxford.

Schwartz, A.J. (1990) 'Secular Price Changes in Historical Perspective' *Journal of Money, Credit and Banking*, Part II, February, 1973, reprinted in Chrystal, K.A. (ed.), *Monetarism*, vol. II, pp. 242–68, Edward Elgar Publishing, Aldershot, Hants.

Senior, N.W. (1992) *Three Lectures on the Value of Money,* reprinted in Schwartz, A.J. (ed.), *Commodity Monies,* vol. 1, pp. 165–244, Edward Elgar Publishing, Aldershot, Hants.

Tobin, J. (1970) 'Money and Income: Post Hoc Ergo Propter Hoc' *Quarterly Journal of Economics*, 84, May, pp. 301–17.

White, L.H. (1984) *Free Banking in Britain: Theory, Experience and Debate, 1800–1845*, Cambridge University Press, Cambridge.

PART III

The Transmission Mechanism

5. Say's Law Extended: An Expository Approach

Martin Bronfenbrenner

SAY'S LAW, SAY'S IDENTITY AND SAY'S PRINCIPLE

Say's Law of Markets says that aggregate supply (of some unspecified bundle of goods and services) creates its own demand, although the converse does not hold. It became in the nineteenth century the *pons asinorum* of conventional macroeconomics. Accepted in full and with inadequate analysis by the orthodox, and even – with doubts and qualifications – by a good many dissidents, it has been supposedly relegated to the dustbin of intellectual history by the "Keynesian Revolution" and the Great Depression. Can it be resurrected in modern dress?

Jean-Baptiste Say (1767–1832) himself stated Say's Law so loosely and ambiguously as to make it difficult to discover precisely what he originally meant by it.[1] In its crudest form, the supporting argument assumes implicitly a world limited to currently supplied and currently demanded goods and services. When one good, say "food," is produced, the motive of its producer is to either consume the good or exchange it for some other good, say "clothing," supplied by other producers in the same economy. In such an economic world, more food may of course be supplied than is demanded by the suppliers of clothing (or vice versa) at current prices or exchange values. Such a situation can be regarded alternatively as a surplus (excess supply) of one good or as a shortage (excess demand) of the other good. No situation can be looked upon as a simultaneous surplus or deficit of both goods taken together. This line of argument is easily extended to three, four, ... *n* goods and services; there can be no general overproduction or "glut."

---

[1] This is the verdict of Joseph Schumpeter (1954) and is accepted generally by historians of economic thought.

This restatement of Say's argument is particularly deficient in its treatment or non-treatment of relative prices. We have spoken only of "at going prices," which may be quite arbitrary; Say sometimes speaks of prices equal to costs of production, which gives away far too much ground to potential opponents. In forms which do not specify prices, Say's Law is now commonly called "Say's Identity"; an assumption of absolute demand-price and supply-price inelasticity is required to support Say's Identity in a macroeconomy limited, like Say's, to aggregate-supply and aggregate-demand functions for current output.

Introducing upward-sloping aggregate-supply and downward-sloping aggregate-demand functions relating what is essentially the national income to indices of output prices, we can raise "equilibrium" questions. Under what conditions, even in a two-commodity world, will any excess supply of food (over and above the demand for own consumption) of the food producers "balance" the excess supply of clothing (over and above own consumption) by the clothing producers? A conventional answer to such questions is to assume, although not to prove, that at any time there is one and only one positive price ratio between food and clothing for which this balance exists at any point in time. Similarly, for n commodities, we conventionally assume a single and unique price level at which aggregate supplies and demands balance for a national income and output composed of these n goods and services at any point in time. This is Say's Law: at any point in time there exists an unique positive price level at which aggregate supply equals or "creates" its own demand.

Say's Law and Say's Identity, taken together, constitute Say's Principle: aggregate supply creates its own demand (but not the reverse), either at any assumed price level whatever (the Identity) or at an equilibrium positive price level which may vary over time (the Law).[2] We may accept the Law but not the Identity, but not the reverse. Acceptance of the Law, with or without the superstructure of the Identity, suffices for acceptance of the Principle.

If the price level is above the equilibrium price level (and only the Law holds), we may indeed have excess supply of goods, "general overproduction," and unemployment at the going level of wages and prices. If the price level is below equilibrium, we have excess demand for goods, "general shortage," and possibly also over-employment.

This essay accepts Say's Principle. For an economic universe expanded or extended to include other important segments in addition to

---

[2] This terminology follows Thomas Sowell's *Say's Law: An Historical Analysis* (1972).

current output, the essay also accepts Say's Identity for the economic universe as a whole – demand creates its own supply – but not for any segment taken individually. Within each segment, again including current output, it accepts Say's Law as an equilibrium condition, while rejecting Say's Identity.

In the sections that follow, I try to explain further and, I hope, more clearly, what I mean by an "economic universe," and identify certain of its principal components in a system of segmentation or partition which seems to me particularly meaningful. With a view to expository clarity and simplicity, the analysis will eschew higher mathematics completely, in favor of prose and two-dimensional diagrams.

ENTER ASSETS, INCLUDING MONETARY ASSETS

Let us return briefly to our initial example, the exchange of food for clothing, this time in a world including durable goods. In this world the goods demanded and supplied include not only the food and clothing currently produced but also the residuals of past periods' production, as well as certain goods not "produced" at all, like Ricardian "land." Suppose in addition that our producers of food and clothing are adequately clothed and fed, respectively, but that each wishes to increase his supply of assets (inventory or "consumers' capital" of past production, along with real estate) at the current prices. In such a world, the argument for Say's Identity falls completely to the ground, and there is overproduction of current output in both its forms.[3] The argument for Say's Law should be expanded to include not only the price level of current production, but also the price level of assets, which may be quite different.

Arguments about Say's Principle – both Say's Law and Say's Identity – should now be expanded to cover increases and decreases in market participants' asset holdings. They should also include the level of asset prices, which (to repeat) may behave quite differently from the level of output prices. (They are not, however, concerned with the total amount of these assets in existence. This is because we cannot add stocks of assets to flows of current output, but increments and decrements of assets are another matter.)

---

[3] In a converse case, the producer of food proposes to obtain clothing by drawing down his supply of assets, and the producer of clothing proposes to obtain food by the same process. The result is a general shortage or "scarcity" of current production. This form of "scarcity" should be distinguished from the microeconomic theorist's technical definition of scarcity in the general case requiring market prices to be non-zero.

Domestic money, moreover, is a special case which merits separate treatment along lines suggested by Oscar Lange (1904–65) under the head of Walras' Law.[4] (Foreign money we shall for the present treat as an ordinary asset.[5]) Domestic money is a special case in that the "price" for expanding one's holdings, and also the reward for contracting them, can be taken (following Keynes) to be the rate of interest rather than the price level of assets as a whole.[6] This is especially true in a regime of credit, with financial intermediaries (banks) which can expand or contract these assets if not precisely "producing" or "consuming" them.

CLASSROOM EXPOSITION: STATIC AND DYNAMIC

A diagrammatic analysis of the above argument is relatively simple, but makes no claims to rigor. Certain pitfalls will be pointed out in passing.

This exposition features a set of three panels, treated as more nearly independent of each other than they are apt to be in the real world. (For example, the demand and supply of current output, including the current output of investment goods and public services, are treated as independent of both the price level of assets and the rate of interest.)

The left-hand panel (Figure 5.1) relates real current production Y per period to the price level of output (the GDP or GNP deflator). Aggregate-demand and aggregate-supply functions D and S are related to this price level p in a form which the late Joan Robinson delighted to call "bastard Keynesianism," but which is common in North American intermediate macroeconomics textbooks.

The middle panel (Figure 5.2) relates to increments in the demand and supply of the community's real non-monetary assets, notably real estate, equities, debt securities, producers' and consumers' capital goods, inventories, and "collectibles." This aggregate is denoted by $\dot{A}$, whose meaning is dA/dt. The demand and supply of $\dot{A}$ are indicated by D^a and

---

[4] Oscar Lange in *Price Flexibility and Employment* (1944) devised the "Walras' Law" terminology a generation after the death of Leon Walras himself in 1910. Lange's expansion of Say's Law, however, did not consider non-monetary assets other than as elements in current output.

[5] In more advanced analyses, changes in domestic holdings of foreign assets and foreign money, and likewise changes in foreign holdings of domestic assets and domestic money, may be treated separately, with exchange rates playing the role of prices. My "Say's Law, Walras' Law, and the International Balances" (1991) is a clumsy attempt in this direction.

[6] This treatment unfortunately sweeps under the rug all our problems of defining money and distinguishing monetary from non-monetary assets. Or to put the matter more mildly, it assumes these problems to have been served to everyone's satisfaction by some future and perhaps unborn winner of the Nobel Prize in Economics!

S^a as functions of the asset-price level, p^a. Since no demander or supplier in the asset markets need either know or care whether the increment demanded or supplied represents a net increment or a mere turnover of A, we cannot tell from Figure 5.2 whether A itself is rising, falling or remaining constant. Equilibrium means only that demand D^a from individuals and firms desiring increments of A balances supply S^a from other individuals and firms desiring to reduce their holdings of A; a rise in $\dot{A}_e$ on the diagram may be caused either by an increase in A itself or by an increase in the "velocity of circulation of (durable) goods" as analyzed by Arthur Marget in the 1930s.

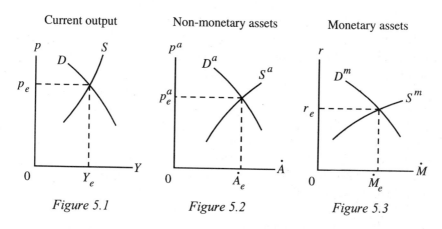

Current output	Non-monetary assets	Monetary assets

Figure 5.1   Figure 5.2   Figure 5.3

The right-hand panel (Figure 5.3) relates in the same way to demand and supply (D^m, S^m) for increments or decrements $\dot{M}$ in the real money holdings M of individuals and firms. These demand and supply curves are drawn as functions of the real rate of interest r. The remainder of the analysis in the preceding paragraph applies here as well, *mutatis mutandis*.

A triplet of equilibrium prices (p_e, p_e^a, r_e) satisfies Say's Law for all three segments simultaneously. Say's Identity, however, is always satisfied for the economy as a whole – for the sum of all three segments taken together – but not for any segment taken singularly. That is to say, excess demand or supply in any one or two segments must be balanced by excess supply or demand in the other segment or segments.

In the case of current output, which was of special concern to Say and his successors, we have this result: at the equilibrium price level p_e, Say's Law is satisfied on this segment regardless of conditions in the other two; at price levels above p_e, there is overproduction and underemployment in this segment, again regardless of conditions in the other two segments; at price levels below p_e, there is general scarcity or over-employment, still regardless of conditions in the asset or monetary segments of the economy.

We may begin a somewhat more dynamic analysis, beginning with a neighborhood-of-full-equilibrium like that indicated by Figures 5.1–5.3. Over time, any or all of the six functions shown on these diagrams can shift, but by Say's Identity, the sum of the demand-side shifts must balance the sum of the supply-side shifts, whether or not equilibrium is maintained in any segment. The sum of either set of shifts (demand or supply) need not, however, be zero. This is because an increase in demand for, say, current output, can be satisfied equally well by reduced demand for assets or by an increased supply of assets: in the first case, the sum of changes in both supply and demand equals zero; in the second case, both these changes are positive.

Turn now to Figures 5.4–5.6. The situation illustrated is a substantial upward shift (increase) in the demand for current output from D to D' on Figure 5.4. Because the shift is substantial, we indicate it by "++" below this figure. This increase must be balanced or "financed" some-how; "if wishes were horses, beggars would ride." The figure supposes the balance to come from increased supplies of both assets and money, indicated by supply-curve shifts and by "+" signs under both Figures 5.5 and 5.6.[7] The combined effect of these three shifts are increases in current output and also in both asset and money-market activity; a rise in the price level of current output is coupled with a decline in the price level of assets and also in the interest rate. This is one but only one possible path of a "natural recovery" from a recession, and the multiplicity of such paths exemplifies the difficulty of framing a business-cycle theory which will fit all cases, either historical or prospective.

---

[7] I work out classroom illustrations and results without numerical manipulations with the aid of only five signs (+, −, ++, −−, 0). The zero implies a mini-shift in either direction, not necessarily a complete constancy. I also present the signs in order (current output, then assets, then money), but this ordering is entirely arbitrary. Thus, for example, in "Black Octobers" like those in 1929 and 1987 in the United States, the configurations

$$D: 0, -, +; \qquad S: 0, +, -$$

represent early financial-crisis phenomena: shifts in demand from assets to money, and shifts in supply in the opposite direction, with demand and supply of current output not (yet) affected. (The diagrams show the accompanying fall in asset prices and rise in interest rates; this shorthand does not.)

Others may prefer to use numerical values for functional shifts. This is not difficult, if one assumes all shifts to be horizontally parallel ones.

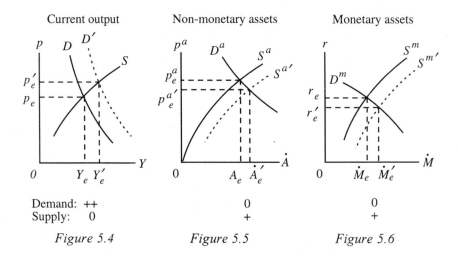

Current output	Non-monetary assets	Monetary assets
Demand: ++	0	0
Supply: 0	+	+
Figure 5.4	*Figure 5.5*	*Figure 5.6*

This procedure counteracts, taking advantage of Say's Identity, an unfortunate tendency of "demand-side" macroeconomic models to omit any explicit indication of the supply-side accompaniments of shifts in public or private demand, especially in demand for current output. The same is true for the equally unfortunate tendency of "supply-side" and "real-disturbance" models to omit adequate consideration of the demand side or to answer the question, "where demand is supposed to come from," especially demand for current output once again.

Our procedure also makes explicit, as we have hinted already, the multiplicity of alternative sources of "cyclical" downturns and upturns, both from "natural" (non-governmental) and "artificial" (public policy) causes.[8] For example, a "natural" recovery from recession or depression may come about from increased demand D for current output, representing replacement of depreciated or obsolete stocks of consumers' capital, industrial equipment, and inventories. In earlier times, there would also occur a rightward shift, or increase, in aggregate supply S, representing falling costs, increased productivity, and technical progress. More important on the current scene seems to be the financing of increased demand by "dishoarding" of money (decrease in D^m, increase in S^m) supplemented by reduction in S^a as the volume of "old" debt instruments is reduced or canceled by repayments, write-downs, and bankruptcies. In

---

[8] Treatments of plateaus of "new era" prosperity, and likewise treatments of sloughs of deflation or stagflation, are considerably simpler. In permanent prosperity, our six basic functions all shift to the right, approximately in tandem. In permanent depression and capitalist crisis, the shifts are to the left.

the notation of Figures 5.4–5.6 and note 7, we might now expect eventually (but not necessarily before the next election!)

$$D: +, 0, -; \qquad S: 0, -, +,$$

whereas the earlier recovery pattern seems to have been

$$D: +, 0, 0; \qquad S: +, -, + .$$

The mechanism of an "artificial" recovery, sparked by monetary and fiscal expansion and with increased demand coming primarily from public civil or military spending, is quite different. Such policies raise input prices and profit margins, tending to reduce S by inflationary pressure. In our symbols:

$$D: +, 0, 0; \qquad S: -, +, + .$$

Manipulations like these may persuade both students and intelligent laymen of the multiplicity of possible causes for any given outcome, and therefore of the difficulty of framing simple "cycle" theories to fill all realistic sequences of prosperity and depression, or if you prefer, of crisis and recovery.

But one may well ask, what of disequilibrium cases, where Say's Law does not apply in one or more segments of the economy? After all, the economy is not a kangaroo, leaping more or less automatically (even if sometimes painfully) from one equilibrium position to another! In such cases I personally argue, in what may seem the remote and unsuitable subjects of American and Japanese economic history, that holding the input and output prices of current production above their equilibrium levels – p_e in Figures 5.1 and 5.4 – has operated to hold aggregate income below its equilibrium value Y_e and thus delay "natural" recovery processes in most or all American recessions and depressions since 1929. (Prior to that date, the principal factor prolonging depressions had been, I should suggest, the "perverse" shift-elasticity of the money supply, M^s, which moved to the left during depressions when recovery would have been accelerated by a shift to the right.) Between recessions or depressions, at the same time, the perverse shift-elasticity of S^m was prolonging and exaggerating intervals of boom.[9]

Applications of our procedure are not limited to the theory and history of business fluctuations. In the remaining paragraphs of this section we may consider two other applications. The first (example 1) is the relation between the growth and proliferation of asset markets and the rate of

[9] Unfortunately, no leading industrial country seems to have combined price-level flexibility with "benign" shifts in its S^m function in any period since the Napoleonic Wars.

physical capital formation. (Do people speculate on existing stocks and shares and real estate when they "should" be investing in the current output of capital instruments?) The second illustration (example 2) is about the result of massive income redistribution in favor of "the poor" or "the working class" and assumes the two categories are not only overlapping but largely identical. (Does such redistribution increase aggregate demand for current output, and if so, with what reactions on other markets?)

Example 1

This is a hoary problem, with which I became acquainted from sampling German-language literature of the 1920s, despite the deficiencies of my school German. If there were (almost) no asset markets in the sense of the present paper, as may be the case in some Third World countries, would wealthy or ambitious savers invest instead of speculating? And would their investments not increase the output of capital goods, and therefore the rapidity of growth in general, including, in the 1920s, the speed of continental European recovery from World War I? It all depends, the apparatus suggests, upon the directions and complementarities of shifts in our hexagonal set of aggregate functions, with Say's Identity looming in the background. What is proposed is in our terms a drastic leftward shift of the D^a function. And what is considered the most "natural" result in "normal" times is a corresponding rightward shift in the D function, with the increment consisting largely of capital instruments and possibly of human capital as well. To me, however, three likely alternatives might have included capital export overseas, luxury consumption and the "hoarding" of money (rightward shift of D^m, following the end of German hyperinflation in 1923). Possible results of the last alternative in particular might have included an undesired run-up of interest rates and a condition we have later learned to call a "credit crunch."

Example 2

This is an even hoarier problem, dating back to Ricardian Socialist precursors of Karl Marx, if not to the British Lollards, Diggers, and Levellers. What would be the economic effect of massive income redistribution from people who, we suppose, spend much of their incomes for assets and cash balances to others who, we also suppose, spend nearly all their incomes on the current output of consumption goods?[10] To simplify our problem somewhat, let us assume that the supply function S for current output is horizontal (perfectly elastic with respect to the price level) and also that it does not shift upward (meaning that higher labor incomes are paid out of gross profits and that the "incidence of collective bargaining" is entirely on "capitalists"). If we accept these "leftist" assumptions, the effects of redistribution become deceptively clear. The national income Y rises without inflation; asset prices fall, and so does the rate of interest. But the realism of these key assumptions is unfortunately open to doubt.

INTERNATIONAL DIMENSIONS

Even in the isolated domestic economy, there is nothing sacred about any three-sector or n-sector partition of the economy. The partition I have used in this essay is no exception. (In the algebraic discussion mentioned in note 5, I used a five-sector partitioning.) In addition, each of our three sectors might – possibly *should* – have been further subdivided. For example, the quantum of current-account exports and imports of goods and services might have been treated separately from purely domestic production. Expansions and contractions of the foreign holdings of home residents, and of domestic asset holdings by foreigners, might also have received separate treatment, in the cases of both non-monetary and monetary assets.

And even in so simplified and expository a treatment as this one, the several prices and price indices considered should perhaps have included several exchange rates as an aspect of attention to the rest of the world. But we propose the simplifying convention of considering only a single foreign country as representing the rest of the world, and therefore of collapsing the spectrum of exchange rates into a single variable p^x. If X is the foreign-currency value of foreign assets held by home residents, less the home-currency value of domestic assets held by foreigners, then $\dot{X}$ is the net exchange of X per period. We may use D^x, S^x) to represent demand and supply $\dot{X}$. The subscript 1 indicates demand or supply arising from import or export of goods and services on current account. The subscript 2 indicates demand or supply arising from net accumulation or decumulation of foreign assets capital account, i.e., capital export or import. The back-to-back diagram of Figure 5.7 is illustrative.

[10] Compare Bronfenbrenner (1971, ch. 5).

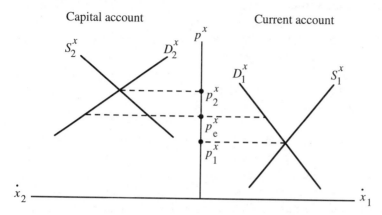

Figure 5.7   Capital and current accounts

Figure 5.7 is designed to indicate exchange-rate determination in a regime including both international trade and capital movements. The right-hand side (subscript 1) shows the demand and supply of foreign exchange on current account only. The exchange rate p_1^x, which would result in the absence of asset transactions, is a purchasing power parity rate, although determined only by the prices of internationally traded goods and services to the exclusion of non-trade or "sheltered" ones.[11]

The left-hand side of Figure 5.7 (subscript 2) shows the demand and supply of foreign exchange from capital buildup and in terms of changed net holdings of foreign assets. (The supply and demand curves of the two sides are treated as mutually independent, an admitted oversimplification.) The exchange rate p_2^x is the one which would result in the absence of current-account transactions. It is sometimes called a rate-of-return or interest parity exchange rate, and is normally different from p_1^x. The purchasing power parity rate is higher for capital-importing countries with negative, passive or "unfavorable" current-account balances, and vice versa.

Combining the two panels of Figure 5.7, which combine the trade and capital markets for foreign exchange, we obtain an overall equilibrium exchange rate, p_e^x, intermediate between the other rates considered. The case illustrated in Figure 5.7 is based on the Japanese-American one of the mid-1980s as seen from Japan, with p_x the number of yen per dollar.

---

[11] The concept of "shelter" from international trade becomes problematic when important suppliers or customers of a non-traded good or service are themselves in international competition.

The equilibrium yen-dollar rate was approximately ¥225, at which an excess supply of dollars on current account represents the Japanese export surplus for goods and services. The balancing excess demand for dollars on capital account represents net capital exports from Japan to the United States. The purchasing power parity rate might have been as low as ¥100 and the interest parity rate as high as ¥300, reflecting the high American interest rates of that period as well as the low Japanese ones.

What are the implications of this procedure with respect to Say's Law and Say's Identity? We have separated out the "international" parts of relationships like those of Figures 5.1–5.2 and 5.4–5.5; at the same time, we have combined them with similar relationships for the rest of the world. The equilibrium exchange rate is one factor in all-round equilibrium in both countries, but it does not require such equilibrium in the current-output markets of either country.

A higher exchange rate than p_e^x would overvalue foreign currency and therefore undervalue domestic money, and vice versa for a lower exchange rate than p_e^x. Say's Law is then invalid for the "international" segments of each economy, but may remain valid for the crucial "current output" segment. Say's Identity continues valid for any exchange rate whatever, if its domain is further extended to include international trade and investment. This extension is combined with redefinition of the domestic segments, both current output and assets, to exclude international transactions.

CONCLUSION

Expansions and extensions of Say's Law are also denials of the law in its original form, which applies only to the market for current output in a single country; this is especially true if Say's Law is identified with Say's Identity. At the same time, the purpose of these expansions and extensions is positive and favorable to Say's Law. They imply that there exists some set of extensions and expansions which may restore some part of its pristine glory, and possibly even render some forms of Say's Identity both true and useful.

This essay is written in such a "compromise" tradition. The extensions follow in the footsteps of Oscar Lange's allowance for domestic money, interpreted as demand and supply for changes in money holdings. The analysis also attempts to allow for changes in the holdings of existing non-monetary assets, and to introduce both current and capital balances of countries' international accounts into the picture. And since the writer is (in old age) more of an economics teacher – still at too abstract a level for public enlightenment – than an original economic thinker, this essay seeks quite deliberately an undergraduate-level exposition, accepting but not welcoming accompanying lapses of both logical rigor and technical fireworks.

REFERENCES

Bronfenbrenner, Martin (1971) *Income Distribution Theory*, ch. 5, Aldine, New York, NY.

Bronfenbrenner, Martin (1991) "Say's Law, Walras' Law, and the International Balances" *Shogaku Ronso* (Fukushima University, Japan), vol. 59, no. 3, March, pp. 3–14.

Lange, Oscar (1944) *Price Flexibility and Employment,* Bloomington, IN.

Schumpeter, Joseph (1954) *History of Economic Analysis,* pp. 617–19, Oxford University Press, New York, NY.

Sowell, Thomas (1972) *Say's Law: An Historical Analysis,* Princeton University Press, Princeton, NJ.

6. Why Do Agents Hold Money, and Why Does It Matter?

David Laidler*

SOME PRELIMINARIES

Let me begin this paper with a confession of academic incorrectness, followed by a plea of mitigating circumstances based on unoriginal methodological considerations, neither of which will disturb Thomas Mayer in the least.[1] The confession: I attach less importance than do most monetary economists to that latest manifestation of methodological individualism, namely 'sound microeconomic foundations' for monetary theory. I am not against deducing conclusions about macroeconomic phenomena from the maximization postulate; and I would treat with extreme scepticism any macroeconomic hypothesis that could be shown to be inconsistent with economic rationality. Even so, maximizing premises are not the be all and end all of economics. They are a commonly used and often useful starting point for generating testable hypotheses, but they are not the only valid starting point.

It is testability, and success or failure when tested, that matter for an economic hypothesis, not its conformity or lack thereof to 'first principles'. For the sake of argument, entertain the possibility that there do indeed exist first principles of economic analysis guaranteed to yield true conclusions about all the phenomena that might interest us, but allow that knowledge of them has not been genetically programmed into us. Suppose also that, by some happy chance, we had nevertheless stumbled upon them. How would we know this? The short answer is that we wouldn't, and couldn't. No matter how many times our predictions succeeded, it would always be possible that they would go wrong tomorrow. We are simply not able to distinguish between ultimate

---

* I am grateful to Fernando Mendez for stimulating conversations on the topic of this paper.

[1] See Mayer (1993) for an eloquent and even-tempered defence of essentially the same position as I take here.

scientific success and a situation in which a set of flawed theories just happen to be helping us to get things right for the time being. That being so, it is appropriate always to allow for the chance that the second possibility is the case, to treat our hypotheses with a touch of scepticism, and keep on comparing them to new data as and when these are generated.

This view of things does not rule out the use of micro-foundations to generate hypotheses. It does, however, require us to take seriously hypotheses generated by other means, including creative conjecture (sometimes called ad hoc guesswork by those discomfited by the means in question), and it also prevents those who derive their hypotheses from micro-foundations claiming that they are, by virtue of having done so, exempt from the discipline of empirical testing. It should also go without saying that a methodological principle whose very foundation is the proposition that, even if we have the truth, we can never know that we have it, offers no guarantee of scientific progress. The best that it offers is the prospect of weeding out a few errors.

THE DEMAND FOR MONEY

The untidy attitude towards generating economic understanding which I have just sketched out underlay the large body of empirical work on the aggregate demand for money function which the 1960s and 1970s produced. Though such work ceased to be fashionable with the rise of new classical economics and its preoccupation with the deep parameters which allegedly define an economy's underlying structure, it did not come to a halt. Indeed it continued to make modest advances, and those advances cast considerable doubt upon the soundness of the micro-foundations which were simultaneously being touted as the *sine qua non* of respectable macroeconomics.

Modern empirical work on the demand for money started in earnest with Milton Friedman's (1956, 1959) papers. Friedman changed the question people usually asked about the subject. Instead of 'Why do agents hold money?', the issues became 'What variables affect the demand for money, and are the parameters of the function stable over time?' Instead of a priori reasoning – 'money is a means of exchange, and therefore it bears a stable relationship to nominal income' or 'money is a liquid asset, and therefore its demand is highly interest-sensitive and sometimes unstable' – the preferred investigative tools became statistical.

The micro-theoretic foundations of Friedman's work were reduced to a bare minimum. The demand for real money balances was modelled 'as if' it were demand for a consumer durable good whose services as 'a temporary abode of purchasing power' yielded a stream of utility to the agents holding it. That was enough to suggest that a constraint variable (wealth measured in some way) and one or more opportunity cost variables (real interest rates and expected inflation) belonged in the demand for money function. To go further was, in the words of one commentator, 'like analysing the "ice cube" and "cold milk" motives for owning a refrigerator' (Laidler, 1969, p. 57, fn.). Whatever one may think of such casual theorizing – and there is no sin against sound micro-foundations more grave than putting money in the utility function – from the point of view of enabling empirical questions to be formulated, it was well up to the task. What we would now term the 'long-run' empirical relationship that emerged from Friedman's own work and those papers which were an immediate response to it (e.g., Meltzer, 1963; Laidler, 1966) has, as Lucas (1988) showed, held up remarkably well in the face of a quarter century of new data.

Friedman's work did not put an end to questions about why agents hold money, but it did change the way in which the questions were addressed. Once we had, as it were, a benchmark demand for money function, we could ask whether the analysis of specific motives for holding money enabled us to formulate alternative, perhaps more precise, versions of the relationship with better empirical characteristics. That was surely a large step forward from the a priori speculation about the empirical nature of the demand for money function that had, up till then, dominated the textbooks – the 'classical' range and the 'Keynesian' range of the relationship, the liquidity trap, and all that. In rather short order, the liquidity trap hypothesis was tested and found wanting (Bronfenbrenner and Mayer, 1960; Laidler, 1966). It was also noted that a pure asset demand for money was difficult to reconcile with large holdings of non-interest bearing cash and demand deposits which were rate of return dominated by such essentially risk-free assets as, for example, savings and loan association shares.[2]

At the end of the 1960s it seemed that those hypotheses about the nature of the demand for money function which were to be had from explicit analysis of the motives which might affect money holding were either wrong in the case of the speculative motive, or essentially

---

[2] And these results have, in my view, held up. For a discussion see the 1993 edition of Laidler, 1969, pp. 150–2, henceforth referred to as Laidler (1969/93).

indistinguishable from Friedman's general postulates in the case of transactions and precautionary motives. Patinkin (1965, ch. V) had demonstrated that one could derive a money-in-the-utility-function model from a precautionary demand model. For such reasons I argued (Laidler, 1969, p. 112) that explicit analysis of the motives prompting the holding of money had 'not produced a model of the demand for money that has made any correct predictions which were not also made on the basis of a simpler approach treating the demand for money in the same way as the demand for any other durable good might be treated.' I am relieved to report that I explicitly labelled this conclusion 'tentative' (p. 113), because it was, with benefit of hindsight, almost surely wrong.

The mid-1970s saw the collapse of most economists' faith in the stability of the demand for money function. I have argued at length (Laidler, 1969/93, pp. 172–5) that this collapse was overdone, just as the previous wave of enthusiasm for the relationship had also been overdone. Suffice it here to note that new empirical techniques based on co-integration analysis, with a little help from taking explicit account of institutional change, have largely rehabilitated the long-run demand for money function. The apparent demise of the relationship nevertheless helped to create an intellectual vacuum in monetary economics which was quickly filled by new classical analysis; however, the work on the demand for money function which continued not only rehabilitated old empirical results, but refined them too. In the process, it also provided a good deal of evidence consistent with the view that money is held because it is a means of exchange.

The well-known Baumol-Tobin inventory-theoretic model of the transactions demand for money (Baumol, 1952; Tobin, 1956) antedates and was widely discussed in the empirical literature on the demand for money to which I have referred above. There was a good deal of scepticism about its empirical value, some of it well based, and some of it not. Perhaps the most compelling argument against the model in question hinges on the fact that it has agents receiving income in money at the beginning of some period, and exhausting that income by the period's end. Even if agents never found it worthwhile to convert cash into bonds and then back again at sub-intervals within the income period, the Baumol-Tobin analysis makes it hard to see why an agent receiving income monthly would ever hold more than 2 weeks' income in the form of cash. And yet the United States economy currently holds close to 2 months' income in M1 balances and well over 6 months' income in M2 balances. It is hard to sustain claims, such as that recently made by Mankiw (1992), that this is still the best available model of the demand for money in the face of evidence like this.

But it was not just, or even mainly, this fact that led to doubts about the empirical validity of this model. It was rather that the economies of scale in money holding that the model was widely believed to predict seemed to fly in the face of Friedman's evidence that the permanent income elasticity of demand for real money balances was well above unity. Here, as it turned out, we were on much more shaky ground, both empirically and theoretically. To begin with, Friedman's initial estimate turned out to be biased upward. When a proper role was accorded to the interest rate in the relationship, the income elasticity fell to about unity (Meltzer, 1963; Laidler, 1966). And when allowance was made for the spread of monetary exchange, particularly in the economies of the late nineteenth century, the elasticity estimate in question was pushed down yet again (e.g., Bordo and Jonung, 1987).

Furthermore, as Brunner and Meltzer (1967) pointed out, the famous 'square root rule' for the demand for money in fact only arises as a limiting special case in the Baumol-Tobin model. Its general prediction for the income elasticity of demand for money is between 0.5 and 1.0. Thus, though it predicts economies of scale except at the upper limit, these need not be particularly pronounced. And to this we may add an observation which originated with Joel Fried (1973): first, the 'brokerage fee' variable which appears in the Baumol-Tobin model is plausibly interpreted as a time and trouble variable for which the real wage, as a measure of the value of time, would be a natural proxy; second, in time-series data, real income (or permanent income, or wealth) is positively correlated with the real wage. Fried concluded that if the real wage were omitted from a time-series regression, then the income-elasticity estimate yielded by that regression would be upward biased.

Now none of this would matter very much if the Baumol-Tobin model were the only one which focused on money's means of exchange role, the only one which predicted that there should be economies of scale in money holding, and the only one which suggested that some real wage measure of the value of time might belong in the function. As I have already noted, agents hold far too much money for this model to be true. But the model in question is in fact representative of a far broader class whose members make the same predictions about economies of scale and the value of time without placing unrealistic upper limits on the size of money holdings. Thus, precautionary demand models, which hark back to Edgeworth (1887) and Wicksell (1898), can easily find room for brokerage fees and also predict economies of scale; while more general 'value of time' models (McCallum and Goodfriend, 1987; Dowd, 1990), though they are not explicit about economies of scale, naturally lead to the inclusion of a wage rate variable in the function. They do, when all is said and done, start from the premise that to hold real balances enables agents to economize on time spent transacting and hence to devote more of it to either work or leisure.

By now the role of wage rates in the demand for money function has been investigated in a number of studies (see Laidler, 1969/93, pp. 168 for references), and it is a fair generalization to say that where their influence has been tested for, it has been found to be statistically significant. Unless this result is a product of publication biases (in the sense that negative evidence on this phenomenon has not been written up, or if written up has failed to find an outlet), it shows that explicit analysis of money's means of exchange role has enabled us to single out an extra variable for inclusion in the demand for money function, a variable that Friedman's approach led us to overlook.[3]

To this we may add another consideration, so obvious once it is pointed out that its neglect must be a cause of some embarrassment. There are, as Faig (1989) and Sumner (1990) have recently noted, well-established seasonal variations in the demand for money, associated with Christmas in particular. It is hard to see how this could be unrelated to the seasonal surge in retail transactions, and hence to money's means of exchange function. And the fact that there were well-documented seasonal fluctuations in the demand for currency in the nineteenth century associated with the harvest (see Jevons, 1866; Sprague, 1910) points in exactly the same direction.

In short, my 1969 conclusion about the empirical fruitfulness of analysing the motives for holding money was probably wrong. It does after all seem worthwhile to analyse the demand for money as a demand for a means of exchange. To do so enables us to make predictions which we would not otherwise have made, and a number of these do have

---

[3] The fact that demand functions in the tradition of Friedman's and Meltzer's work continue to hold up in tests such as those of Lucas (1988), even though they omit a real wage variable, surely stems from the close correlation between this variable and permanent-income and wealth variables in long runs of time-series data.

empirical content.[4] The relevance of this conclusion in the context of theorizing about the demand for money is obvious enough, but as I shall now go on to argue, it is potentially relevant in a broader context too. It suggests that those who attach high value to micro-foundations have been looking for them in the wrong place when they have turned to Walrasian general equilibrium analysis.

MONEY AND MICRO-FOUNDATIONS

It is instructive to consider the properties of the two most widely used methods of introducing money into the economic models which currently dominate the 'micro-foundations' tradition, namely to resort to an overlapping generations framework or to impose a 'cash in advance' constraint on an otherwise Walrasian economy.

The former approach involves modelling the demand for money as the demand for a pure store of value, and it should not therefore be surprising that it yields some predictions that look remarkably like those of Keynes's model of the speculative demand for money. If money is a store of value pure and simple, then it is almost by definition a close, and in some cases perfect, substitute for other assets that perform the same function. Hence, if money is dominated in rate of return, it will not be held. But empirical evidence, even of the most casual kind, makes it hard to take this prediction seriously. Defenders of this approach are aware of the problem and therefore resort to stories about money's 'backing' (i.e., its prospect of being redeemed in the form of utility-yielding goods or direct claims thereon at some time in the future) or about 'legal restrictions' that force agents to hold rate of return dominated cash.

The key prediction of the 'backing' hypothesis, as developed, say, by Bruce Smith (1985), is that the demand for money will be highly elastic with respect to the expected opportunity cost of holding it, so that changes in the nominal quantity of well-backed money will be absorbed in cash balances rather than affect the price level. This prediction is hard

---

[4] In Laidler (1990, pp. 13, 21, 47–8) I have argued that a precautionary approach to modelling the demand for money predicts that there are externalities in money holding: if agent A holds more cash, he is more likely to be able to pay a debt when called upon to do so; therefore his creditors, B, C, etc. need to hold less money to achieve a given degree of security. This argument implies that the cross-section permanent-income elasticity of demand for money should exceed the time-series elasticity. This prediction remains to be tested, though the results of Mulligan and Sala-i-Martin (1992), showing an unusually high income elasticity of demand for money arising from cross-section estimates on data drawn from US states, are intriguing.

to reconcile with an enormous body of evidence about the rather low interest elasticity of demand for money found in modern economies, not to mention the absence of a liquidity trap. More to the point, the evidence which Smith produces to suggest that the hypothesis had content in eighteenth century North America has been severely, and in my view convincingly, criticized by Michener (1987) and McCallum (1992) for neglecting the presence of components other than colonial government paper in the money supplies of the economies studied.

As to 'legal restrictions', these are and often have been in place, and undoubtedly affect the demand for money. It is uncontroversial that many of the institutional changes which have underlain recent disturbances to empirical demand for money functions have been direct and obvious consequences of changes in the regulatory environment.[5] But this observation stops far short of supporting the claim that legal restrictions per se explain the very existence of a demand for money. As Carl Menger (1892) noted long ago, legal tender laws and the like have usually been introduced in order to codify already existing customs in the monetary sector, rather than to establish new and previously non-existent norms of behaviour. Neil Wallace (1988) was surely right, therefore, when he characterized the legal restrictions idea as a means of 'oversimplifying the theory of money'.

What then, of the cash in advance constraint? It is much used by the exponents of 'sound micro-foundations', yet these same exponents offer no micro-foundations for it. Rather they treat it as a convenient but admittedly ad hoc device that enables them to get on with their monetary economics. They are right to do so, and, as should already be apparent, I do not think that this alone should be grounds for condemnation. The trouble is empirical: the constraint yields what amounts to the degenerate special case of the Baumol-Tobin model discussed above, a case in which agents receive income in cash and then spend it, without resort to trips to the bank in the interim; and actual money holdings are far too large to be explained by it. If one is going to abandon explicit micro-foundations in order to get money into one's model, why stop with the cash in advance constraint when the literature is full of empirically more satisfactory models which are, at least, no less ad hoc?

It must certainly be admitted that models of the demand for money, based upon explicit consideration of its means of exchange role, cannot be reconciled with a strict application of the tenets of methodological individualism as they are conventionally applied in economics. These

---

[5] See Laidler (1969/93, pp. 174–5 and 186–7) for discussion of this point.

tenets would have us start with the economy's primitive characteristics (the tastes of individuals, their endowments and available technology) and proceed from there, by way of the maximizing choices of the individuals in question to predictions about market outcomes when those individuals interact in accordance with well-defined rules of market behaviour. If these injunctions are taken seriously, it simply will not do to put money in the utility function, either directly, or indirectly as a creator of time. This can be seen most clearly by considering that special-case economy inhabited by Robinson Crusoe.

One might put all manner of arguments into Crusoe's utility function, but a means of exchange would not be one of them. Nor would the appearance of Man Friday change matters. As we all know, it takes at least three agents and three goods before it becomes physically possible to move away from barter. Monetary exchange itself imbues money in value-of-time models with the capacity to generate utility. And monetary exchange is an inherently social phenomenon. If we model the demand for money in this way, we must presume that a market experiment is already in progress before we analyse the individual experiment. That individual experiment cannot be treated as having logical priority.

Something must give way: either that body of theorizing about the demand for money which has kept reasonably close contact with empirical evidence and leads us to conclude that the demand for money stems from its means of exchange role, or some rather widely held notions of what constitutes sound theoretical procedure. Obviously, I would opt for giving up the latter. To argue that some social phenomena cannot be reduced to the behaviour of individuals, but also seem to derive from relationships among individuals, might disturb those who believe that scientific knowledge must be derived from a set of true and strictly individualistic first principles, but it is an innocuous position to take for someone who is content to believe that our most primitive premises can never be more than a set of tentative working hypotheses that are always likely to be superseded. In short, if methodological individualism does not permit us to cope with monetary phenomena, then so much the worse for methodological individualism.

From this point of view, much of the fuss that is made about the impropriety of putting money in the utility function seems to arise from looking for the micro-foundations of the demand for money in the wrong place. If we are permitted to treat the 'rules of the market game' as a starting point for economic theorizing, and monetary exchange, like property rights, as a component of those 'rules', then it makes perfectly good sense to think of agents receiving a flow of services from the asset which permits them to participate in an already ongoing market game.

It is worth noting that economic theorists have not entirely neglected questions about the origins of monetary exchange. Menger (1892), Brunner and Meltzer (1971), Jones (1976) and Kiyotaki and Wright (1993), among others, have all provided analyses, characterized by varying degrees of mathematical rigour, of why monetary exchange exists, and how it might evolve. The fact that the end-point of such analysis (typically the emergence of some pre-existing commodity as the economy's means of exchange) stops short of enabling us to move on directly to deal with the more traditional questions addressed by monetary theory (the determination of the price level, the influence of monetary policy on output and employment, etc.) tells us not that it is unhelpful, or that the models which do enable us to deal with these issues are inherently and fatally flawed, but only that there currently exists a gap in the body of knowledge that we call monetary theory.

MONEY AS A BUFFER STOCK

In the last few pages, I have argued that the models of the demand for money which emphasize its means of exchange function, and sometimes take the short-cut of placing real balances in the utility function, are not quite as devoid of theoretical foundations as is sometimes suggested. If we do not insist on deriving *everything* from the analysis of the maximizing individual, if we are willing instead to treat the facts of monetary exchange as standing in the same logical relationship to individual behaviour as those characterizing the structure of property rights, that is as describing the pre-existing rules of the market game which we are analysing, then the 'value of time' approach does provide an intellectually respectable basis for theorizing about the demand for money, and, as I have already argued, an empirically fruitful basis too.

Indeed, I would go further than this. The approach in question, and particularly that variation of it that stresses precautionary behaviour, also yields new insights about monetary analysis which have both theoretical and empirical implications. I have written about these matters elsewhere (e.g., Laidler, 1990, chs 1 and 3), under the label 'Buffer Stock Approach'.[6] It will suffice therefore to summarize these insights

[6] I do not claim to have originated the 'buffer stock' terminology. The earliest usage of which I am aware is that of Friedman and Schwartz (1963).

here, while highlighting their subversive implications for much recent macroeconomic analysis.

To begin with, if it really is the case that the demand for real money balances which we observe in any actual economy has a strong precautionary element to it, then this has immediate implications for the way in which we treat both expectations formation and price flexibility. For the last two decades, the advocates of sound microeconomic foundations for macroeconomics have usually insisted upon modelling agents' behaviour on the assumption that they make 'full' use of 'all available' information in formulating their market strategies. They have also – albeit with less insistence lately – preferred to model the macroeconomy 'as if' markets are continuously cleared by flexible nominal prices. In each case, the relevant postulate has been defended as the only one consistent with basic maximizing assumptions. A moment's consideration, however, of a typical precautionary demand for money model leads one to suspect that this need not be the case, because both nominal price stickiness and expectations that, while 'sensible', fall short of being 'rational', can be compatible with maximizing behaviour.

To generate a precautionary demand for money on the part of the individual agent, one must begin by postulating some random element in the pattern of payments and receipts. Money is then held as a buffer against such fluctuations, in order to reduce the costs that they impose. The point is, though, that the degree of randomness in this pattern is usually under the agent's control to some extent. Resources can be devoted to gathering and processing information – to forming expectations – and in the case of a price-setting agent, to responding to that information by altering prices in order to influence flows of revenue and expenditure. But if data processing is subject to rising marginal cost, if it is costly to vary prices, and, crucially, if holding precautionary balances reduces the costs of encountering imbalances in payments and receipts, then a maximizing agent will balance these costs on the margin. It is thus possible that, in an economy where monetary exchange is one of the 'rules of the market game', this very fact might give rise not just to precautionary inventories of cash, but also to nominal price stickiness and less-than-rational expectations.

This possibility is surely intriguing. It is now 10 years since Boschen and Grossman (1982) showed that contemporaneously observable changes in the money supply seemed to have systematic consequences for real variables. It is hard to reconcile this observation with the idea that agents make full use of all available information and operate in markets where prices are free to vary in response to new data as and when they appear. But if maximizing agents do not use all available information, and do not continuously adjust nominal prices, because it is uneconomic to do so, there is nothing here to puzzle us, and certainly nothing that should make us despair of the predictive power of the basic postulate of maximizing behaviour.[7]

This particular insight, namely that rigidities of prices and expectations are not necessarily signs of irrationality on the part of agents, is also valuable in another area of applied macroeconomic analysis, namely that which goes under the label 'the short-run demand for money function'. It is beyond question that theorizing of the type described in the second section of this paper, though it has a great deal of empirical content, still leaves much to be explained. The theory yields a 'long-run' relationship. When this relationship is confronted with time-series data, it generates complex patterns of serial correlation that vary from sample to sample. To cope with them requires the skilful deployment of some sort of distributed lags.

Laidler (1982, ch. 2) and Lane (1990) have shown, however, that the most usually advanced economic rationalization of such distributed lags, namely the existence of private portfolio adjustment costs that create a distinct and essentially Marshallian 'short-run' demand function, is not satisfactory in the presence of price flexibility. Such flexibility enables the market to adjust real balances to a new equilibrium value without individual agents ever encountering adjustment costs, and its existence would ensure that the economy is always on its long-run demand for money function. In that case, unless we have the wrong long-run model of the demand for money, we will not encounter serially correlated residuals.

On the other hand, price stickiness and expectations which, though 'sensible', nevertheless are sometimes systematically in error, can easily be deployed to generate a pattern of money holding that deviates systematically from that predicted by a correctly specified long-run demand for money function. However, if we interpret matters this way, we must be careful to note that the parameters which describe short-run fluctuations in money holding do not characterize structural characteristics of any demand for money function. Rather they appear to be unidentified quasi-

---

[7] In a review of Laidler (1990), Peter Hartley (1992) has suggested that we need not take Boschen and Grossman's results seriously, because the data upon which they are based may not represent the true variables to which new classical predictions apply. Testing data by comparing their characteristics with the predictions of theory seems to me to put things exactly the wrong way round!

reduced forms of the structure which links variations in the money supply
to the arguments of the long-run demand for money function, of what is
generally described as the transmission mechanism of monetary policy.

   Now a claim that the above interpretation of the evidence is well
established cannot be defended.[8] One of its earliest formulations, that of
Carr and Darby (1981), suggested that the so-called 'Goldfeld equation'
(see Goldfeld, 1973), which transformed the long-run demand for money
function into a short-run one by adding a lagged dependent variable, was
simply a price level adjustment equation in disguise. As MacKinnon and
Milbourne (1988) showed, this interpretation does not withstand careful
scrutiny. But other, more sophisticated formulations of the same 'buffer
stock' approach to the short-run dynamics of money holding behaviour
seem to be more robust.[9] This approach also helps to explain the
apparent instability of the demand for money function whose appearance
in the 1970s did so much to render unfashionable the work I have been
dealing with in this paper. Ought we not to expect a relationship which
describes the long and variable lag linking monetary changes to real
income and prices to display instability?

CONCLUSIONS

The title of this paper consists of two questions, and we are now in a
position to answer both of them. Why do agents hold money? – probably
because money is a means of exchange, and because holding a
precautionary stock of money enables agents to economize on the time
and trouble it takes to transact in markets. Why does it matter? –
because, if the foregoing answer turns out to be valid, first, it forces us
to confront the fact of monetary exchange as an alternative to the
Walrasian market as a means of co-ordinating economic activity;
second, it seems to undermine the methodological individualism upon
which the currently fashionable quest for 'sound' microeconomic
foundations for monetary economics is based; and third, it seems to
point us towards some interesting and potentially fruitful lines of
enquiry, both theoretical and empirical.

   [8] Once again, the reader is referred to Laidler (1969/93, pp. 175–8, 186–8) for further
discussion.
   [9] See, for example, the formulations of Cuthbertson and Taylor (e.g. 1990, which contains
extensive references to related work) or Davidson (1987).

REFERENCES

Baumol, W.J. (1952) 'The Transactions Demand for Cash: an Inventory Theoretic Approach' *Quarterly Journal of Economics*, 66, November, pp. 545–56.

Bordo, M. and Jonung, L. (1987) *The Long Run Behaviour of the Velocity of Circulation: The International Evidence*, Cambridge University Press, New York, NY.

Boschen, J. and Grossman, H.I. (1982) 'Tests of Equilibrium Macroeconomics using Contemporaneous Data' *Journal of Monetary Economics*, 10, pp. 309–33.

Bronfenbrenner, M. and Mayer, T. (1960) 'Liquidity Functions in the American Economy' *Econometrica*, 28, October, pp. 810–34.

Brunner, K. and Meltzer, A.H. (1967) 'Economies of Scale in Cash Balances Reconsidered' *Quarterly Journal of Economics*, 81, August, pp. 240–83.

Brunner, K. and Meltzer, A.H. (1971) 'The Uses of Money: Money in the Theory of an Exchange Economy' *American Economic Review*, 61, December, pp. 784–805.

Carr, J. and Darby, M. (1981) 'The Role of Money Supply Shocks in the Short-Run Demand for Money' *Journal of Monetary Economics*, 8, September, pp. 183–99.

Cuthbertson, K. and Taylor, M. (1990) 'Money Demand, Expectations and the Forward Looking Model' *Journal of Policy Modeling*, 12, Summer, pp. 289–316.

Davidson, J. (1987) 'Money Disequilibrium: Some Further Results with a Monetary Model of the U.K.' in Goodhart, C., Llewellyn, D. and Currie, D. (eds), *The Operation and Regulation of Financial Markets*, Macmillan, New York, NY.

Dowd, K. (1990) 'The Value of Time and the Transactions Demand for Money' *Journal of Money, Credit and Banking*, 22, February, pp. 51–64.

Edgeworth, F.Y. (1887) 'The Mathematical Theory of Banking' *Journal of the Royal Statistical Society*, 51, March, pp. 113–26.

Faig, M. (1989) 'Seasonal Fluctuations and the Demand for Money' *Quarterly Journal of Economics*, 104, November, pp. 847–61.

Fried, J. (1973) 'Money, Exchange and Growth' *Western Economic Journal,* 11, September, pp. 653–70.

Friedman, M. (1956) 'The Quantity Theory of Money – a Restatement' in *Studies in the Quantity Theory of Money*, pp. 3–21, University of Chicago Press, Chicago, IL.

Friedman, M. (1959) 'The Demand for Money – Some Theoretical and Empirical Results' *Journal of Political Economy*, 67, June, pp. 327–51.

Friedman, M. and Schwartz, A.J. (1963) 'Money and Business Cycles' in Friedman, M. (1969) *The Optimum Quantity of Money*, pp. 189–235, Macmillan, London.

Goldfeld, S.M. (1973) 'The Demand for Money Revisited' *Brookings Papers on Economic Activity*, 3, pp. 577–638.

Hartley, P.R. (1992) 'Review of D. Laidler: *Taking Money Seriously*' *Journal of Money, Credit and Banking*, 24, August, pp. 405–7.

Jevons, W.S. (1866) 'On the Frequent Autumnal Pressure on the Money Market and the Action of the Bank of England' reprinted in Foxwell, H.S. (ed.) (1884) *Investigations in Currency and Finance,* Macmillan, London.

Jones, R.A. (1976) 'The Origin and Development of Media of Exchange' *Journal of Political Economy*, 84, August, pp. 756–75.

Kiyotaki, N. and Wright, R. (1993) 'A Search-Theoretic Approach to Monetary Economics' *American Economic Review*, 93, March, pp. 63–77.

Laidler, D. (1966) 'The Rate of Interest and the Demand for Money – Some Empirical Evidence' *Journal of Political Economy*, 74, December, pp. 545–55.

Laidler, D. (1969) *The Demand for Money: Theories and Evidence*, International Textbook Company, Scranton, PA; 1993, 4th edn, Harper Collins, New York, NY.

Laidler, D. (1982) *Monetarist Perspectives*, Philip Allan, Oxford.

Laidler, D. (1990) *Taking Money Seriously*, Philip Allan, Hemel Hempstead.

Lane, T.D. (1990) 'Costly Portfolio Adjustment and the Demand for Money' *Economic Inquiry*, 28, July, pp. 466–87.

Lucas, R.E. Jr. (1988) 'Money Demand in the United States: a Quantitative Review' in Brunner, K. and McCallum, B.T. (eds), *Money, Cycles and Exchange Rates: Essays in Honour of Allan Meltzer*, Carnegie Rochester Conference Series, vol. 29, North Holland, Amsterdam.

MacKinnon, J.G. and Milbourne, R.D. (1988) 'Are Money Demand Equations Really Price Equations on Their Heads?' *Journal of Applied Econometrics*, 3, pp. 295–305.

Mankiw, G. (1992) 'Comment and Discussion' *Brookings Papers on Economic Activity*, 2, pp. 330–4.

Mayer, T. (1993) *Truth versus Precision in Economics*, Edward Elgar, Aldershot.

McCallum, B.T. (1992) 'Money and Prices in Colonial America: a New Test of Competing Theories' *Journal of Political Economy*, 100, February, pp. 143–61.

McCallum, B.T. and Goodfriend, M. (1987) 'Demand for Money – Theoretical Studies' in Eatwell, J., Millgate, M. and Newman, P. (eds), *The New Palgrave. A Dictionary of Economics,* Macmillan, London.

Meltzer, A.H. (1963) 'The Demand for Money: The Evidence from the Time Series' *Journal of Political Economy*, 71, June, pp. 219–46.

Menger, C. (1892) 'On the Origin of Money' *Economic Journal*, 2, June, pp. 239–55.

Michener, R. (1987) 'Fixed Exchange Rates and the Quantity Theory in Colonial America' in Brunner, K. and Meltzer, A.H. (eds), *Empirical Studies of Velocity, Real Exchange Rates, Unemployment and Productivity*, Carnegie Rochester Conference Series, vol. 27, North Holland, Amsterdam.

Mulligan, C.B. and Sala-i-Martin, X. (1992) 'U.S. Money Demand: Surprising Cross-Sectional Estimates' *Brookings Papers on Economic Activity*, 2, pp. 285–329.

Patinkin, D. (1965) *Money, Interest and Prices*, 2nd edn, Harper and Row, New York, NY.

Smith, B. (1985) 'Some Colonial Evidence on Two Theories of Money: Maryland and the Carolinas' *Journal of Political Economy*, 93, December, pp. 1178–1211.

Sprague, O. (1910) *A History of Crises under the National Banking System*, Government Printing Office, Washington, DC.

Sumner, M. (1990) 'Demand for Money in the U.K.: Breadth, Scale and Seasonality', University of Sussex (mimeo).

Tobin, J. (1956) 'The Interest Elasticity of Demand for the Transactions Demand for Cash' *Review of Economics and Statistics*, 38, August, pp. 241–7.

Wallace, N. (1988) 'A Suggestion for Oversimplifying the Theory of Money' *Conference Papers*, supplement to the *Economic Journal*, 98, March, pp. 25–36.

Wicksell, K. (1898) *Interest and Prices*, Tr. R.F. Kahn for the Royal Economic Society, Macmillan, London, 1936.

7. Money Supply Control: Base or Interest Rates?

C.A.E. Goodhart

A ANALYTICAL ANTECEDENTS TO THE COURSE OF THE MONEY SUPPLY CONTROL DEBATE

Commercial bankers have traditionally seen themselves as playing a passive role in the money supply process. Bankers argued that, in general, they only lent out money that had first been deposited with them. There were two major flaws in this argument. First, the loan made on the basis of cash initially deposited generally led to the funds being redeposited in another bank. Creation of deposits was restrained by the banks' need to keep reserves in the form of specie and/or central bank notes and deposits, in order to maintain the convertibility of their own liabilities into cash. Thus, *assuming* a constant desired deposit/reserve ratio (D/R), the initial injection of one unit of reserves into the banking system would, if there were no subsequent drains of such cash reserves from the system, lead to an ultimate multiple increase in deposits of D/R, in reserves of 1, and in other bank assets (e.g., loans) of $D/R - 1$.

Second, a banker could choose to behave in a more, or less, aggressive fashion, in particular by altering the bank's reserve/liquidity ratio. Many banking cycles and panics of the last two centuries have been ascribed to cycles of optimistic over-lending, followed by liquidity crises with bank runs, and subsequent retrenchment.

People use cash as well as commercial bank liabilities as money. Central banks in virtually all countries came to monopolize the provision of bank notes. Where this is not so (e.g., Scotland and Hong Kong), both the conditions of note issue and seigniorage are controlled by the monetary authorities. An expansion of the money supply leads to some increase in the non-bank public's demand for cash, a reduction in

101

reserves and further attenuation of the money multiplier. These factors are formalized in the famous monetary multiplier:

$$M = \frac{H(1 + C/D)}{(C/D + R/D)} \tag{7.1}$$

where M is the money stock, H is high-powered money (reserves and currency), C is currency in the hand of the public and D is commercial bank deposits.

If there are differing kinds of deposits, or financial intermediaries with differing reserve ratios, the multiplier formula can become complex and messy. Moreover, the cash drain is *not* the only drain of reserves from the banking system. In a monetary expansion, reserves may drain abroad, at least in an open economy with a fixed exchange rate. Similarly, if the monetary expansion leads the non-bank private sector to buy government debt or to incur higher taxes, cash will be transferred to the government. Such drains of cash reduce the high-powered money (H) available to the private sector.

Equation (7.1) is an identity, which must hold at all times.[1] One cannot quarrel with an identity. Analytical differences arise when, first, we ascribe a direction of causation to an identity which, of itself, implies no presumption of causation and, second, when we attempt to embed such an identity into a choice-theoretic analysis in which banks, the non-bank public and the monetary authorities try to maximize their utilities subject to market constraints.

In particular, in earlier descriptions of the money multiplier process, the banking system and the non-bank public react to an exogenous change in the high-powered money (H), which, in turn, drives changes in M. The influence of the banks and of the non-bank public appears limited to their choices of desired R/D and C/D ratios. But what happens if, for example, the public's demand for bank loans rises? There are two sides to a commercial bank's balance sheet; Why should the interest rate that equilibrates the money market, with the money supply equal to money demand, also equilibrate the demand for credit, bringing the demand and supply of loans into equilibrium?

Is it correct, in current institutional circumstances, to treat H as exogenously given? If not, then causation may run from M to H. If so, what determines M? What part, irrespective of the exogeneity of M or H,

---

[1] It can be obtained by a simple manipulation of the identities $M = C + D$ and $H = R + C$, which hold at all times. The equilibrium condition, however, is that R/D (actual) = R/D (desired) and C/D (actual) = C/D (desired).

do the behavioural decisions of the banks and non-bank public play in this? And what are the adjustments that ensure that the assets and liabilities of banks are both at their desired levels and that, simultaneously, the balance sheet identity is respected?

To start answering these questions, it may be helpful to give a shortened, simplified reprise of the historical regimes of money supply determination during the last 150 years.

B   AN HISTORICAL REPRISE

Under a specie standard, the monetary base consists primarily of the available stock of monetary gold or silver (ignoring distinctions between a full metallic standard, an exchange standard, a 'limping' standard, etc.). The central bank under a specie standard aims to maintain convertibility of local money into specie according to 'the rules of the game' (see Bloomfield, 1959). These rules were simple: the central bank should raise interest rates, when 'the Proportion' of metallic reserve to its own notes and deposits was falling, and vice versa. (For an account of the importance attached by the Bank of England to 'the Proportion' as a key indicator, see Beach, 1935; Goodhart, 1972; Dutton, 1984; Pippenger, 1984.)

Because of its strong and privileged position as the government's bank, the central bank was the last available source of liquid funds when other potential lenders were seeking to conserve their liquidity in a crisis. Following Bagehot (*Lombard Street*, 1873), the central bank also came to accept a duty for maintaining the stability of the banking system, determining to whom it would lend and on what terms.

Under the gold standard the causal relationships between H and M could be complex. There could be exogenous shocks in H driving M. There could be shocks to M (e.g., a reduction in the R/D ratio), which could affect H inversely, and/or shocks to M (e.g., via changes in the central bank's interest rate) which could bring about a positive change in H. Either way, the influence of the central bank on H was indirect: a central bank, under such a metallic standard, cannot create gold (or silver), but it can attract reserves by using its open market operations to adjust relative interest rates. Indeed, a central concern of central banks under the gold standard was to ensure their effective power to control interest rates (Sayers, 1936).

A further objective of the central bank was to help finance the government on acceptable, but non-inflationary, terms. During the decades of low government expenditures before World War I this objective was not much of a burden. During the World Wars and the immediate post-war years government finance became an overriding concern for virtually all European countries, though much less so for the USA.

The government financing identity implies that the growth of high-powered money depends on the size of the borrowing requirement (i.e., fiscal policy) and the extent to which this can be funded without recourse to the 'printing press' (i.e., funding policy). Facing *massive* government deficits, the central bank can hardly 'control' H. Rather, it adjusts interest rates and otherwise attempts to encourage the non-bank public to hold public sector debt directly in order to limit excessive growth in the monetary base and the money stock. In so far as the non-bank public did not absorb sufficient public sector debt, the banking system would provide residual finance. Central banks tried to ensure that bank funding of the public sector did not lead to an excessive buildup of bank liquidity and multiple expansion of loans and deposits. Central banks then used direct controls: first, banks were required to hold a large proportion of their assets in government paper; second, direct controls were placed on bank lending to the private sector, so banks had no alternative but to use excess funds to purchase government paper.

In so far as credit controls then effectively constrained bank lending, interest rates were largely influenced by three considerations: first, the need to keep long-term rates high enough to encourage public sector debt sales to the non-bank public; second, to keep short-term interest rates high enough to maintain the exchange rate; third, to keep interest rates low in order to finance the government deficit cheaply.

There was no attempt under such circumstances to vary interest rates as a means of influencing either the demand for money or the demand for bank loans. Nor, despite the money multiplier identity, would it be sensible to describe that system as one of monetary base control. Instead, the three main credit counterparts to a monetary expansion, viz. the budget deficit, public sector debt funding and bank lending to the private sector, were each influenced by three specific policies – fiscal policy, funding policy and credit control.

The subsequent abandonment of direct credit controls threw greater weight on the use of interest rates to control monetary expansion. At this stage it might have been possible, *in theory*, to have moved towards a true system of monetary base control, in which the authorities control the amount of available bank reserves, letting the market determine the level of interest rates. As we shall see, with a few possible exceptions, no central bank did so in practice. Instead, they sought to control the level of interest rates in order to affect the rate of monetary expansion indirectly.

As already noted, commercial banks were largely force-fed public sector debt during major wars and their immediate aftermaths. They therefore entered the 1950s with an 'excessive' holding of such debt. With the combination of low real interest rates, active funding policies and the relaxation of credit control then leading to the demand for money growing slower than private sector demand for credit, the banks ran down their portfolio of such Treasury bills and bonds to meet the excess loan demand, at the level of interest rates determined by the authorities.

This asset management mechanism could last only so long as the banks were prepared to allow their holdings of public sector debt to decline as a proportion of total assets. Once their holdings were reduced to the level where they were positively desired for their liquidity attributes, this buffering mechanism became exhausted. Commercial banks, starting in the USA in the mid-1960s, then turned to managed liabilities (i.e., to wholesale money market instruments, such as CDs and euro-deposits) to finance any excess of desired lending over the available inflow of retail deposits.

So long as monetary control was focused on a narrow aggregate like M1, consisting primarily of retail deposits with pegged own interest rates, e.g., pegged at zero for demand deposits (current accounts), liability management initially caused no additional control problems. Interest rates on alternative assets, including wholesale bank liabilities, could be raised by the central bank, causing substitution out of retail deposits and thereby allowing the growth of M1 to be reined back.

A combination of worsening inflation in the 1970s, deregulation and enhanced competition led to market-related interest rates being offered on an increasing range of retail deposit instruments. This led to major shifts in liquid asset holdings both within and between the somewhat arbitrary definitions of the various monetary aggregates. This posed a serious problem for monetary control using interest rates. The key variable within the demand function for money is no longer just r_{st} (the general level of short-term interest rates that the authorities can control); it is now $r_{st} - r_{bd}$ (the differential between the general level and the rates offered by banks on their various deposit liabilities). The authorities *cannot* control that differential. So long as there is sufficiently strong demand for bank loans by the private sector, the banks will go on bidding for funds to meet that demand. Consequently, the central bank must now use interest rates either directly to reduce the demand for loans, or indirectly to reduce nominal incomes and, *hence,* the demand for both loans and deposits, if it is to limit the rate of monetary expansion.

Both these routes are fraught with uncertainty. The demand for loans appears to be, in the UK at least, highly inelastic to changes in the general level of interest rates, perhaps because most such loans are on a variable rather than a fixed-rate basis. Instead, such demand appears to be more responsive to interest rate differentials; but, once again, the central bank cannot control these in a regime of liability management. Furthermore, if nominal incomes are the ultimate target, and the monetary aggregates an *intermediate* target, it seems an ungainly method to control monetary aggregates via the effect of interest rates on nominal incomes. Why not just concentrate on the interest rate/nominal income nexus?

C   PROBLEMS OF INTEREST RATE MANAGEMENT

The use of interest rates as the main mechanism of monetary control, therefore, entails several serious problems. First, as noted above, while the central bank can control the general level of interest rates, it cannot control *differentials* between rates on deposits and rates on other assets/liabilities, notably the loan/deposit spread (Miller and Sprenkle, 1980; Cuthbertson, 1993; Chowdhury et al., 1989). Furthermore, variable rate mortgage/deposit rates reduce intertemporal substitution effects and enhance income effects on borrowers/depositors. Under a variable rate system, it is less important to time the moment of making the loan or deposit correctly; conversely, the change in the interest rates will affect the cash flow of a larger number of agents and may, therefore, make interest rate adjustments more politically sensitive.

Second, lags between changes in interest rates and in the response of either monetary or wider economic variables are long and variable. In so far as substitution effects act more quickly than income effects on general expenditures, a variable rate system may lengthen the lag between the change in interest rates and its observed effect on the economy.

Why such lags exist is uncertain. McCallum (1985, pp. 583–4) notes that

> past values of interest rates should not have *any* direct effect on asset demands. That is because interest rates (or other prices) prevailing in the past would seem to fall clearly in the category of bygones – and the irrelevance of bygones is of course one of the most fundamental principles of monetary economics.

There may be several reasons why such lagged effects nevertheless appear. McCallum suggests possible mis-specification, for example of the demand for money function. Another reason, already noted above, is that the indirect income effects of interest rate changes may be the more powerful.

A more likely explanation is, perhaps, that during a boom, prices and expectations of future inflation may be revised upwards. Confidence in future real profits, incomes, employment, etc. will be increasing. Against that background some increase in *nominal* interest rates is necessary just to hold correctly calculated real interest rates constant.

If nominal interest rates are raised far enough to halt the boom, price expectations and confidence will become dented, and a given nominal level of interest rates may have an increasing real effect. Without having any clear measure either of expectations or confidence, and of what expectations and whose confidence is most important, we cannot measure 'real' interest rates accurately, and changes in nominal interest rates may then appear to have long and variable lags. Nevertheless, all this leads to great uncertainty. The impact effect of interest rates is generally found to be low on real expenditures and asset demands. The long-run effect is now widely believed to be considerable and important (whereas this was doubted in the 1950s and 1960s), but it is not clearly quantified.

Such uncertainty has caused political hesitation in using this instrument expeditiously and vigorously. Increases in interest rates cause immediate dismay to large segments of the population, for example recent house buyers on variable-rate mortgages, small businessmen who rely on bank credit, etc. It is therefore politically unpopular. Against such patent unpopularity, the economist or central banker cannot state with any confidence how any level of interest rates will affect the monetary aggregates or the economy over any particular period. So, action tends to be deferred until the need is more clearly discerned, with the natural result that interest rates are varied 'too little, too late'.

D   THE DEBATE INTENSIFIES

The consequence of 'too little, too late' was that the monetary aggregates have generally varied procyclically. With stagflation in the 1970s, governments became increasingly disillusioned with discretionary demand management. Following the example of West Germany in 1975, most developed countries then adopted monetary aggregate targets.

Targets were, of course, predicated on the belief that econometric estimates of the relationship between the targeted monetary variable and nominal incomes would remain stable. The intermediate target would then give an early indication of where nominal incomes were heading; and the deviation of actual money growth from its target might provide a quicker, clearer signal for counter-cyclical policy.

But this just transferred the problem of the uncertainty about the effect of interest rates on the economy as a whole to their effect on the monetary target. Monetarists argued that the uncertainties involved were so great that interest rate control mechanisms could never work effectively (e.g., Friedman, 1980). Moreover, they demonstrated in the 1970s that many countries failed to hit their targets using such control mechanisms.

In particular, the adoption of monetary targets in the USA from 1975 did *not* reduce monetary growth by mid-1979. In the early years, the target base was allowed to drift continuously. More fundamentally, the Fed chose to vary the Federal Funds rate, its key instrument, only in discrete steps of 25 basis points (see Lindsey, 1986, figure 5.1, and Friedman, 1982). This, of course, internalized 'too little, too late'.

With the economic crisis of 1979, the Fed accepted some of these criticisms and changed its control regime. On 6 October 1979, Chairman Volcker introduced the non-borrowed reserve base system. Its name suggests a move towards monetary base control; in practice, however, features such as lagged reserve requirements and an administered discount rate meant that it was more a quasi-automatic mechanism for forcing quicker and larger adjustments in interest rates whenever actual M1 growth deviated from desired growth.

Non-borrowed reserve control introduced volatility in interest rates four or five times as great as under the previous regime (see Walsh, 1982, 1984). Moreover, the average level of interest rates (1980–82) was much higher. Such high and volatile interest rates, however, succeeded in reducing monetary growth, inflation and nominal incomes.

But it was a bumpy ride. Short-term volatility in monetary growth increased to the highest level for any 3 years during the post-war period (Friedman, 1984). Some argued (e.g., Mascaro and Meltzer, 1983) that volatility in money growth increased the volatility of short-term and long-term interest rates, strengthened their positive correlation and altered the relationship between M1 (which went on growing rapidly in 1982) and nominal incomes (whose growth rate declined sharply).

A 'purer' method of monetary base control, they argued, would allow more predictable and steadier growth of the monetary aggregates. The debate in the USA focused on whether alternative versions of monetary base control could improve monetary control. All sides agreed that the pre-1979 regime had led to 'too little, too late'.

In the UK in 1971 financial deregulation, part of the Competition and Credit Control reform, led to a surge in bank lending and broad money (£M3). Unlike M1, £M3 did not seem to respond much to (politically acceptable) increases in interest rates. Rates were nonetheless raised to 13 per cent in 1973, but no one could be confident what further increase might be required to halt the expansion. In the event the authorities reverted to a revised form of credit control, 'the corset', which, in effect, penalized banks which used liability management to fund additional lending. (On these episodes, see Bank of England, *Development and Operation of Monetary Policy, 1960–83*, especially chapters 2 and 6.) The 'corset', a downturn in the economy (1974/75), and an external sterling crisis in 1976, which brought in the IMF, restrained monetary growth until 1978. Sterling M3 and inflation had both begun to accelerate ominously again before the Conservatives were returned to power in May 1979. As they had pledged, the Conservatives abolished exchange controls (an adjunct to direct credit controls, needed to avoid external disintermediation) in October 1979 and the 'corset' in June 1980.

Without the 'corset', how was the new government to achieve control over £M3, the centrepiece of its medium-term financial strategy?[2] The experience of 1971–73 did not augur well for control by interest rate variation. Several influential advisers of the incoming Conservative government, notably Griffiths and Pepper, were monetarist by inclination (Griffiths and Wood, 1981) and favoured adoption of some form of monetary base control. Pepper was then editor of the *W. Greenwell Special Monetary Bulletin*, an influential monthly survey of monetary matters, published by a City firm. He wrote several issues advocating a switch to monetary base controls in January and February 1977 and July 1979.

The Bank of England opposed monetary base control. Foot, Goodhart and Hotson outlined the major arguments against monetary base control in a *Bank of England Quarterly Bulletin* article in June 1979. The Bank

---

[2] The advent of the Reagan government in the US in 1980 had less of a catalytic effect on the debate there. This was partly due to Volcker having preempted and shaped the discussion by shifting to NBR in October 1979, and also partly due to the constitutional separation of powers in the monetary policy field between the Fed and the Treasury.

was supported by much of the City and also most, predominantly Keynesian, economists in the UK. Caught, on the one hand, between the proposals of its own academic advisers and its preference for a rule-based approach, which leaves interest rate determination to market forces, and, on the other hand, the opposition of the Bank and most of the City, the Government asked for an internal study, a Green Paper on 'Monetary Control', which appeared in March 1980, Cmnd 7858 (H.M. Treasury and Bank of England).

E   ELEMENTS IN THE DEBATE

It is difficult to isolate the main elements in the monetary base control debate in an uncontroversial manner, partly because there are several variants of monetary base control mechanisms.

One variant uses movements in the monetary base as an indicator guiding subsequent adjustments in interest rates, either according to discretion or to a rule (e.g., if the base deviates by X per cent, vary interest rates by Y per cent). No attempt is made to control movements in the base directly. The Deutsche Bundesbank (1980, 1985 and 1987; also see Dudler, 1980a,b and 1984) viewed its central bank money target in this light. The evidence is more mixed on the operating procedures of the Swiss National Bank: Rich and Schiltknecht (1980) reads as implying pure monetary base control, but Rich and Beguelin (1985) and Kohli and Rich (1986) suggest a monetary base indicator system. After abandoning broad money targets in 1985, the UK government targeted the monetary base (MO); but, unlike the Germans and Swiss, the British government did not take the path of their base money targets seriously as a guide to interest rate adjustment. In these circumstances there is no change in the control mechanism, which continues to use discretionary adjustments in interest rates. As indicator mechanisms, targets for central bank money or MO are no different than intermediate targets for M1 or M3 or any other M. Here, however, we wish to concentrate on monetary base *control* proposals, not monetary base indicator (target) systems.

A preliminary issue is the connection between monetary base control mechanisms and the reserve requirements system. Most countries calculate reserve requirements using data on the deposit base over some *past* period. Such lagged reserve requirements were usually introduced for prudential reasons. But lagged reserve requirements present a severe hurdle for monetary base control. Since the deposits on which the reserve requirements are based are history, the banks cannot possibly reduce the amount of reserves that legally they must hold. Consequently the authorities must either connive at banks missing their requirements or provide the needed bank reserves at a price of their own choosing. The latter amounts once again to a discretionary choice of interest rates by the authorities.

The Green Paper on 'Monetary Control' (1980) in the UK emphasized the difficulties of adopting any system of *mandatory*[3] base control (pp. 10–11, 23–6). Henceforward I focus mainly on a comparison of discretionary interest rate control with a *non-mandatory* monetary base control. Even with a non-mandatory system we must still consider problems of net shortages of reserves within the system that may force a commercial bank into borrowing from the central bank. The central bank in that case must decide what interest rate it would charge on such an overnight overdraft. We assume that the central bank charges a severely penal rate. We also assume that commercial banks cannot avoid incurring penal rates through the use of cosmetic accounting devices.

It is easier to analyse historical experience than to judge what might occur hypothetically. Thus, the problems of using interest rates as a major instrument for monetary control and the 'too little, too late' syndrome are generally understood. Furthermore, the actual time path of the C/D and R/D ratios is known. In the United States and West Germany, these ratios have generally been stable and predictable (Johannes and Rasche, 1979, 1981; Rasche and Johannes, 1987; Dewald and Lai, 1987; von Hagen, 1988). They have been less so in the UK and Australia (Capie and Wood, 1986; Macfarlane, 1984). Where the base is non-mandatory, the R/D ratio can, however, become more variable, weakening the link between changes in H and the targeted M, at least in the short run. Nevertheless, given the ability of the central bank to vary H in the short run, and sophisticated statistical techniques (e.g., Kalman filtering) for predicting the levels of the R/D and C/D ratios, their variability might not prove, if best practice is followed, a serious handicap to the adoption of monetary base control.

In the USA under the non-borrowed reserve system there was an increase in the short-run (quarter by quarter) volatility, both of monetary growth and of short-term and *long-term* interest rates. Over the *medium term*, M1 was fairly well controlled; interest rates were on average much higher; and a strong deflationary shock was applied to the USA (and

---

[3] Pepper (1990, especially p. 61, note 1) also prefers a non-mandatory system for its flexibility and lack of distortion in response to shifts between deposits with differing ratios.

world) economy. Was this vastly increased short-run volatility (1) the chance effect of a series of unconnected shocks (e.g., the imposition and removal of the Carter credit controls, financial innovation) (see, e.g., Wenninger and Radecki, 1986); (2) the direct consequence of moving towards monetary base control, which might be further exacerbated by a 'purer' form of monetary base control (i.e., in which total H, or total bank reserves, not just non-borrowed reserves, were strictly controlled); or (3) the consequence of failure to control total bank reserves, or H, sufficiently closely? These issues have never been convincingly resolved.

Five questions remain about how a system might operate under a (non-mandatory) monetary base control system.

1 What Would Happen to Interest Rates?

Within any system, to each equilibrium price corresponds an equilibrium quantity. To try to control monetary aggregates, the authorities had to accept large variations in interest rates. In 1979–81 they reached the limits of political tolerance. Would forcing monetary control upon a system, seemingly unresponsive to variations in the general level of interest rates, make interest rates even more volatile? If so, by how much?

2 How Might the Control Mechanism Itself Change?

In the UK, opponents of monetary base control argued that monetary policy operated through interest rates. Consequently, they saw monetary base control just a means of forcing more violent interest rate adjustments on the system. Proponents of monetary base control argued that, if banks knew in advance that additional reserves would not be made available or made available only at extremely penal interest rates to accommodate an 'excessive' expansion, they would be less aggressive during boom times. Proponents saw the regime change as stabilizing the behaviour pattern of the banks themselves.

3 Would Closer Control of H Deliver Closer Control of M?

Proponents of monetary base control pointed to the past predictability of the monetary base multiplier. Opponents attributed this stability of the R/D ratio to the confidence of banks that they could always obtain additional reserves at a predictable, non-penal, rate. A regime change that shattered this confidence might shift the level and increase the volatility of R/D. To a lesser extent, volatile interest rates and doubts about the convertibility of deposits into cash might also shift in the C/D ratio.

4 Would Monetary Control be Achieved Cosmetically?

A non-mandatory system would be less prone to disintermediation than certain other variants of mandatory monetary base control, e.g., forward reserve requirements (see Laurent, 1979; Kopecky, 1984). Even so, a system that caused short-term volatility in interest rates might develop mechanisms for shifting financing flows between banks and non-bank intermediaries. In consequence, monetary growth rates might be stabilized while inducing greater variability in the relationship between money and nominal incomes. Proponents of monetary base control dismiss this possibility.

5 How Would the Structure and Stability of the Monetary System Change?

Opponents of monetary base control claim that the structure of the present system (e.g., the overdraft system, money market arrangements, and bank desired asset portfolios) presumes that additional cash reserves will always be made available on reasonable terms, and that circumstances when interest rates are adjusted abruptly (e.g., foreign exchange crises) are few, widely understood, and often predictable (e.g., the Exchange Rate Mechanism crisis in September 1992). Opponents claim that there could be severe transitional problems in a regime change. During the transition the banking system might be unstable and, even after the new system had settled down, it might be more fragile. Proponents claim that this is just scare-mongering.

Recall, however, that both proponents and opponents of monetary base control more or less agree that discretionary interest rate control is fallible and problematic. So, acceptance of some of the points made by opponents does not necessarily settle the argument.

F THE DEBATE RECEDES

Quite remarkably, and unusually, there actually were *formal debates* over monetary base control in the UK and the USA. In the UK, the

Green Paper on 'Monetary Control', prepared by Bank and Treasury officials, argued strongly against the adoption of any system of monetary base control. It concluded (para. 1.9): 'Using the basic weapons of fiscal policy, gilt-edged funding and short term interest rates, the monetary authorities can achieve the first requisite of control of the money supply – control, say, over a year or more'.

British proponents (e.g., Pepper, 1980) were neither convinced nor impressed by the analysis in the Green Paper. To see if any meeting of minds could be achieved, an official debate was held on 29 September 1980. As might have been expected, the protagonists stuck to their prejudices, and the event created more heat than light.

Nevertheless the government had to reach a decision on whether to change the monetary control system. They decided *not* to do so, although many of those closely influential in reaching that decision (e.g., both Lawson and Walters) were sympathetic to the case for change. The prospective difficulty of steering the system clearly through the transitional period seemed to be the deciding factor: 'we in the UK have very little idea of the size of cash balances the banks would wish to hold if we were to move to a system of monetary base control' (Lawson, 1981); moreover, the ratio of £M3 to base money was not stable or predictable, so there was 'little or no point in trying to use the monetary base control system to control £M3' (Walters, 1986, p. 123). These considerations, combined with opposition from the Bank of England, commercial bankers, and the City of London, persuaded the monetarists not to push more strongly for monetary base control.

In the USA, in addition to several conferences held on the monetary control regime (e.g., the American Enterprise Institute Conferences in February 1982 and February 1985; see *Journal of Money, Credit and Banking* (*JMCB*) November 1982 and November 1985), a formal debate was held on 30 April 1981 on the motion 'Is the Federal Reserve's Monetary Control Policy Misdirected'. Rasche and Meltzer were for the affirmative, arguing for the adoption of a 'purer' form of monetary base control, and Sternlight and Axilrod were for the negative, arguing for persisting with non-borrowed reserve control (*JMCB* February 1982).

In the event, the Fed's monetary control system was to be changed again, in the early autumn of 1982, but away from, rather than towards, a purer monetary base control. The Fed adopted a 'borrowed reserve base' target (see Wallich, 1984). Since borrowed reserves were largely a function of the differential between the Federal Funds rate and the discount rate (Goodfriend, 1983), the borrowed reserves target implied a reversion to targeting interest rates.

Among the reasons for abandoning non-borrowed reserve control were the LDC crisis and its potential implications for banking fragility in the USA, and the recession in nominal incomes. Inflation ceased to be enemy number one. But more important, the growth of M1 no longer behaved consistently with the time path of nominal incomes and interest rates.

In both the USA and the UK in the early 1980s, nominal incomes declined sharply, more or less as planned, while the intermediate monetary aggregates (£M3 and M1) continued to grow faster than targeted. Both countries unsuccessfully sought alternative monetary targets with more predictable characteristics, and by the mid-1980s to late 1980s monetary targetry was effectively abandoned in most Anglo-Saxon countries (see B. Friedman, 1988), though not in West Germany or Switzerland.

That effectively ended the monetary control debate. If the links between monetary aggregates and nominal incomes were loose and unstable, intermediate monetary targets seemed pointless. Whereas interest rates remained important, irrespective of the collapse of monetary targetry, because of their direct links with exchange rates, incomes and expenditures, the only function and purpose of the monetary base multiplier was to link movements in H and M.

Only sporadic calls are still made for a reconsideration of monetary base control. Central banks have been left to run their traditional operational mechanism of discretionary adjustments in short-term interest rates. Although interest rate control remains subject to all the same technical problems noted earlier, economists now appear less concerned about such operational problems.

G MAY THE DEBATE REVIVE?

In the absence of monetary targets the debate over monetary base control appears historical. But in an analytical sense the debate also mirrors a fundamental, continuing discussion about the process of money supply determination. Central bankers, and their supporting economists, see the driving force of monetary expansion as deriving from the demand from the public and private sectors for *credit*. While narrow monetary growth remains best explained within the context of a demand for money function, broad money growth in this view is, in the short run, a consequence of the credit counterparts via liability management (and buffer stock adjustments). Again, on this view, the monetary base multiplier is not a particularly important identity.

All this remains anathema to many American monetary economists (much less so to monetarists in other countries). To them the essential causal direction remains from the creation of base money by the central bank, via the multiplier, to the determination of M. They accept that, in practice, the discretionary choice of short-term interest rates by the Fed makes H an endogenous variable, but for analytical purposes they still tend to focus on its movements to help to explain changes in M.

REFERENCES

American Enterprise Institute Conference (1982) 'Current Issues in the Conduct of US Monetary Policy' 4–5 February 1982, with papers by William Poole, Ralph Bryant, William Fellner, William Arnett, Bejamin Friedman, Stanley Black, James Pierce, Robert Anderson, Robert Rasche, and Peter Tinsley et al., reproduced in *Journal of Money, Credit and Banking*, vol. 14, no. 2, pt 2, November.

American Enterprise Institute Conference (1985) 'Monetary Policy in a Changing Financial Environment' 8 February 1985, with papers by Bennett McCallum, Vance Roley, Gerald Dwyer Jr, John Merrick and Anthony Saunders, *Journal of Money, Credit and Banking*, vol. 17, no. 4, pt 2, November.

Bagehot, Walter (1962) *Lombard Street*, Richard D. Irwin Inc., Homewood, IL, reprinted, with minor editorial changes, from the 1873 edn, Scribner, Armstrong & Co., New York, NY.

Bank of England (1984) *Development and Operation of Monetary Policy, 1960–1983*, Clarendon Press, Oxford.

Beach, W.E. (1935) *British International Gold Movements and Banking Policy, 1881–1913*, Harvard University Press, Cambridge, MA.

Bloomfield, A.I. (1959) *Monetary Policy under the International Gold Standard, 1880–1914*, Federal Reserve Bank of New York, monograph.

Capie, Forrest H. and Wood, Geoffrey E. (1986) 'The Long Run Behaviour of Velocity in the UK' Centre for Banking and International Finance, City University Business School, Discussion Paper, no. 23, May.

Chowdhury, G., Green, G. and Miles D.K. (1989) 'Company Bank Borrowing and Liquid Lending' *National Westminster Bank Review*, pp. 45–52.

Cuthbertson, Keith (1993) 'Monetary Control: Theory, Empirics and Practicalities' in Arestis, P. (ed.), *Money and Banking Issues for the 21st Century*, Macmillan, London.

Deutsche Bundesbank (1980) 'Control of the Money Supply in the Federal Republic of Germany' Memorandum no. 14, to the Treasury and Civil Service Committee of the House of Commons on Monetary Policy, vol. 11, Minutes of Evidence, pp. 290–7, 24 February, 163-11.

Deutsche Bundesbank (1985) 'The Longer-term Trend and Control of the Money Stock' *Monthly Report*, vol. 37, no. 1, January, pp. 13–26.

Deutsche Bundesbank (1987) *The Deutsche Bundesbank: Its Monetary Policy Instruments and Functions*, Special Series, no. 7.

Dewald, William C. and Lai, Tsung-Hui (1987) 'Factors Affecting Monetary Growth: ARIMA Forecasts of Monetary Base and Multiplier' *Kredit und Kapital*, vol. 20, no. 3, pp. 303–16.

Dudler, Hermann-Josef (1980a) 'Money-Market Management, Supply of Bank Reserves and Control of Central-Bank Money Stock', in *The Monetary Base Approach to Monetary Control*, BIS, Basle, September.

Dudler, Hermann-Josef (1980b) Evidence to Treasury and Civil Service Committee on *Monetary Policy*, vol. 11, Minutes of Evidence, pp. 297–307, 10 November.

Dudler, Hermann-Josef (1984) *Geldpolitik und ihre Theoretischen Grundlagen*, Fritz Knapp Verlag, Frankfurt am Main.

Dutton, John (1984) 'The Bank of England and the Rules of the Game under the International Gold Standard: New Evidence', ch. 3 in Bordo, M.D. and Schwartz, A.J. (eds), *A Retrospective on the Classical Gold Standard*, University of Chicago Press, Chicago, IL.

Foot, Michael D.K.W., Goodhart, Charles A.E. and Hotson, Anthony C. (1979) 'Monetary Base Control' *Bank of England Quarterly Bulletin*, June, reproduced in ch. 6 of Bank of England (1984), *Development and Operation of Monetary Policy, 1960–1983*, Clarendon Press, Oxford.

Friedman, Benjamin (1988) 'Monetary Policy without Quantity Variables' *The American Economic Review*, AEA Papers and Proceedings, vol. 78, no. 2, May, pp. 440–5.

Friedman, Milton (1980) Memorandum to Treasury and Civil Service Committee on *Monetary Policy*, Session 1980-81, H C (1979–80) 720, Memorandum 9, HMSO, London.

Friedman, Milton (1982) 'Monetary Theory: Policy and Practice' *Journal of Money, Credit and Banking*, vol. 14, no. 1, pp. 98–118.

Friedman, Milton (1984) 'Lessons from the 1979–82 Monetary Policy Experiment' *The American Economic Review*, AEA Papers and Proceedings, vol. 74, no. 2, May, pp. 397–400.

Goodfriend, Marvin (1983) 'Discount Window Borrowing, Monetary Policy, and the Post-October 6, 1979, Federal Reserve Operating Procedure' *Journal of Monetary Economics*, 12, pp. 343–56.

Goodhart, Charles A.E. (1972) *The Business of Banking, 1891–1914*, Weidenfeld and Nicolson, London.

Griffiths, Brian and Wood, Geoffrey E. (eds) (1981) 'Introduction' in *Monetary Targets*, Macmillan, London.

Johannes, James M. and Rasche, Robert H. (1979) 'Predicting the Money Multiplier' *Journal of Monetary Economics*, 5, pp. 301–25.

Johannes, James M. and Rasche, Robert H. (1981) 'Can the Reserves Approach to Monetary Control Really Work?' *Journal of Money, Credit and Banking*, 13, August, pp. 289–313.

Kohli, U. and Rich, G. (1986) 'Monetary Control: The Swiss Experience' *Cato Journal*, vol. 5, no. 3, Winter, pp. 911–26.

Kopecky, Kenneth J. (1984) 'Monetary Control Under Reverse Lag and Contemporaneous Reserve Accounting: A Comparison' and 'A Reply' by Robert D. Laurent, *Journal of Money, Credit and Banking*, vol. 16, no. 1, pp. 81–92.

Laurent, Robert D. (1979) 'Reserve Requirements: Are They Lagged in the Wrong Direction?' *Journal of Money, Credit and Banking*, vol. 11, August, pp. 301–10.

Lawson, Nigel (1981) 'Thatcherism in Practice: A Progress Report' Speech to the Zurich Society of Economists, 14 January, H.M. Treasury Press Release.

Lindsey, David E. (1986) 'The Monetary Regime of the Federal Reserve System' Chapter 5 in Campbell, C.P. and Dougan, W.R. (eds), *Alternative Monetary Regimes*, Johns Hopkins University Press, Baltimore, MD.

Macfarlane, Ian J. (1984) 'Methods of Monetary Control in Australia', paper presented at the New Zealand Association of Economists Annual Conference, Massey University, August.

Mascaro, Angelo and Meltzer, Allan H. (1983) 'Long and Short-Term Interest Rates in a Risky World' *Journal of Monetary Economics*, vol. 12, November, pp. 485–518.

McCallum, Bennett T. (1985) 'On Consequences and Criticisms of Monetary Targeting' *Journal of Money, Credit and Banking*, vol. 17, no. 4 (November, pt 2), pp. 570–97.

Miller, Marcus and Sprenkle, Case M. (1980) 'The Precautionary Demand for Narrow and Broad Money' *Economica*, vol. 47, no. 188, November.

Pepper, Gordon (1977) 'A Monetary Base for the UK' *W. Greenwell Special Monetary Bulletin*, January.

Pepper, Gordon (1977) 'The Mechanism for the Control of the Money Supply – Further Thoughts' *W. Greenwell Special Monetary Bulletin*, February.

Pepper, Gordon (1979) 'A Monetary Base for the UK – A Practical Proposal' *W. Greenwell Special Monetary Bulletin*, July.

Pepper, Gordon (1980) 'Monetary Base Control' *W. Greenwell Special Monetary Bulletin,* April.

Pepper, Gordon (1990) *Money, Credit and Inflation*, Institute for Economic Affairs, London, Research Monograph, no. 44, April.

Pippenger, John (1984) 'Bank of England Operations, 1893–1913' in Bordo, M.D. and Schwartz, A.J. (eds), *A Retrospective on the Classical Gold Standard, 1821–1931*, University of Chicago Press, Chicago, IL.

Rasche, Robert H. and Meltzer, Allan H. 'For the Affirmative' and Sternlight, Peter D. and Axilrod, Stephen H. 'For the Negative' in the Journal of Money, Credit and Banking debate on 30 April 1981, 'Is the Federal Reserve's Monetary Control Misdirected', reproduced in *Journal of Money, Credit and Banking* (1982), vol. 14, no. 1, February, pp. 119–47.

Rasche, Robert H. and Johannes, James M. (1987) *Controlling the Growth of Monetary Aggregates*, Kluwer Academic Publishers, Amsterdam.

Rich, Georg and Beguelin, Jean-Pierre (1985) 'Swiss Monetary Policy in the 1970s and 1980s' *Monetary Policy and Monetary Regimes,* Graduate School of Management, University of Rochester Center Symposia Series, CS17.

Rich, Georg and Schiltknecht, Kurt (1980) 'Targetting the Monetary Base – The Swiss Approach' in *The Monetary Base Approach to Monetary Control,* ed BIS, Basle, September.

Sayers, Richard S. (1936) *Bank of England Operations, 1890–1914,* P.S. King & Son Ltd, London.

Treasury, H. M. and Bank of England (1980) *Monetary Control*, Cmnd 7858, HMSO, London.

von Hagen, Jurgen (1988) 'Alternative Operating Regimes for Money Stock Control in West Germany: an Empirical Evaluation' *Weltwirtschaftliches Archiv*, vol. 124, no. 1, pp. 89–107.

Wallich, Henry C. (1984) 'Recent Techniques of Monetary Policy' *Federal Reserve Bank of Kansas City Economic Review*, May, pp. 21–30.

Walsh, Carl E. (1982) 'The Federal Reserve's Operating Procedures and Interest Rate Fluctuations' *Federal Reserve Bank of Kansas City Economic Review*, pp. 8–18.

Walsh, Carl E. (1984) 'Interest Rate Volatility and Monetary Policy' *Journal of Money, Credit and Banking*, vol. 16, no. 2, pp. 133–50.

Walters, Alan (1986) *Britain's Economic Renaissance,* Oxford University Press, New York, NY.

Wenninger, John and Radecki, Lawrence J. (1986) 'Financial Transactions and the demand for MI' *Federal Reserve Bank of New York Quarterly Review*, Summer, pp. 24–9.

8. Monetary Policy, Wealth Effects and the Transmission Mechanism

Richard J. Sweeney[*][1]

Since the Keynesian revolution, there has been voluminous and often acrimonious debate on the role of money in business cycles. The debate has focused on different issues at different times; many issues in the debate remain unresolved even as the participants turn to new issues. This paper discusses the evolution of the debate about the price-induced effect on wealth.[2] It also summarizes the current state of knowledge about the price-induced effect on wealth and discusses the adequacy of how current empirical models handle effects on wealth.

1 MONETARISTS VERSUS KEYNESIANS

Leijonhufvud (1992) argues that a key distinction between monetarists and Keynesians is where the disturbances that drive the economy arise. Keynesians view output market disturbances as the important disturbances; the key disturbances, in size and frequency, are to private sector investment demand, though consumption-function shifts may be important in particular episodes. Monetarists view money demand and supply disturbances as the important disturbances, with money-stock fluctuations the key disturbances, though money demand shifts may be

[*] For stimulating discussion over many years, thanks are due to Axel Leijonhufvud. Part of the work on this paper was supported by summer grants from the Georgetown University School of Business.

[1] Thomas Mayer has done the economics profession, and the discussion of public policy, great service in advancing the debate over the role of monetary policy for stabilizing the economy and in clarifying the Keynesian-monetarist debates that preoccupied monetary economists into the 1970s and still dominate policy discussions. This paper focuses on monetary issues where Mayer has made such an important mark.

[2] Pesek and Saving (1967) refer to the price-induced effect on wealth rather than the real balance effect. Because the "real balance effect" is often taken as referring to effects proportional to the monetary base, I use the "price-induced effect on wealth" (Sweeney, 1988) to leave open the issue of how various components of the money stock enter the effect.

important in particular episodes; the simple prescription is for government, in its central banker role, to refrain from causing money-stock disturbances.[3] Both Keynesians and monetarists tend to use the same transmission mechanism: sluggish price or wage adjustment.[4] Sluggish prices or wages allow money-stock changes to affect such real variables as output, employment and the real interest rate. Prices and wages eventually adjust; in the typical monetarist view, the long-run effect of money-stock changes is on prices.

The Keynesian revolution was immensely successful. Economists who saw important insights in the old Quantity Theory of Money often had to make their case in the Keynesian aggregate demand-supply framework to sow doubts and make converts. Price-induced effects on wealth played a key role in these controversies; money-stock changes can affect aggregate demand on which Keynesians concentrate.

Price-Induced Effects of Wealth

An early Keynesian-monetarist debate was whether self-equilibrating forces would pull the economy out of a recession, in particular, the Great Depression. Pigou (1943) argued that price deflation would eventually so raise the money stock's real value that people would be wealthy enough to return aggregate demand to the full-employment level. Pigou argued that the required deflation might be substantial and take a long time;[5] he offered his view as a matter of economic logic and explicitly disavowed waiting on price/wage adjustments to cure the Depression.[6]

Discussions of wealth effects in the transmission mechanism focused on the size and sign of excess demands that a disturbance causes, with

[3] There is a large literature on monetary instruments and targets. In principle, stabilizing the appropriate money-stock measure may be difficult because of unstable relationships between variables the central bank can control directly and the money-stock measure it wants to control. Many monetarists argue that this may be a problem in practice, but not an insuperable one. On a related issue, the relationship between price-level stability and the money-stock measure that the central bank attempts to control may be unstable. Since the early 1980s, many observers have argued that past relationships between any particular money-stock measure and inflation or growth of nominal income no longer hold. Others argue that the appropriate money-stock measure changes over time. Some argue that the items included in a particular money-stock time-series change over time, and old relationships hold but with regard to a money-stock measure with a new name (see Darby, Mascaro and Marlow, 1989).

[4] Leijonhufvud (1992) argues that Keynes's transmission mechanism was a sluggish (nominal and real) interest rate; later Keynesians (but not New Keynesians) almost always use sluggish prices or wages (or real wages) as the transmission mechanism (Bailey, 1971).

[5] Between the start of the Great Depression in August 1929, and its nadir in 1933, prices in the US fell by roughly 30 percent as measured by most aggregate price indices.

[6] Similarly, Haberler (1937, 1952) argued for the existence of self-equilibrating forces but rejected doing nothing and waiting for the economy to right itself.

excess demands evaluated at the current price vector.[7] These excess demands were assumed to cause adjustment of the endogenous variables to new equilibrium values, the speed depending on the excess demands times a vector of adjustment coefficients. For much of the period, the vehicle for analyzing this issue was the real balance effect (the old Pigou effect), and the *locus classicus* was Patinkin's (1965, 1972) analysis. The level of real balances in this approach is the ratio of the relevant money stock to the aggregate price level, M^S/P; Patinkin mainly focuses on base money,[8] though Pesek and Saving (1967) argue for inclusion of some part of bank money.[9] In this analysis, money-stock and price-level changes have symmetric effects; halving the price level has the same effect on real balances as doubling the money stock. Adjustment can be achieved painfully through sluggish price decreases or painlessly through money-stock increases. If the real balance effect is important, money matters; equilibration through the Pigou effect is not a curiosum but an invitation to rely on the money rather than price part of real balances.[10]

In Patinkin's formulation, the real balance effect necessarily enters the excess demands for output, bonds or money, and likely enters all three. If base money is part of wealth, a halving of the price level doubles the real value of the money stock and thus raises wealth. If the increased wealth is used wholly to accumulate more real balances, then it has no effect in the excess demands for output or bonds; the price level is

[7] This is the "true" dynamic stability analysis in Samuelson (1947) and Metzler (1945) as opposed to Hicks's (1946) stability analysis. This literature was active into the 1960s; Patinkin used this type of analysis (1965). This analysis assumes that excess demands are based on desired purchases at the given current vector regardless of whether the desired transactions could take place. As opposed to this *tâtonnement* stability, literature on non-*tâtonnement* stability took some account of whether transactions could be made in the face of non-zero excess demands. Barro and Grossman (1976) can be thought of using a type of non-*tâtonnement* stability model; see also Sweeney (1974).

[8] Patinkin (1965) allows for the possibility of the numerator including some fraction of the stock of government bonds if the associated tax liabilities are not fully discounted.

[9] A key issue is the relevant money stock. In the early part of the Great Depression, the US stock of high-powered money was relatively stable, but the M1 money stock fell substantially (see Friedman and Schwartz, 1963).

[10] This discussion typically assumed a closed economy (but see Meinich, 1968 and Sweeney, 1975). It is closely related, however, to the monetary approach to the balance of payments that enjoyed great vogue from the early 1970s. In the long run, an exogenous doubling of one country's money stock produces a doubling of the country's price level. Similarly, under freely floating exchange rates, its exchange rate (the number of units of its currency needed to buy one unit of foreign currency) doubles; while under fixed exchange rates an outflow of reserves induces money-stock adjustments that leave the levels of real balances in both countries, as well as the level of the real exchange rate between the country and the rest of the world, the same as before. With sluggish adjustment of prices and also of trade flows, money-stock changes can have major and long-lasting effects on real output; an example of this is Dornbusch's (1976) overshooting model where expectations are rational but price levels are sluggish, leading to protracted output and real exchange rate changes as the price level adjusts to its long-run value, and output and the real exchange rate adjust to their unchanged long-run levels.

indeterminate because any change in the stock of real balances is met by an equal change in the demand for real balances. For the price-level determinacy, the price-induced change in real balances must affect non-monetary excess demands. This spillover may affect only the excess demand for bonds, or may affect the excess demand for output; if output is a superior good, the spillover affects the excess demand for output.

Many monetarists argued that in the short run an increase in the money stock affects all three excess demands – for output, bonds and money. If the real balance effect works only in the money and bond markets, it affects excess demand for output only through first affecting the interest rate, and then output through the dicey channel of investment demand.

Quantitative Importance of the Priced-Induced Effect on Wealth

Monetarists attacked the view that "money doesn't matter," which they ascribed to Keynesians. By the late 1960s, many Keynesians saw "money doesn't matter" as a straw man.[11] In a common Keynesian view, money matters but is not very important quantitatively; similarly, the real balance effect perhaps enters aggregate demand, but has minor importance. Many Keynesians view the time required to return to equilibrium as quite long if only the economy's self-equilibrating forces are relied on (a common property of the large-scale Keynesian macroeconometric models of the 1960s, one that continues in such models to today). In terms of the price-induced effect on wealth, this was because the deflationary gap might be very substantial relative to the money stock and because prices adjust sluggishly. After substantial debate, many Keynesians adopted the view that the priced-induced effect on wealth works only on base money, which is small relative to nominal GDP; furthermore, prices are sluggish enough in the Keynesian view to take a very long time even to cut the price level in half.

Some early Keynesians argued that the economy could be in an unemployment equilibrium. Pigou's argument was a convincing refutation of this Keynesian view,[12] though it took some time to be

---

[11] Keynesian books from the 1950s and early 1960s pay relatively little attention to money; monetarists shifted the profession enough to make "money doesn't matter" a straw man. Typically, Keynesians integrated money into their analyses through emphasis on the IS-LM analysis; see Leijonhufvud (1983) for a critique of IS-LM analysis.

[12] Pigou's argument was highly informal, as was the Keynesian view he was refuting. "New Keynesian" models beginning in the 1980s often stress microfoundations that lead to multiple equilibria, with some equilibria showing less wealth and lower employment than others (e.g., Rowe, 1987 and the papers he cites or Mankiw, 1989).

recognized.[13] Another Keynesian view was that price deflation might lead to expectations of more deflation, with these expectations causing the private sector to spend less now in anticipation of future bargains, thus offsetting any effect on aggregate demand of the increase in the real value of the money stock (the so-called Tobin effect[14]). Later there seemed to be agreement that eventually the price-induced effect on wealth would dominate, but that the time required might be long. Thus, the stability issue became part of the question of how long the economy requires to return to equilbrium. This leads back to the size of the price-induced effect on wealth.

Pesek and Saving (1967) argued that, in addition to base money, some part of bank money enters the price-induced effect on wealth, thus increasing the effect. Patinkin (1969, 1972) argued against including bank money. Indeed, Johnson (1961) noted that even base money might be an overstatement; government might increase the stock of money in response to increases in the price level, thereby reducing the effect, or in the case of proportionate changes in the price level and the money stock, reducing the effect to zero. Patinkin (1965) argued that inclusion of base money depends on the government not responding to economic forces in the same way as the model's other actors, but he considered this to be reasonable.

By the late 1960s, Keynesians acknowledged that money is more important than some had thought. The 1970s' protracted bouts of high inflation coupled with high unemployment and low growth of output destroyed the credibility of the "1975 version" of Keynesianism. "New Keynesian" models typically do not require a stable Phillips curve or the earlier Keynesian elasticities assumptions. Similarly, rational expectations monetarism from the 1970s on does not require the early monetarist elasticities assumptions.

By the mid-1970s, discussion of wealth effects and their role in the transmission mechanism had wound down. Much Keynesian energy went into reformulating a New Keynesianism rather than fighting the old Keynesian-monetarist battles; similarly, much monetarist energy went into developing and elaborating rational expectations monetarist models. Discussions of wealth effects settled into agreement to disagree. Pesek and Saving (1967) argued that at least part of bank money entered the

---

[13] In the literature discussed here, the question of the existence of equilibrium in a monetary economy is better thought of as the question of the determinacy of the price level. In particular, at a full-employment equilibrium, will a displacement of the price level create excess demands? Stability of equilibrium is the issue of whether the vector of excess demands will move the system towards or away from the presupposed equilibrium.

[14] The Tobin effect plays a main role in some recent suggestions that price and wage flexibility might be destabilizing (Delong and Summers, 1986); but see Kandil (1993) for empirical evidence against this view.

price-induced effect on wealth; Patinkin (1969, 1972) argued that only the monetary base entered the real balance effect.[15] Rather than reaching resolution, the argument petered out.

Early rational expectations macro models (Lucas, 1973, 1975; Sargent, 1973, 1976) were clearly monetarist in orientation; these models, however, did not rely on sluggish price adjustment as the transmission mechanism from money-stock disturbances to the real economy,[16] but instead focused on money-stock surprises. If expected and actual money stocks differ, expected and actual price levels differ, with the gap between the expected and actual price levels having real effects on the economy. Presumably, the effects depend in part on wealth effects.[17] Most rational expectations monetarist models ignore these wealth effects; if rational expectations monetarists accept the old Keynesian argument that such effects on wealth are small, neglecting them does little quantitative harm. Indeed, if wealth effects do not enter output demand or labor demand, and if production decisions do not depend on the rate of inflation, consistent with typical 1960s Keynesian views, then the model displays superneutrality. In this case, fully anticipated changes in the sequence of money stocks have no real effects, but also the real effects of unanticipated changes in the money stock are independent of the effects on wealth of money-stock surprises.[18]

2   CURRENT STATUS OF THE PRICE-INDUCED EFFECT ON WEALTH

My previous work (Sweeney, 1988) analyzes effects on wealth in terms of Hicksian equivalent variations, for consistency with micro analysis.[19]

---

[15] Patinkin (1965) allows for the possibility of the numerator in the real balance effect including some fraction of the stock of government bonds if the associated tax liabilities are not fully discounted.

[16] Rational expectations models need not assume market clearing, even those rational expectations models that preserve the "policy irrelevance" proposition that anticipated monetary policy has no real effects (see, for example, McCallum, 1986).

[17] Lucas (1975) notes the omission of price-induced effects on wealth in his model but argues that they complicate without changing the important results.

[18] Even in models where changes in the steady-state rate of inflation do not affect real variables such as output and the capital stock, variable money-stock growth may cause fluctuations of real variables around their steady-state levels (Sweeney, 1984; Fischer, 1979).

[19] Of course a number of other measures of effects on wealth can be used in micro analysis, for example, compensating variation. The equivalent variation has the virtue of being independent of preferences. Using the equivalent variation, the wealth effect in the output market of a rise in the price level is price-induced effect on wealth times the marginal propensity to consume out of changes in wealth.

The equivalent variation measure asks how wealth must change in the face of a disturbance to allow all of the economic actor's purchases and sales to remain as before; thus, the equivalent variation can be found from the actor's budget constraint, not preferences. Under the assumption that distribution effects are unimportant, the economy-wide effect on wealth is found from the aggregate budget constraint. Important results follow from the assumptions that holdings and supplies of money of all types (government money, bank money, bank money with various restrictions on withdrawal, etc.) are all chosen to satisfy optimization conditions, and all nominal costs and benefits are homogeneous of degree one in money and the price level (so that only real balances of all types matter for real decisions and activities).

A Zero Price-Induced Effect on Wealth

This result supposes that it is real balances that are of use, or that an increase of every actor's money holdings in every period along with a proportional rise in all periods' price levels has no real effect.[20] Each actor chooses the level of real balances in every period that sets his indirect intertemporal welfare W at a constrained maximum; this implies setting $W_{mt} (1/P_t) = W_{mt} = 0$, where W_{mt} is the marginal net benefit of an increase in the individual's real balances (m_t) in period t (the partial derivative of W with respect to m), P_t the price level, and $(1/P_t)$ the derivative of period t real balances with respect to a change in nominal money holdings (M). Suppose there is a proportional rise in the price level in every period; this changes welfare by $-W_{mt} M_t /(P_t)^2 = W_{mt} = 0$. Because all actors are optimizing and none changes his/her choice of m, there is no price-induced effect on wealth; if there were a price-induced effect on wealth, some actor would have to change his behavior.

Non-zero effects arise when some actor is not satisfying optimization conditions. Suppose government pays interest on its money, and sets the interest rate r^* equal to the marginal cost of supporting whatever level of nominal money it plans on in every period (costs include wear and tear, protection against counterfeiting, etc.). In particular, hold constant the sequence of government money stocks $\{ M_{g,t}^s \}$ and let all current and future price levels rise proportionately. With higher prices, government costs of supporting the nominal stocks of its money in each period fall

---

[20] Conventionally, the price-induced effect on wealth is found by assuming that all current and future price levels are proportionately displaced, with no change in any one-period interest rate, thus holding constant intertemporal relative prices. In previous work (Sweeney, 1988) I consider some cases where relative prices vary.

because the real stocks are lower with higher prices (real costs are assumed homogeneous of degree zero in the price level and the nominal stock; a fall in real balances reduces government costs). The government passes this benefit on to consumers in the form of lower taxes. Consumers must now devote more resources to accumulating government money if they are to hold constant in every period their stock of real balances of government money, but their taxes are reduced just enough to allow this extra accumulation. The conventional Pigou or real balance effect arises because government money does not pay a competitively determined rate of interest.[21] The fact that there is no price-induced effect on wealth when government pays a competitive rate of interest on its money does not come from the government having a wealth effect that makes it want to spend more on output as a consumer might (as in the Johnson–Patinkin conundrum discussed above), or from government making the sequence of its money stocks unit-elastic with respect to the price levels. Alternatively, even if the government does not operate under an optimizing marginal condition, it may plausibly be taken to vary the time path of the stock it will supply more or less proportionately with the current price level; if the government responds to the current price level by exactly proportionate changes in future money stocks, the price-induced effect on wealth is again zero, as Johnson and Patinkin note.[22]

Although there is no price-induced effect on wealth through government money when the government pays a competitive rate of interest on its money, in future periods there will be non-zero excess demands for government money when government holds constant the sequence of its money stocks, because consumers will hold constant their desired real balances of government money though the stocks available are reduced. If the auctioneer currently chooses a market-clearing price

[21] If banks are prevented by regulation from paying a competitively determined rate of interest, there is also a price-induced effect on wealth through bank money, in a way parallel to the price-induced effect on wealth through government money.

[22] Many discussions focus on a world where the money stock is exogenous and fixed, with government having no ongoing role in maintaining the money stock, and hence not in the position to pay interest. This case is often identified with the gold standard. In fact, governments were often heavily involved with managing metallic money stocks. With a fixed stock of metal, the weight of the average coin fell over time. Money stocks were often "renewed" by calling in all coins and reminting with a lower weight (this was particularly common in England); sometimes the mint kept only enough metal to pay the costs of reminting, but much more often kept more as government seignorage. Further, it is thought that there was a tendency for a net drain of metal (and high-quality coins) in both ancient and medieval times; this caused fluctuations in the nominal money stock. In medieval Europe there were sometimes bullion shortages lasting for decades. One source is thought to be variations in production of new metal; government was often deeply involved in mining, through taxes, requirements for minting, and giving incentives for exploration and mining.

vector for all periods, this doubling of all price levels cannot be a new equilibrium; in this context, the price levels are determinate in the sense that arbitrary price-level displacements cause non-zero excess demands. If the government varies its future money stocks in proportion with the current price level, the future stocks of real balances are unchanged; in this case there are not even future excess demands to make the current price level determinate.

The Initial-Condition Effect

Many economists are reluctant to rely on future excess demands to render determinate the current price level if the government sets an optimizing condition; furthermore, the Johnson–Patinkin worry over determinacy remains when future government money stocks vary proportionately with the current price level. The doubling of all price levels – the current level and all future levels – will create non-zero excess demands in the current period. These excess demands arise not through wealth effects but through the "initial-condition effect." Even if there is no price-induced effect on wealth, the amount of real government money held at the start of the current period falls with an increase in all periods' price levels.[23] In many models of money holdings, an actor accumulates money balances over the current period to have them available at the start of next period to make transactions; the actor would not forego the interest lost by building up money balances in this period if it were possible to acquire costlessly the desired money balances in the first instant of the following period. In these models, a doubling of the price level reduces the adequacy of initial money holdings, necessarily creating non-zero excess demands in some current markets. Thus, the current price level is determinate even without price-induced effects on wealth.

The initial-condition effect is small compared to the usual real balance effect. Suppose a typical consumer holds money balances to reduce transactions costs; let nominal transactions costs be $T = T(M_g^s, P) = PT^*(m) = PT(M_g^s/P, 1)$, where T is homogeneous of degree one in the money stock and the price level expected for next period, and real transactions costs are T^*. In each period, he sets the marginal real benefit of an extra unit of real balances for the next period equal to the interest rate, the opportunity cost of carrying wealth into next period in the form of

---

[23] A parallel initial-condition effect through bank money (and other liquid assets) also exists, but to save space is not discussed here.

money rather than bonds, or sets $dT^*/dm = -i$. A rise in the price level changes the consumer's transactions costs at his initial income-expenditure program by $-(dT^*/dm)\,(M_g^s/P^2) = i\,(M_g^s/P^2)$ or changes wealth by $-i\,(M_g^s/P^2)$. The conventional real balance effect is $-(M_g^s/P^2)$; the initial-condition effect through government money is only a fraction of the usual real balance effect.[24] Though the initial-condition effect suffices to make the price level determinate, it is even less important quantitatively (or an even weaker reed) than the conventional real balance effect.

3   EMPIRICAL WORK ON WEALTH EFFECTS

The intuition of the result that government money has a zero contribution to the price-induced effect on wealth is that with a rise in price, consumers must incur higher costs over time to accumulate the same sequence of real balances as before, but government has lower costs, with the two changes in costs offsetting; when the government reduces its taxes, the consumers are left just as well off as before. This emphasizes that the researcher must take care to look at actors on both sides of the market.

Another illustration is the old issue of the interest-rate-induced effect on wealth.[25] When all one-period interest rates rise, what is the effect on wealth? Borrowers lose, lenders gain. Indeed, if all current and future-period excess demands are initially zero, an increase in interest rates hurts borrowers and helps lenders by exactly the same amount, or the aggregate effect on wealth is zero; assuming no redistribution effects, there is no change in aggregate behavior due to wealth effects. The value of bonds (or more generally, debt) outstanding has fallen, however.

Many econometric models purport to estimate the role of changes in wealth. They often include measures of wealth, for example, the value of the stock market plus the values of outstanding business and government bonds, in behavioral functions. Under the Ricardian Equivalence Hypothesis, the stock of government bonds should not be included if the researcher is looking for effects on wealth; any change in the value of this stock is matched by an offsetting change in the value of private-sector discounted future tax liabilities.

[24] The size of the initial-condition effect relative to the conventional real balance effect is i. The value of i depends on the rate of inflation, through the Fisher effect, and on the duration in calendar time of the Hicksian "week." If low inflation gives a nominal interest rate of 5 percent per annum, and if the calendar-time for the "week" is 7 days, then the ratio is 0.000962 (= 0.05/52), and if a calendar month is 0.00417.
[25] See Pesek and Saving (1967) and Sweeney (1988).

Many changes in the value of the stock market should not be included either. For example, suppose that all current and future markets are clearing, and say unions manage to force a proportionate increase in current and future real wage rates. This reduces the value of firms and thus causes a reduction in wealth as measured by the value of the equity market. On the other side of the labor market, workers are richer. In terms of equivalent variations, the effect on the household sector's wealth nets to zero; as stockholders, consumers are worse off, as wage recipients better off, and by offsetting amounts. Assuming no distribution effects, there is no wealth effect. Thus the movement in the value of the stock market may give important information, but the movement is not an effect on wealth. Similarly, a rise in interest rates reduces the value of corporate bonds outstanding, but under the assumptions above, this fall is not an effect on wealth.

Some movements in the value of the stock market are effects on wealth. For example, suppose that innovations make the capital stock more productive, and that for convenience leave firms' demand for labor unchanged. This leads to a rise in the value of firms, with the effect on wealth equal to this rise in value; there is no one on the other side of the market to be hurt by the increase in the wealth of stockholders.

Applied econometricians may put what variables they like into their models. They may, for example, enter the value of the stock market or the sum of the values of equity plus corporate bonds, and perhaps some fraction of the stock of government bonds. They may not, however, treat all movements in this sum as effects on wealth in the sense of equivalent variations. To the extent that misunderstandings about which movements are changes in wealth leads to misunderstandings of how the economy works, current econometric practice leaves much to be desired.

REFERENCES

Bailey, Martin J. (1971) *National Income and the Price Level*, McGraw-Hill, New York, NY.

Barro, R. and Grossman, H. (1976) *Money, Employment and Inflation*, Cambridge University Press, Cambridge.

Darby, Michael R., Mascaro, Angelo R. and Marlow, Michael L. (1989) "The Empirical Reliability of Monetary Aggregates as Indicators" *Economic Inquiry*, 27, October, pp. 555–86.

Delong, Bradford and Summers, Lawrence (1986) "Is Increased Price Flexibility Destabilizing?" *American Economic Review*, 76, pp. 1031–44.

Dornbusch, Rudiger (1976) "Expectations and Exchange Rate Dynamics" *Journal of*

Political Economy, 84, December, pp. 1161–76.

Fischer, Stanley (1979) "Capital Accumulation on the Transition Path in a Monetary Optimizing Model" *Econometrica*, 47, November, pp. 191–205.

Friedman, Milton, and Schwartz, Anna (1963) *A Monetary History of the United States*, National Bureau for Economic Research, New York, NY.

Haberler, Gottfried (1937) *Prosperity and Depression*, 1st edn, League of Nations, Geneva.

Haberler, Gottfried (1952) "The Pigou Effect Once More" *Journal of Political Economy*, 60, June, pp. 240–46.

Hicks, John R. (1946) *Value and Capital*, Oxford University Press, London.

Johnson, Harry G. (1961) "The General Theory After Twenty-five Years" *American Economic Review*, Supplement 51, May, pp. 1–17.

Kandil, Magda (1993) "Price Flexibility and Aggregate Stability: New Evidence and Implications" *Economic Inquiry*, forthcoming.

Leijonhufvud, Axel (1983) "What was the Matter with IS-LM?" in Fitoussi, J.-P. (ed.), *Modern Macroeconomic Theory*, Blackwell, New York, NY.

Leijonhufvud, Axel (1992) "Keynesian Economics: Past Confusions, Future Prospects" in Vercelli, A. and Dimitri, N. (eds), *Macroeconomics: A Survey of Research Strategies*, Oxford University Press, Oxford.

Lucas, Robert E., Jr. (1973) "Some International Evidence on Output-Inflation Trade-offs" *American Economic Review*, 63, June, pp. 326–34.

Lucas, Robert E., Jr. (1975) "An Equilibrium Model of The Business Cycle" *Journal of Political Economy*, 83, December, pp. 1113–44.

Mankiw, N. Gregory (1989) "Real Business Cycles: A New Keynesian Perspective" *Journal of Economic Perspectives*, 3, pp. 79–90.

McCallum, B.T. (1986) "On 'Real' and 'Sticky-Price' Theories of the Business Cycle" *Journal of Money, Credit and Banking*, 18, November, pp. 397–414.

Meinich, Per (1968) *A Monetary General Equilibrium Theory for An International Economy*, Scandinavian University Books, Copenhagen.

Metzler, Lloyd (1945) "Stability of Multiple Markets: The Hicks Conditions" *Econometrica*, 13, pp. 272–92.

Patinkin, Don (1965) *Money, Interest and Prices*, Harper & Row, New York, NY.

Patinkin, Don (1969) "Money and Wealth: A Review Article" *Journal of Economic Literature*, 7, December, pp. 1140–60.

Patinkin, Don (1972) *Studies in Monetary Economics*, Harper & Row, New York, NY.

Pesek, Boris P. and Saving, Thomas R. (1967) *Money, Wealth and Economic Theory*, Macmillan, New York, NY.

Pigou, A.C. (1943) "The Classical Stationary State" *Economic Journal*, 53, December, pp. 343–51.

Rowe, P. Nicholas (1987) "An Extreme Keynesian Macroeconomic Model with Formal Micro-economic Foundations" *Canadian Journal of Economics*, 20, pp. 306–20.

Samuelson, Paul A. (1947) *Foundations of Economic Analysis*, Harvard University Press, Cambridge, MA.

Sargent, T. (1973) "Rational Expectations, the Real Rate of Interest and the Natural Rate of Employment" Brookings Papers on Economic Activity, 2 , pp. 429–72.

Sargent, T. (1976) "A Classical Macroeconometric Model for the United States" *Journal of Political Economy*, 84, April, pp. 207–37.

Sweeney, Richard J. (1974) *A Macro Theory With Micro Foundations*, South-Western, Cincinnati, OH.

Sweeney, Richard J. (1975) "Inflation, the Balance of Trade, and the Effects of Exchange Rate Adjustments" in Clark, Peter B., Logue, Dennis E. and Sweeney, Richard J. (eds), *The Effects of Exchange Rate Adjustments*, US Treasury Department, Washington, DC.

Sweeney, Richard J. (1984) "Anticipated Countercyclical Monetary Policy" *Economic Inquiry*, 22, January, pp. 28–36.

Sweeney, Richard J. (1988) *Wealth Effects and Monetary Theory*, Basil Blackwell, New York, NY.

9. Using Existing Financial Repression to Blunt the Dutch Disease: A Missed Opportunity in Indonesia

Wing Thye Woo

1 INTRODUCTION

The international financial community was rudely shocked on 15 November 1978 when Indonesia devalued its currency, the Rupiah, by 50 percent. The oil boom that started with the quadrupling of oil prices in 1973 was still going strong. Indonesia's foreign reserves were at an all-time high and there had been no deterioration in the balance of payments. Just a few months before the devaluation, the newspapers were actually speculating about an appreciation of the Rupiah.[1] Furthermore, the just-released November 1978 issue of the respected *Bulletin of Indonesian Economic Studies* offered the assessment that "The overall picture for Indonesia's balance of payments in the current fiscal year is thus still reasonably reassuring. On a longer view, it is difficult to resist the traditional balance of payments pessimism of economists everywhere, official and unofficial alike" (Arndt, 1978).

With the benefit of hindsight, it is now recognized that the 1978 devaluation was the correct remedy for the "Dutch disease" that began with the 1973 oil price increase. The Dutch disease is the phenomenon of the traditional export sector being decimated after the discovery of new minerals. The surge of new mineral exports would appreciate the real exchange rate (defined as the ratio of prices of nontradeables to

---

[1] For example, "Revaluation is not the Solution," *Warta Berita* 6 April 1978; "Would a Revaluation be More Beneficial?" *Merdeka,* 5 May 1978; "A Suggestion that the Rupiah Should be Revalued," *Merdeka* 24 May 1978; "Again, it is not necessary to devalue or revalue," *Suara Karya* 24 June 1978; and "Weak US Dollar Upsets Indonesia's Balancing Act," *Far Eastern Economic Review,* 21 July 1978.

prices of tradeables[2]) and render the production of traditional tradeables unprofitable. The Dutch disease, in essence, is the emergence of new mineral exports that cause relative price changes that shift factors of production from the traditional tradeable sector to the nontradeable sector.

In the case of Indonesia, the 1973 OPEC oil price increase and the rapid development of the oil and gas sectors constituted the equivalent of the discovery of new minerals. The oil boom enabled large increases in government expenditure, and the big balance of payments surpluses increased the money supply. This expansion in aggregate demand caused an inflation that was mainly confined to nontradeable goods and services. This is because the openness of the Indonesian economy allowed international goods arbitrage to keep the Rupiah prices of tradeables to

$$p_R = p_\$ * e * (1 + t),$$
where
p_R = Rupiah price of tradeables in Indonesia,
$p_\$$ = dollar price of tradeables in international markets,
e = Rupiah–dollar exchange rate,
t = tariff rate equivalent if tradeable is importable, and export subsidy rate if tradeable is exportable.

So the export-led demand expansion caused the prices of nontradeables to increase with respect to the prices of the traditional tradeables. Since a major portion of nontradeables were services, which were labor-intensive by nature, wages rose; this reduced the profitability of the traditional tradeable sector. Because Indonesia was an overwhelmingly agricultural country and agricultural products are highly homogeneous tradeables, this relative price shift reduced the benefits of the oil boom for most Indonesians. The 1978 devaluation[3] was an attempt to reverse the relative decline in the prices of traditional tradeables in order to maintain the economic viability of that sector.

The aim of this paper is to take even greater advantage of hindsight and argue that the Dutch disease could have been remedied in a less disruptive manner than the abrupt 50 percent devaluation. Specifically, a tighter monetary policy would have been a less painful way of

---

[2] See Wing Thye Woo (1991a) for a discussion on the various definitions of the real exchange rate and their interrelationships.
[3] In terms of the above equation, the devaluation raises p_R by raising e.

combatting the Dutch disease. Under the financially repressed system of that time, where most credits were allocated administratively at controlled interest rates, the tighter monetary policy could have been concentrated on reducing private consumption and would have had little impact on capital formation.[4] We make our argument by outlining the economic mechanism of the Dutch disease in section 2; recasting the economic mechanism within the familiar IS-LM framework in section 3 to introduce monetary policy into the analysis; and, finally, using simulation in section 4, to show the superiority of tight monetary policy over devaluation as the cure for the Dutch disease.

2 THE MECHANISM OF THE DUTCH DISEASE

The curve AA' in Figure 9.1a represents Indonesia's production possibility frontier before the sharp rise of the oil sector. By abstracting from growth and assuming that the economy is initially at a long-run equilibrium, the production possibility frontier also becomes the consumption possibility frontier of the economy – that is, the net saving of this constant population is zero. The slope of the curve is the ratio of the price of tradeables to the price of nontradeables. We assume that the composition of aggregate demand is unaffected by the distribution of income between the public and private sectors. These assumptions generate the consumption bundle at point W (Q_0 units of tradeables and N_0 units of nontradeables). If the social indifference function is homothetic, the straight line OE is the income expansion path of the relative price given at W.

Indonesia's oil industry is capital-intensive and most of the capital has been supplied by foreign oil companies. Expansion of the industry therefore drew little labor and capital away from the nonoil sectors. The growth of the oil industry and the first price shock can be modeled as oil exports bringing a net income equivalent to f units of tradeables. This is represented in Figure 9.1a by curve BB', which is a rightward shift of AA' by the amount f, making the production possibility frontier now ABB', with the length of AB equal to f. The new production possibility frontier has the same slope as the old one for a given value of nontradeables. The slope at point X is the same as at point W.

---

[4] See Woo (forthcoming) for details of the financial repression.

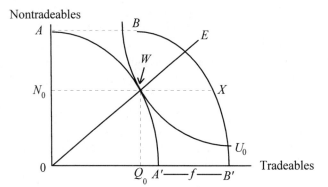

Figure 9.1a

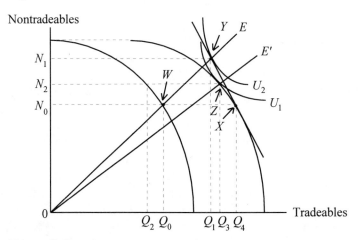

Figure 9.1b

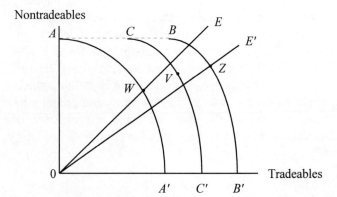

Figure 9.1c

Assuming that relative prices adjust with a lag, this means that at the time of the oil boom the output mix is denoted by point X, and the desired consumption mix is denoted by point Y (Figure 9.1b). The results are an excess demand for nontradeables, given by $N_1 - N_0$, and an excess supply of tradeables, $Q_4 - Q_1$. Disequilibrium then causes the prices of nontradeables to rise and the prices of tradeables to fall. The lowering of the relative prices of tradeables shifts the new output mix to the left of X and the new demand mix to the right of OY. The new equilibrium is at point Z with output consisting of Q_3 units of tradeables (of which Q_2 units are traditional tradeables) and N_2 units of nontradeables. This shrinkage of traditional tradeables (from Q_0 to Q_2) along with increased output of nontradeables is known as the Dutch disease.

The welfare implications of an oil boom are straightforward as long as the increase in income from oil exports, f, is permanent. The movement from W to Z is efficient, and the decline of the traditional tradeable industries is not a cause for concern. The only way to keep the output of the traditional tradeables at Q_0 is for the country to shift its consumption possibility frontier *back* to the old production possibility frontier by accumulating foreign reserves worth f every period. But a return to the past would be irrational. There would then be no welfare gain from the greater prosperity, since consumption would not change.[5]

The Dutch disease is a disease only if the increase in income is temporary. The "disease" is the result of the adjustment costs incurred in the shift from W to Z during the boom and then back to W after the boom ends. The economics literature has so far focused only on these back-and-forth adjustment costs. We want to point out that the Dutch disease involves another cost when the revenue from the resource boom goes to the government rather than to the private sector. This additional cost comes from intertemporal inefficiency in consumption.

Consumption theory holds that temporary increases in income result in less than equivalent increases in consumption because private consumers realize that the increase in income is temporary and hence spread the temporary income over the rest of their lifespans. In terms of Figure 9.1b, this means that the consumption possibility frontier is found between the old and the new production possibility frontiers. The costs incurred in changing the product mix mean that private consumers will

---

[5] If f goes to the government, another way to keep the product mix at W is to spend the new revenue on tradeables, but our assumption that the government mimics private expenditure in order to maximize consumer welfare rules out this possibility.

further contract the consumption possibility frontier from ABB'. In general, the shorter the duration of the increase in income and the larger the adjustment costs, the closer the consumption possibility frontier will be to the original production possibility frontier. Figure 9.1c shows curve CC' to be the efficient consumption possibility frontier and point V to be the sustainable equilibrium if the oil income had accrued to private agents.

In Indonesia, however, all oil income net of payments to the foreign oil companies and net of the (insignificant) payments to domestic labor goes to the government. It was natural for the various interest groups to argue for a consumption possibility frontier higher than CC' because no group could be assured that the future distribution of power (and hence income) would be to its advantage.[6]

There is a second major political reason for the Indonesian government's inability to reduce public absorption, viz., government expenditure. When the present government took power in 1966, it pledged to observe a balanced budget from 1967 onward as its commitment to macroeconomic stability. Thus, when the oil revenue started gushing in from 1972 onward, state spending went up accordingly. The political benefits of the increased spending, of course, made observance of the balanced budget pledge an easier task.

As a result of political pressures and the balanced budget practice, Indonesia's absorption level was much closer to, if not actually at, ABB'. The two costs imposed by the oil boom were a consumption inefficiency due to distortion of intertemporal allocation and the costs of adjusting to shifts in the product mix. These two costs were positively correlated. The farther away from CC' the actual consumption possibility frontier was, the larger the intertemporal inefficiency and the larger the adjustment costs.

The lesson from the above analysis is that intertemporal consumption and production efficiency requires that national (private and public) absorption during the oil boom be lower than the maximum level possible. Herein lies the point of this paper: despite the inflexibility in fiscal policy due to the balanced budget practice and myopic political lobbying, the government could have attenuated the severity of the Dutch disease by using monetary policy to lower private absorption.

[6] See Woo (1991b) for details of the political economy of policy-making in Indonesia.

3 THE MONETARY FACTORS IN THE DUTCH DISEASE

During the 1970s, the Indonesian monetary authorities had little control over the money supply in the short run. The chief instrument of monetary control before April 1974 was direct central bank credit to state and private enterprises. Since these credits were extended for a *contractually fixed period of time*, there was no way to reduce the money supply quickly. So when the oil boom began, and the government financed its increased expenditure by converting the dollar earnings of the oil exports into rupiahs at the fixed exchange rate, the domestic money stock exploded.

When oil revenue in 1972 increased by 90 billion rupiahs over 1971 (a 64 percent increase), reserve money growth was 46 percent compared to the 29 percent of the previous 2 years. Then the price of oil quadrupled at the end of 1973, encouraging the government to increase its spending. Reserve money grew 57 percent in 1974 and the inflation rate for that year was 41 percent.

The central bank responded to this monetary anarchy in April 1974 by setting lending ceilings on the banking system. However, the credit ceilings were not able to cut the link between the reserve base (which is directly affected by the oil export earnings) and the money supply. When reserve money grew 33 percent in 1975, M1 grew 35 percent. Further evidence for this conclusion is the upsurge in money growth in 1979 (32 percent) and 1980 (36 percent) when the OPEC-2 price increase occurred.

The main reason why the credit ceilings did not control the money supply effectively was because they were extremely cumbersome to change. It was almost impossible to reset the aggregate credit ceiling at short notice. Quick ceiling changes were difficult because there were separate ceilings for each kind of credit; the ceiling for the same credit category varied across banks; and changes were made only after consultation with each bank. The consultation with each bank was necessary because most bank loans were extended for a fixed period of time. Any unilateral action by the central bank to lower the total amount of credit could potentially bankrupt some banks or automatically make criminals out of them (because the banks could not for contractual reason reduce their outstanding loans). The standard operating procedure which emerged from this complicated situation was to change the credit ceilings at the beginning of the year.

There was also an asymmetry in the management of bank credits. Banks could request, and many times received, higher ceilings during the year; but the central bank shied from lowering the credit ceilings in response to economic events during the year. It is thus misleading to say that the central bank had three instruments of monetary control (credit ceilings, reserve requirements and central bank credit) because the first two cannot be frequently used to reduce credit on short notice.

During times of low credit demand, the credit ceilings were operative by default; demand was lower than supply. But whenever the total domestic credit demand was higher than the aggregate credit ceiling, the excess demand would be partially relieved by some rise in the interest rates,[7] occasionally some relaxation of the ceilings and *by credits from abroad*. The last mechanism is possible because there has been no control on capital account transactions since 1967. The result was that big Indonesian firms could supplement their domestic credit with credit from international banks stationed in Singapore and Hong Kong whenever domestic bank lending was reduced. The conversion of the private external credit through the balance of payments automatically increased the domestic money supply since the credit ceilings could not be constantly reset to offset the capital inflows. Furthermore, sterilization through open-market operations was not possible because of the absence of developed financial markets. It is crucial to note that private capital inflows increased the money supply only by the amount of the increase in the monetary base when the credit ceiling is binding. *The money multiplier had a value of one because the credit ceiling prevented the banks from expanding credit in line with the rise in deposits.*[8]

It is a well-known theoretical result that if private agents regard domestic and foreign financial assets to be imperfect substitutes, then domestic interest rates would not equal foreign interest rates even when there are no barriers to borrowing from abroad under a fixed exchange regime. In this imperfect asset substitutability case, the private capital flow equation is a positive function of the domestic interest rate and a negative function of the foreign interest rate.

We want to make the point here that *even if private agents regarded Indonesian and foreign financial assets to be perfect substitutes, there*

---

[7] The deposit and lending rates of the state banks were controlled by the government and those of private and foreign banks were not. The state banking system dwarfed its competitors both in business volume and number of branches.

[8] The Indonesian banks would often deposit these excess reserves with the international banks in Singapore and Hong Kong. This meant that the foreign debt incurred by domestic private agents became the foreign exchange reserves of the commercial banks.

would not have been sufficient private capital flow in the 1970s to enforce interest rate equalization. The reasons for this phenomenon are the domestic banks had no interest in borrowing cheaper funds from abroad because of the credit ceiling; the small and medium firms did not have access to the international credit market; and the big firms which did have access were not willing to risk taking on large-scale intermediation activities for the small firms. The proof of small Indonesian firms being unable to get locally intermediated international credit during the 1970s can be seen by the lending rates of secondary banks in the rural areas being two and a half times those of commercial urban banks, and by the lending rates of the curb market being six times those of the organized sector.

In short, tight credit policy could still deflate the Indonesian economy even if perfect substitutability were true because of the inability of small Indonesian business to obtain international credit. So even in the perfect substitutability case, private capital flows in Indonesia during the 1970s can also be modeled as a positive function of the domestic interest rate and as a negative function of the foreign interest rate. The result of the Indonesian central bank being reluctant to reset credit ceilings downward during the calendar year was that private capital flows endogenized the money supply, but due to financial market fragmentation these flows were not large enough to equalize the domestic interest rate with the foreign interest rate.[9]

One rigorous way to decide the degree of endogeneity in the money supply is to investigate whether capital flows have been able to systematically offset changes in the volume of domestically created credits, i.e., to estimate the offset coefficient.[10] Maxwell Fry (1988) has done this but his evidence is only suggestive because he grouped Indonesia with Korea, Malaysia, Philippines and Thailand in the estimation. He found the offset coefficient of the group to be 0.6, a sign that the credit ceilings were not able to fully shelter the money supply from capital flows.

Another indirect piece of evidence in favor of the ineffectiveness of the credit ceilings comes from the finding by Anwar Nasution (1983) that the Indonesian data during this period are very well characterized by a model which assumed a positive relationship between the money supply and the balance of payments. The government was capable of

[9] Balino and Sundarajan (1986) also concluded that structural features segmented the domestic financial market from the foreign ones.

[10] A zero value connotes total control over the money stock and a unity value connotes complete lack of control. In a fixed exchange rate setting, a non-unity value also means that the home financial assets are not regarded as perfect substitutes for foreign financial assets.

controlling the money supply, but it chose not to when it did not actively manage the amount of central bank credit outstanding. The result was that the money supply became endogenous during the Dutch disease period. Either because of small Indonesian firms being unable to get foreign credit or because of imperfect asset substitutability, Indonesian interest rates did not move in lock-step fashion with foreign interest rates.

We now use the preceding discussion to explicitly show the link between monetary control and the Dutch disease. This link can be formally represented by the following money supply equation:

$$\dot{m} = 1/M_0 \, (\, k + x + d \,) \tag{9.1}$$

where

m = money supply, expressed as a logarithm,

$\dot{m}$ = derivative of m with respect to time,

M_0 = the level of money supply at beginning of period,

k = capital account position in the balance of payments with private capital flows responding positively (negatively) to increases in domestic interest rate r (foreign interest rate r^*), i.e., $k(r,r^*)$,

x = trade account balance, detailed in equation (9.4) below, and

d = increase in money due to central bank action.

There is a limit to the use of d to offset the monetary consequences from the balance of payments position given the finite stock of foreign reserves. The money supply, m, can be kept constant only as long as the *sustained* balance of payments disequilibrium is the result of *surpluses* and not deficits. Given the inability to conduct open-market operations, to reset credit ceilings quickly, and to change direct central bank credit in response to capital flows, $d = 0$. The result is that the domestic money supply is endogenous.

The relation between the controllability of money supply and the Dutch disease can be analyzed by supplementing equation (9.1) with the following model:

aggregate supply,	$y^s = y_n + f$	(9.2)
aggregate demand,	$y^d = a(r, y_n) + g + x$	(9.3)
trade balance,	$x = x_0 + x_1(e + p^* - p)$	(9.4)
money market equilibrium,	$m - p = b(r, y_n)$	(9.5)

Equation (9.2) is GDP by sector – y_n from the nonoil sector and f from the oil sector. Since the oil sector employs very little labor, we assume that all labor was engaged in producing y_n. In light of the extreme flexibility of the Indonesian labor market as evidenced by large swings in the real wage series, we take y_n to be exogenous. Aggregate demand, equation (9.3), is the sum of private absorption, government expenditure and the trade balance. Private absorption, $a(r, y_n)$, is a function of the interest rate and nonoil income. Oil income does not affect private absorption directly because it goes to the government.

The first component of equation (9.4), x_0, is a convenient way to model increases in (price-insensitive) government expenditure on imports ($dx_0 < 0$) and increases in oil exports ($dx_0 = df > 0$). The second component of equation (9.4) represents the response of the private sector to the relative price of home goods and foreign goods. In the analytical exercises below, this second component of equation (9.4) represents the net export of *nonoil* goods. The term e is the nominal exchange rate (rupiahs per unit of foreign currency), p^* is the foreign price level, and p is the domestic price level, all expressed in log forms. The terms e and p^* are exogenous. The demand for money in equation (9.5) depends on y_n and not $y_n + f$ because oil is mined by foreign companies and exported. The bulk of the demand for the rupiah comes from transactions to produce y_n.

This one-good macroeconomic model cannot reproduce the structural details of sectoral resource allocation in the real model. The Dutch disease has to be interpreted as the shrinkage of the traditional export industries and the expansion of imports, i.e., a diminution of the traditional net exports. The real exchange rate in this model is the national terms of trade rather than the sectoral terms of trade.[11] This macroeconomic model highlights the role of fiscal and monetary policies in determining national absorption, and the path of adjustment.[12]

We will now establish two propositions.

Proposition 1: If the government were to increase its spending by the amount of oil revenue, the ability (or willingness) to cut the link between the balance of payments position and the money supply would permit amelioration of the Dutch disease.

Proof. Step 1: Either with the existence of domestic financial markets, (which makes open-market operations possible) or with the constant changing of credit ceilings, the money supply could have been kept constant. We get

---

[11] The national terms of trade and sectoral terms of trade are obviously not identical. In Woo (1991), I show that these two definitions of the terms of trade have a one-to-one relationship under the modern definition which assumes the law of one price.

[12] For dynamic analysis, the additional assumptions are that $p = c(y^d - y^s)$ and that equation (9.5) always holds.

$(dr)_1 = -df/(a_r + x_1 b_r) > 0$
$(dp)_1 = b_r df/(a_r + x_1 b_r) > 0$
Shrinkage of net traditional exports $= x_1 df/(a_r + x_1 b_r)$.

Step 2: When the balance of payments position influences the money supply, we get

$(dm)_2 = df/x_1$
$(dr)_2 = 0$
$(dp)_2 = df/x_1$

As $(dp)_2 - (dp)_1 = a_r df/[x_1(a_r + x_1 b_r)] > 0$, the Dutch disease is more serious when the domestic money stock cannot be controlled.

Step 3: If there is good control over the money stock, an aggressively contractionary policy can be used to completely offset the Dutch disease effects caused by the expanded public spending. To prevent the shrinkage of net traditional exports, the money supply can be varied to keep p constant. It can be easily shown that $dm = -(b_r/a_r)df$ will reduce private absorption by the amount of the increase in public absorption, df.

Q.E.D.

Proposition 2: A nominal exchange rate devaluation will not result in a long-run real exchange rate depreciation only if the money supply is endogenous.

Proof. Step 1: When money supply is endogenous we get:

$(dm)_3 = (df + x_1 de)/x_1 > 0$
$(dr)_3 = 0$
$(dp)_3 = (df + x_1 de)/x_1 > 0;$
therefore
$d(e-p) = -df/x_1.$
The net real exchange rate movement is the same as $de = 0$.

Step 2: When money supply is held constant,

$(dr)_4 = -(df + x_1 de)/(a_r + x_1 b_r)$
$(dp)_4 = b_r(df + x_1 de)/(a_r + x_1 b_r).$

Therefore, if we set $de = b_r df/a_r$, then $d(e-p) = 0$; we get complete elimination of the Dutch disease.

Q.E.D.

An objection may be raised to our suggested method of ameliorating the Dutch disease effects by crowding out private absorption. Since the crowding out is through the interest rate mechanism, the decrease in private absorption would mainly take the form of a decline in private investment. In short, our suggested method would involve a trade-off between maintaining the economic viability of the nonoil export sector and economic growth.

However, in the case of Indonesia in the 1970s, such a trade-off could have been avoided. This is because a large part of the credit was allocated by government directives rather than by the market mechanism. Since only about 30 percent of outstanding credit was investment credit and since more than 90 percent of investment credit was extended by the state banks, the government could have directed the state banks to simultaneously increase the amount of investment credit (hence boosting private investment) *and* reduce the total amount of credit. In short, the repressed financial system of the 1970s would have allowed the government to channel all the direct negative effects of the credit crunch on private consumption spending.

4   ASSESSING THE RELATIVE EFFICACY OF DEVALUATION AND TIGHT MONETARY POLICY IN BLUNTING THE DUTCH DISEASE

We now investigate how the loose monetary policy had affected the production mix between tradeables and nontradeables. We do this by considering the counterfactual scenario of an annual 20 percent money growth rule over the 1973–80 period *with the effects of (nominal) credit availability on investment kept the same in the counterfactual case as in the actual case*.[13] The counterfactual analysis is conducted using a macroeconometric model of Indonesia estimated by economists at the State Planning Board (BAPPENAS) (Kobayashi, Tampubolon and Ezaki, 1985).

Column II of item (a) in Table 9.1 shows that if a 20 percent money growth rule had been implemented, the price level in 1980 would have been less than half of its actual value. The lower inflation would have boosted exports and discouraged imports. Throughout the 1975–79 period, real nonoil nongas exports would have been at least 12 percent higher each year, with the counterfactual figure in 1980 being 21 percent higher; see column IV of item (b) in Table 9.1. Real imports would also have averaged an annual 26 percent lower in the 1975–80 period.

---

[13] The imposition of this requirement does not mean that the counterfactual level of investment would equal the actual level. Private investment spending depended on other variables besides the amount of allocated credit; see equation R.12 of the BAPPENAS model.

Table 9.1   Effects of a 20 percent money growth rule on the trade sector

Year	I Baseline[a]	II Tight money[b]	III Tight money with no devaluation[c]	IV Effect of tight money (% of baseline)	V Effect of tight money and no 1978 devaluation (% of baseline)
(a) GDP deflator					
1973	100.0	83.1	83.1	−16.9	−16.9
1974	120.3	83.3	83.3	−30.8	−30.8
1975	135.2	85.7	85.7	−36.6	−36.6
1976	152.6	90.3	90.3	−40.9	−40.9
1977	159.9	99.5	99.5	−37.8	−37.8
1978	168.4	106.6	106.1	−36.7	−37.0
1979	198.2	113.7	110.2	−42.6	−44.4
1980	257.3	123.8	117.0	−51.9	−54.5
(b) Real nonoil nonLNG exports					
1973	651.3	684.9	684.9	5.2	5.2
1974	721.6	793.1	793.1	9.9	9.9
1975	719.8	809.7	809.7	12.5	12.5
1976	767.6	881.2	881.2	14.8	14.8
1977	849.7	961.5	961.5	13.2	13.2
1978	871.8	983.7	968.1	12.8	11.0
1979	1,022.9	1,183.2	1,068.8	15.7	4.5
1980	972.3	1,180.4	1,071.8	21.4	10.2
(c) Nonoil nonLNG exports in US$ million					
1973	1,569.4	1,650.3	1,650.3	5.2	5.2
1974	2,333.3	2,564.5	2,564.5	9.9	9.9
1975	2,105.5	2,368.4	2,368.4	12.5	12.5
1976	2,739.3	3,144.6	3,144.6	14.8	14.8
1977	4,022.5	4,551.8	4,551.8	13.2	13.2
1978	4,114.2	4,642.1	4,568.4	12.8	11.0
1979	7,007.7	8,105.7	7,321.9	15.7	4.5
1980	7,418.6	9,006.2	8,177.4	21.4	10.2

Table 9.1 continued

(d) Real imports

1973	1,268.6	1,095.5	1,095.5	−13.6	−13.6
1974	1,352.6	1,032.3	1,032.3	−23.7	−23.7
1975	1,382.2	1,036.6	1,036.6	−25.0	−25.0
1976	1,675.0	1,270.8	1,270.8	−24.1	−24.1
1977	4,022.5	1,596.3	1,596.3	−60.3	−60.3
1978	2,346.0	1,911.6	1,963.8	−18.5	−16.3
1979	2,566.7	2,071.7	2,416.7	−19.3	−5.8
1980	3,331.3	2,628.0	3,003.3	−21.1	−9.8

[a] Actual money growth; actual exchange rate.
[b] Tight money growth; actual exchange rate.
[c] Tight money growth; exchange rate set at 415 for 1978–80.

We next extend the counterfactual analysis to ask whether Indonesia would have been better off if it had maintained a tight monetary policy with *no subsequent devaluation*. Column III of Table 9.1 gives the counterfactual consequences of this type of tight monetary policy. It shows that the volume and dollar earnings of nonoil nongas exports under the "tight money – no devaluation" scenario would have been higher than the actual levels in the 1978–80 period. The additional nonoil nongas exports of the 1973–80 period would have increased the foreign exchange reserves by $3,037 million, which is 56 percent of Indonesian nongold reserves in 1980. Counterfactual real imports in 1978–80 would still have been lower than the actual level achieved with the devaluation.

What would have been the cost of this strengthening of the trade sector through tight monetary policy? Specifically, by how much would growth have been stunted? Table 9.2 suggests that the economic costs would have been small. Annual real GDP would have been only half a percent lower, and the *number of unemployed* (not the unemployment rate) would have increased by 1 percent. Because of the maintenance of investment credit availability, the reduced absorption caused by the 20 percent money growth rule would have come from the fall in private consumption. For example, in 1976 the counterfactual private consumption was Rp 340 billion lower (1973 prices) while counterfactual private investment was only Rp 20 billion lower (1973 prices). (Real public consumption and real public investment are assumed exogenous in the model.) The total real capital stock in 1980 would have at most been 0.8 percent lower than the actual value; see columns IV and V of item (e) in Table 9.2.

Table 9.2   The costs of a 20 percent money growth rule

Year	I Baseline[a]	II Tight money[b]	III Tight money with no devaluation[c]	IV Effect of tight money (% of baseline)	V Effect of tight money and no 1978 devaluation (% of baseline)
(a) Real GDP (1973 prices)					
1973	6,464.3	6,464.3	6,464.3	0.0	0.0
1974	6,941.6	6,912.2	6,912.2	−0.4	−0.4
1975	7,456.6	7,420.3	7,420.3	−0.5	−0.5
1976	8,031.3	8,002.2	8,002.2	−0.4	−0.4
1977	8,724.1	8,689.4	8,689.4	−0.4	−0.4
1978	9,497.9	9,471.1	9,471.1	−0.3	−0.3
1979	10,362.0	10,320.0	10,320.0	−0.4	−0.4
1980	11,276.0	11,234.0	11,236.0	−0.4	−0.4
(b) Number of unemployed (in thousands)					
1973	1,103.5	1,103.5	1,103.5	0.0	0.0
1974	1,145.9	1,155.8	1,155.8	0.9	0.9
1975	1,166.2	1,178.4	1,178.4	1.0	1.0
1976	1,161.9	1,171.7	1,171.7	0.8	0.8
1977	1,131.0	1,142.6	1,142.6	1.0	1.0
1978	1,078.9	1,088.0	1,088.0	0.8	0.8
1979	999.4	1,013.6	1,013.6	1.4	1.4
1980	913.7	927.7	927.1	1.5	1.5
(c) Real private consumption					
1973	4,437.3	4,343.9	4,343.9	−2.1	−2.1
1974	4,839.3	4,438.2	4,438.2	−8.3	−8.3
1975	5,078.4	4,571.1	4,571.1	−10.0	−10.0
1976	5,413.2	4,877.1	4,877.1	−9.9	−9.9
1977	5,689.0	5,110.5	5,110.5	−10.2	−10.2
1978	6,444.4	5,915.8	5,982.9	−8.2	−7.2
1979	7,178.9	6,462.7	6,916.2	−10.0	−3.7
1980	7,994.6	7,095.5	7,569.5	−11.2	−5.3

Table 9.2 continued

(d) Real private investment

1973	828.7	713.1	713.1	−13.9	−13.9
1974	821.7	795.2	795.2	−3.2	−3.2
1975	852.3	879.2	879.2	3.2	3.2
1976	987.9	966.5	966.5	−2.2	−2.2
1977	1,023.4	1,051.4	1,051.4	2.7	2.7
1978	1,213.8	1,156.9	1,157.5	−4.7	−4.6
1979	1,283.8	1,285.2	1,290.5	0.1	0.5
1980	1,506.6	1,427.9	1,437.9	−5.2	−4.6

(e) Real capital stock

1973	16,893.0	16,777.0	16,777.0	−0.7	−0.7
1974	17,792.0	17,653.0	17,653.0	−0.8	−0.8
1975	18,845.0	18,735.0	18,735.0	−0.6	−0.6
1976	20,212.0	20,083.0	20,083.0	−0.6	−0.6
1977	21,753.0	21,654.0	21,654.0	−0.5	−0.5
1978	23,494.0	23,340.0	23,341.0	−0.7	−0.7
1979	25,251.0	25,103.0	25,108.0	−0.6	−0.6
1980	27,587.0	27,363.0	27,378.0	−0.8	−0.8

[a] Actual money growth; actual exchange rate.
[b] Tight money growth; actual exchange rate.
[c] Tight money growth; exchange rate set at 415 for 1978–80.

Tables 9.1 and 9.2 clearly show that the loose monetary policy during the oil boom hurt the tradeable sector. The 1978 devaluation was a much needed move. The comparison of columns II and III in Table 9.2 reveals that the costs in 1979 of using devaluation to strengthen the tradeable sector were a 6 percent drop in real private consumption and a 0.4 percent drop in real private investment.

5   CONCLUSION

The main lesson of this paper is an old one. In a world where distortions already exist, the correction of some types of distortions can be made easier by using a solution that uses the remaining distortions to enhance its effectiveness. In the Indonesian situation in the 1970s, the existing financial repression could have been used to enable tight monetary policy to eliminate the Dutch disease. The 50 percent devaluation of November 1978 was the correct policy response, but its abruptness meant that it was also a more disruptive cure.

The fundamental problem of the Dutch disease in Indonesia was the intertemporal distortion of consumption. Myopic political lobbying and the adherence to the balanced budget principle meant that Indonesia, from the permanent income perspective, was consuming too much of the proceeds of the *temporary* oil windfall. A tight monetary policy implemented within the existing financial repression would have reduced the intertemporal distortion by cutting private absorption to accommodate the increased public absorption.

REFERENCES

Arndt, Heinz (1978) "Survey of Recent Developments" *Bulletin of Indonesian Economic Studies*, vol. 14, no. 3, November, pp. 1–28.
Balino, Tomas and Sundarajan, V. (1986) "Financial Reform in Indonesia: Causes, Consequences, and Prospects" in Cheng, Hang-Sheng (ed.), *Financial Policy and Reform in Pacific Basin Countries*, Lexington Books, Lexington, MA.
Fry, Maxwell (1988) *Money, Interest, and Banking in Economic Development*, Johns Hopkins University Press, Baltimore, MD.
Kobayashi, Kasumi, Tampubolon, Hasdungan and Ezaki, Mitsuo (1985) "Indonesia Model" in Ichimura, Shinichi and Ezaki, Mitsuo (eds), *Econometric Models of Asian Link*, Springer-Verlag.
Nasution, Anwar (1983) *Financial Institutions and Policies in Indonesia*, Institute of Southeast Asian Studies, Singapore.
Woo, Wing Thye (1991a) "Integrating the Real Exchange Rate into Growth-Oriented Macroeconomic Management" Working Paper No. 375, February, Economics Department, University of California, Davis, CA.
Woo, Wing Thye (1991b) "Using Economic Methodology to Assess Competing Models of Economic Policy-Making in Indonesia" *ASEAN Economic Policy*, vol. 7, no. 3, March, pp. 307–21.
Woo, Wing Thye (forthcoming) "The Structure of Indonesia's Financial System and its Consequences" in Haggard, Stephen and Lee, Chung (eds), *Government, Financial Systems, and Economic Development: Allocation and Efficiency*, Cornell University Press, Ithaca, NY.

10. Identifying Monetary and Credit Shocks

Steven M. Sheffrin

1 INTRODUCTION

In recent years there has been increased interest in using novel sources of a priori information in econometric work. Econometricians, of course, have always stressed that a priori information is required to proceed from reduced forms to structural equations. They traditionally have emphasized using economic theory which leads to either exclusion restrictions or cross-equation restrictions to provide the necessary a priori information.

Both of these sources of a priori information have been challenged. Sims (1980) emphasizes that dynamic economic theory typically implies that exclusion restrictions will be rare to the extent that expectations of endogenous variables (rational or not) enter into the behavioral equations of the model. Since these expectations are likely to be functions of the exogenous variables in the model, it is difficult to rationalize the exclusion of exogenous variables from any equation. Lucas and Sargent (1981) have advocated using the cross-equation restrictions that emerge from dynamic rational expectations models to provide the necessary identification restrictions. However, this approach is very sensitive to the precise dynamic specification of the model and has not been very successful to date.

Macroeconomists have attempted to cope with these difficulties in two ways. First, they have tried to use what they view as only limited a priori information. Examples of this include assuming a recursive structure in traditional vector autoregressions (VARs), restrictions on only contemporaneous variables in structural VARs (Bernanke, 1986), and restrictions on the long-run properties of economic systems. A second approach has been to bring institutional or historical information into macroeconomic debates. This paper explores the interface of these two strategies.

There have been two distinct approaches to integrating historical a priori information into macroeconomic analysis. Hoover (1991) and Hoover and Sheffrin (1992) use historical information to identify potential structural breaks and then determine the nature of the causal relations of economic variables. The emphasis in this work is on determining causal structure without having to achieve identification of structural equations.

A second approach to incorporating historical information has been taken by Romer and Romer (1989). Following in the tradition of Friedman and Schwartz (1963), they first identify periods in which they believe that the Federal Reserve has changed policies (specifically, tightened monetary policy to reduce inflation). They then conduct univariate, dynamic simulations for unemployment and industrial production and view the downturns in these series as evidence for the efficacy of contractionary monetary policy. Essentially, the monetary policy episodes are associated with the error terms in the univariate models for unemployment and industrial production. A priori information is thus used to identify structural "shocks" or structural disturbances to econometric equations.

Before proceeding it is important to note that these are two very distinct methods for utilizing a priori information. Under the "structural break" approach, history is used to isolate periods of institutional change. These changes are assumed to be important enough so that the underlying structural equations actually change. The "shock" approach is quite different. This method uses history to identify periods in which, controlling for other factors, economic policy is seen to be extreme. However, it is not so extreme as to change the underlying structural equations. In other words, history is used to find large residuals in an otherwise unchanged structure.

Hoover and Perez (1994) have questioned the approach taken by Romer and Romer on other grounds. Among their several points, they emphasize that disturbances in univariate equations can represent a variety of factors from other variables in an entire system. In this case, using historical methods to associate monetary policy changes with a residual in a univariate equation may produce misleading results.

Residuals in equations can also be extremely sensitive to the econometric specification. As an example, Thomas Mayer (1978) found that an unexplained "shock" to consumption identified by Peter Temin (1976), which Temin viewed as a cause of the Great Depression, disappeared when the estimation period was changed.

This paper examines whether historical methods that identify a priori shocks with residuals to equations produce results which are consistent with commonly used macroeconomic time-series methods. Specifically, are the structural residuals from vector time-series models consistent with the shocks as identified by historical analysis? To address this question, we first use several prior studies to identify periods in which there allegedly were shocks to money or shocks to credit. We then use several alternative methods to obtain structural residuals from reduced-form residuals in vector autoregressions. Finally, we compare the structural residuals to the historical episodes.

Section 2 presents a summary of the results of several studies that attempted to identify shocks to money or credit from historical or institutional analysis. Section 3 discusses our statistical methods and several econometric issues. Econometric results are presented in section 4, followed by an overall assessment of this approach in section 5.

2   HISTORICAL EPISODES OF MONEY AND CREDIT SHOCKS

This paper uses one source of historical research to identify monetary shocks and two sources for credit shocks. The econometric work uses quarterly data so that all monthly dates are converted to the corresponding quarters. For the monetary shocks, we rely on the work of Romer and Romer. They read the Records of Policy Actions of the Federal Open Market Committee (FOMC) as well as the minutes of these meetings, when they were available, to determine when the Fed decided to slow economic growth substantially to reduce inflation. Their dates have been widely used in empirical work and have not been challenged on a historical basis. However, they do appear to conflict with the rational partisan business cycle literature that argues that monetary-induced downturns occur at the beginning of Republican administrations. This point is discussed more fully in Sheffrin (1989).

For credit shocks, we rely on Eckstein's work (1983) on the Data Resources, Inc. (DRI) model with Alan Sinai and a recent paper on credit crunches by Owens and Schreft (1992). Eckstein and Sinai define a credit-crunch period as follows: (1) there is a sharp increase in the Federal Funds rate; (2) the banking system has high net borrowed reserves; (3) there is an inverted term structure; (4) there is a weakening of business cash flow; and (5) there is a deterioration of balance sheets.

Owens and Schreft took a different approach. They reserved the term "credit crunch" to refer to periods when there is explicit credit rationing. They proceed in a fashion similar to Romer and Romer, examining the historical record to find periods of sharply increased credit rationing. Their main source is lenders reports of non-price credit rationing.

Table 10.1 lists the quarterly dates from 1962 to 1984 for all the credit and money shocks as well as National Bureau of Economic Research (NBER) peaks for reference. The time period corresponds to the econometric work reported below. The Romer and Romer shocks occur at different times than shocks to credit. Owens and Schreft find fewer episodes of credit shocks than Eckstein and Sinai. In their interpretation, some of the Eckstein-Sinai periods are not times of increasing non-price rationing.

Table 10.1   Quarterly dates of monetary and credit shocks in 1962–84

Credit		Money	NBER Peaks
Eckstein-Sinai	Owens-Schreft	Romer-Romer	
	1966.2–1966.3		
1966.4			
		1968.4	
	1969.2–1969.4		1969.4
1970.1			
			1973.4
		1974.2	
1974.3			
		1978.3	
		1979.4	
1980.1	1980.1–1980.2		1980.1
			1981.3
1982.2			

3   ECONOMETRIC METHODS

The econometric analysis will take place within the context of vector autoregressions. We will assume that the reduced form of all the models can be written as:

$$\mathbf{Y}_t = \sum_{i=1}^{n} \mathbf{B}_i \mathbf{Y}_{t-i} + \gamma \bullet \mathbf{X}_t + \mathbf{U}_t \qquad (10.1)$$

where Y_t is a column vector of endogenous variables, X is a vector of exogenous or predetermined variables, and U_t is a vector of reduced-form disturbances with a covariance matrix Ω. A structural specification will be a transformation of the reduced-form system and, in particular, a transformation of the disturbances.

The models under consideration will contain measures of credit, money, prices and output. For output and prices, the measures will be real GNP and the GNP deflator. Choosing measures for credit and money are more difficult. For credit, we use the sum of commercial and industrial loans plus nonfinancial commercial paper and deflate this measure by the GNP deflator. This is a relatively broad measure of credit in that it contains commercial paper which is a substitute for bank credit. Since we are concerned with the impact of credit shocks on the entire economy, a broad measure is appropriate.

Choosing the proper measure of money is more difficult. We are seeking a measure of monetary policy so that narrow measures such as M1 are perhaps appropriate. Recent work by Bernanke and Blinder (1992) has stressed the federal funds rate as a measure of monetary policy. But there are some econometric difficulties with using the funds rate. In particular, there are significant periods in which the funds rate is unchanged from period to period. In this case, the error terms from regressions explaining the funds rate are likely to have unusual statistical properties. For this reason, M1 is chosen as the measure of monetary policy.

The sample period for estimation of the VARs is 1962.1–1984.1. A quarterly sample period is chosen in order to use GNP data as a measure of output and to allow a sufficient length of time so that M1 is a reasonable proxy for monetary policy. The starting date is dictated by the credit series, which is only available beginning in 1960.1. The ending date of 1984.1 was chosen because after that time financial innovations led to drastic changes in M1 which made the series not comparable with earlier periods. Finally, the money and credit series were converted to quarterly data using the average of the values during the month.

After taking the logarithms of all four series, we checked for the non-stationarity of the time series. Using Dickey-Fuller tests with a constant and a time trend, the hypothesis of nonstationarity could not be rejected. The test statistic for the logarithm of money, GNP, prices and credit were -1.38, -2.52, -2.36 and -1.93, whereas the critical 10 percent value (the MacKinnon statistic as reported on Micro TSP) was -3.15.

Since all the series exhibited nonstationarity, we checked for the existence of one or more cointegrating vectors using the Johansen tests. Both the trace and eigenvalue tests (as reported using Microfit) strongly indicated the presence of one cointegrating vector. The hypothesis that there was one (or fewer) cointegrating vector was marginally close to rejection at the 5 percent level. Allowing for a second cointegrating vector had little effect in the empirical work; therefore, we used only a single cointegrating vector.

Based on these statistics we estimated VARs in growth rates of the variables (differences in logarithms) including error-correction terms as calculated from the estimates of the cointegrating vector. Four lags of the endogenous variables were used in all the estimates. Only the error-correction term from the first cointegrating vector was significant in any of the regressions, and the covariance matrix of the residuals did not change substantially even with the introduction of this extra variable. In the results below, we use the covariance matrix of the residuals of the VARs for the variables in growth rates, with and without the addition of the error-correction term.

The first method used to find structural residuals is to examine recursive orderings for the model. First, order the variables according to the prespecified recursive ordering. Let the covariance matrix of the reduced-form residuals be denoted by Ω. The Choleski factorization of Ω is an upper triangular matrix Z such that $Z'Z = \Omega$. Premultiply both sides of equation (10.1) by $(Z')^{-1}$. The covariance matrix of the transformed residuals will be the identity matrix. The left-hand side will be $(Z')^{-1}Y$ and will produce a recursive ordering of the variables in Y_t. Dividing both sides of each equation i by the coefficient of the ith endogenous variable produces the standard normalization of a unit coefficient with a resulting covariance matrix of the residuals that is diagonal. The structural residuals implied by this transformation is the vector $V_t = (Z^{*\prime})^{-1}*U_t$, where $Z^{*\prime}$ is the matrix Z' normalized by dividing each row by the value on its main diagonal.

The second method used to determine the structural residuals follows Bernanke (1986) in specifying exclusion restrictions among the contemporaneous relations of the endogenous variables. Writing a structural model in the form

$$Y_t = B^*Y_t + \sum_{i=1}^{n} B_i Y_{t-i} + \gamma \bullet X_t + V_t, \qquad (10.2)$$

this method requires specifying the matrix **B** and assuming that the covariance matrix of V_t, Σ, is diagonal. We employed an exactly identified model:

$$C = b_1 P + b_2 Y + u_1$$
$$M = b_3 P + b_4 Y + u_2$$
$$P = u_3$$
$$Y = b_5(C - P) + b_6(M - P) + u_4,$$

where C, M, P and Y are the measures of credit, money, prices and output, and the b_i are parameters to be estimated. The six b_i terms plus the four variances of the u_i are the 10 parameters to be estimated from the 10 independent covariances of the sample covariance matrix of the reduced-form residuals from the VAR. These coefficients can be estimated by solving the nonlinear system of equations

$$\Sigma = (\mathbf{I} - \hat{\mathbf{B}}) \; \hat{\Omega} \; (\mathbf{I} - \hat{\mathbf{B}})'. \qquad (10.3)$$

This particular structural specification places credit and money on an equal a priori footing. Both variables can be influenced contemporaneously by prices and output and structural shocks. Output is determined by real credit and real money plus a shock. The only contemporaneous determinant of prices is a structural shock. Lagged terms in all variables enter into the structural specification given in equation (10.2). Finally, the structural residuals will be given by the equation $V_t = (\mathbf{I} - \hat{\mathbf{B}})U_t$.

4   ECONOMETRIC RESULTS

The VARs in growth rates, with and without error-correction terms, were run for the period 1962.1–1984.1. Table 10.2 contains the variance–covariance matrix for the residuals for both versions. In both versions, money and GNP are positively correlated while credit and GNP are negatively correlated. Money and credit shocks are negatively correlated in both models. Variance decompositions under alternative orderings indicate that both money and credit have some influence on output. In the ordering [money, GNP, prices, credit], after 10 quarters money explains 18 percent of the variance of GNP while credit explains 6 percent. Reversing money and credit in the ordering raises the contribution of credit shocks to 8 percent and lowers the contribution of money to 12 percent.

Table 10.2   Variance–covariance matrix of residuals

Variables: money, GNP, prices, credit (in order)

I.   Standard model (four lags)

$$\begin{bmatrix} 13.8 & 3.2 & -0.55 & -9.6 \\ 3.2 & 17.7 & -2.9 & -5.9 \\ -0.55 & -2.9 & 5.3 & -1.6 \\ -9.6 & -5.9 & -1.6 & 89.2 \end{bmatrix}$$

II.   Error-correction model (four lags plus error-correction terms)

$$\begin{bmatrix} 3.5 & 2.3 & -0.2 & -7.6 \\ 2.3 & 13.8 & -1.1 & -5.8 \\ -0.2 & -1.1 & 3.19 & -4.1 \\ -7.6 & -5.8 & -4.1 & 74.1 \end{bmatrix}$$

Although the variance–covariance matrices with and without error-correction terms were similar, the coefficients in the exactly identified structural model did differ. The estimated models were:

Case I (no error-correction terms)

	Variance of error
$C = -0.85P - 1.0Y + u_1$	63.9
$M = 0.0004P - 0.10Y + u_2$	11.7
$P = u_3$	5.3
$Y = 0.12(C - P) + 0.35(M - P) + u_4$	11.6

Case II (error-correction terms)

	Variance of error
$C = -1.57P - 0.80Y + u_1$	52.8
$M = 0.04P - 0.05Y + u_2$	10.3
$P = u_3$	3.2
$Y = 0.04(C - P) + 0.22(M - P) + u_4$	8.9

In both models, the contemporaneous effects of prices and income on credit were negative. Price shocks increased the money supply while income shocks led to a contemporaneous decrease. In both models, real money and real credit were positively related to output. This latter finding demonstrates the importance of considering structural models. Recall that in the reduced-form covariance matrix, money and GNP were positively correlated while credit and GNP were negatively correlated. This could have led a researcher to infer that money and credit shocks had qualitatively different effects on output. However, in the context of this particular structural model, their effects on output were similar. Nonetheless, it is true that in both models the impact of monetary shocks is stronger.

The structural residuals will be linear combinations of the reduced-form residuals. In the two structural models, the structural residuals for the money shocks are very close to the reduced-form shocks. The structural credit shocks differ distinctly from the reduced-form residuals. The specific linear combinations in these cases (where the terms on the right-hand side of the equation refer to reduced-form residuals) are:

Case I
  Structural $M = M + 0.10P$
  Structural $C = C + 1.0Y + 0.85P$

Case II
  Structural $M = M - 0.04Y + 0.05P$
  Structural $C = C + 0.80Y + 1.57P$

The structural residuals under the alternative methods – traditional and structural VARs, with and without error-correction terms – were highly correlated. For the monetary shocks, the empirical results can be best summarized by presenting three series: a traditional VAR with money ordered first without an error-correction term, the same VAR with money ordered last, and a structural model with the error-correction terms. For the credit shocks, three models also best convey the results. These models are a traditional VAR with credit ordered first without error-correction terms and two structural models with and without the error-correction terms.

The structural residuals for the monetary shocks are presented in Table 10.3. The residuals are also presented for the quarter before and after the Romer dates. The results do not suggest that the information contained in the Romer series can be associated with shocks from estimated models. None of the structural errors in the quarters during or

surrounding these dates have negative values whose absolute value
exceeds the standard error; the within-quarter sums in the first and
second cases are positive, and in the third case it is negative and
insignificant. Of the four dates considered, two have negative residuals
near the Romer dates but two do not.

Table 10.3   Monetary shocks

Date (quarter before and after)	VAR (money ordered first, no error-correction terms)	VAR (money ordered last, no error-correction terms)	Structural model (with error-correction terms)
	2.39	2.44	2.66
1968.4	1.38	2.99	1.31
	3.46	4.33	3.37
	1.60	1.103	2.08
1974.2	−1.37	0.088	−1.80
	−2.61	−1.27	−2.44
	0.33	−0.83	−0.32
1978.3	2.53	3.15	1.63
	1.56	1.20	0.36
	3.02	3.81	1.83
1979.4	−0.37	0.46	−1.68
	−1.79	−1.82	−3.40
	Sum in quarter = 2.16	Sum in quarter = 6.69	Sum in quarter = −0.54
	Std deviation = 3.71	Std deviation = 3.50	Std deviation = 3.64

The results for the credit shocks are given in Table 10.4. Eckstein and
Sinai (ES) and Owens and Schreft (OS) identify periods that are fairly
close to one another, so it is more useful to look at the residuals during
the intervals of alleged credit crunches. During the classic 1960s crunch,
the residuals are nearly uniformly positive. No transformations indicate a

negative shock to credit during this period. In the period 1969.2–1970.1, the OS dates are also associated with positive shocks, while the 1970.1 ES date has a negative shock which, in one case, exceeds the standard error of the residual. ES also identify a credit shock in 1974.3. The residuals for this date are small in absolute value and of mixed sign. In the two-quarter period 1980.1–1980.2, the first quarter has small residuals in absolute value but the second quarter, claims OS, has a large negative residual. Finally, ES also identify 1982.2 as a credit crunch period, but it has a large positive residual that greatly exceeds the standard errors. Overall, the econometric residuals are not closely related to the a priori structural credit shocks.

Table 10.4   Credit shocks

Date	VAR (credit ordered first, no error-correction terms)	Structural model (no error-correction terms)	Structural model (with error-correction terms)
1966.2 (OS)	6.92	3.38	−2.27
1966.3 (OS)	10.91	10.37	4.46
1966.4 (ES)	11.83	10.09	7.23
1969.2 (OS)	11.11	8.27	5.79
1969.3 (OS)	3.56	3.17	2.26
1969.4 (OS)	10.94	5.82	6.28
1970.1 (ES)	−5.44	−9.84	−5.71
1974.3 (ES)	−1.65	−3.36	0.18
1980.1 (OS/ES)	0.13	3.33	1.63
1980.2 (O/S)	−0.16	−9.85	−6.94
1982.2 (ES)	15.40	12.88	21.69
	Std deviation = 9.17	Std deviation = 9.28	Std deviation = 8.06

OS: see Owens and Schreft, 1992.
ES: see Eckstein, 1983.

5   EVALUATING THE PROCEDURE

There are two different ways of viewing these results which perhaps are complementary. First, the results suggest that there is not a close correspondence between structural residuals from econometric equations and shocks identified on a priori grounds. The alternative parameterizations of the structural models did not seem to matter very much. The story was contained in the data and the reduced-form regressions. This suggests that in this case, issues of sample period and variable definition are more important than the precise VAR ordering or structural equation specification. In this exercise, the message was carried in the reduced form.

If we believe that the a priori information is important, then we would want to check the robustness of our model. There are several different avenues that could be explored to check the robustness of the model and data used in this paper. There are many alternatives to the measure of monetary policy used in this paper; in particular, the federal funds rate has been widely used as an indicator of monetary policy. However, as noted above, movements in the federal funds rate tend to be discrete, which will cause difficulties in interpreting residuals from an equation containing the funds rate. The sample period in this paper was dictated largely by the credit measure that was employed. Alternative credit measures would allow the use of different time periods. One response to the results of this study would be to re-focus attention on choices for variables and time periods and not devote our attention exclusively to clever ways of teasing results out of the same reduced form.

A second response to these results would be to use the findings of the empirical investigation to re-think our criteria for identifying historical episodes. For example, it is somewhat surprising that the classic credit crunch in the 1960s was associated with positive residuals. Why were borrowers and banks complaining about the shortage of credit when the econometric results show that, controlling for the usual variables, more credit was being offered than usual? Could the statements simply reflect a desire to have even more credit than normal in extremely robust economic times? Would we want to call this phenomenon "credit rationing"?

Similarly, the fact that the monetary shocks did not coincide with the Romer dates should raise many questions. Hoover and Perez (1994) have already challenged the Romer methodology. The results here suggest that the intentions they alleged to have uncovered have not been translated into actual monetary shocks. However, to avoid jumping to conclusions too quickly, we should heed the warnings of Tom Mayer that econometric results are fragile and must be used judiciously with other evidence.

REFERENCES

Bernanke, Ben (1986) "Alternative Explanations of the Money-Income Correlation" in Brunner, Karl and Meltzer, Alan H. (eds), *Carnegie-Rochester Conference Series on Public Policy*, vol. 25, pp. 49–100, North Holland, Amsterdam.

Bernanke, Ben and Blinder, Alan (1992) "The Federal Funds Rate and the Channels of Monetary Transmission" *American Economic Review*, 82, pp. 901–21.

Eckstein, Otto (1983) *The DRI Model of the U.S. Economy*, McGraw Hill, New York, NY.

Friedman, Milton and Schwartz, Anna J. (1963) *A Monetary History of the United States, 1867–1960*, Princeton University Press, Princeton, NJ.

Hoover, Kevin D. (1991) "The Causal Direction Between Money and Prices: An Alternative Approach" *Journal of Monetary Economics*, 27, pp. 381–423.

Hoover, Kevin D. and Perez, Stephen J. (1994) "*Post Hoc Ergo Propter Hoc* Once More: An Evaluation of 'Does Monetary Policy Matter?' in the Spirit of James Tobin" *Journal of Monetary Economics,* 34, pp. 47–73.

Hoover, Kevin D. and Sheffrin, Steven M. (1992) "Causation, Spending, and Taxes: Sand in the Sandbox or Tax Collector for the Welfare State?" *American Economic Review*, 82, pp. 225–48.

Lucas, Robert E. and Sargent, Thomas J. (1981) "Introduction" in Lucas, Robert E. and Sargent, Thomas J. (eds), *Rational Expectations and Econometric Practice*, pp. xi–xl, University of Minnesota Press, Minneapolis, MN.

Mayer, Thomas (1978) "Consumption and the Great Depression" *Journal of Political Economy*, 86, pp. 139–45.

Owens, Raymond E. and Schreft, Stacey L. (1992) "Identifying Credit Crunches" Federal Reserve Bank of Richmond, VA (unpublished paper).

Romer, Christina D. and Romer, David H. (1989) "Does Monetary Policy Matter? A New Test in the Spirit of Friedman and Schwartz" in Blanchard, Olivier and Fischer, Stanley (eds), *NBER Macroeconomic Annual*, vol. 4, MIT Press, Cambridge, MA.

Sheffrin, Steven M. (1989) "Evaluating Rational Partisan Business Cycle Theory" *Economics & Politics*, 1, pp. 239–59.

Sims, Christopher A. (1980) "Macroeconomics and Reality" *Econometrica*, 48, pp. 1–48.

Temin, Peter (1976) *Did Monetary Forces Cause the Great Depression?* Norton, New York, NY.

PART IV

The Political Economy of Monetary Policy

11. Monetary System for a Free Society

Milton Friedman*

The past three decades have seen a major change in both international and domestic monetary arrangements: the end of the Bretton Woods system and of any pretense to maintaining a pseudo gold standard, increased recognition in domestic policy of the urgency of controlling inflation, and increased emphasis in domestic monetary policy on controlling the quantity of one or another monetary aggregate. These changes in arrangements, needless to say, have not been accompanied by any comparable change in performance – though there are some notable and important exceptions, of which Japan is one, and Chile, another.

In the intellectual arena, there has been far less change than in institutions. Yet even here, there has been a shift in emphasis and a widening of the arrangements considered, in no small measure because of Professor Hayek's writings in support of competitive moneys.

I propose in this paper to consider, first, the objectives of a liberal monetary system, and then alternative approaches to achieving these objectives: through gold, competitive money, constitutional rules, and, for smaller countries, links with other countries.

1 OBJECTIVES OF A LIBERAL MONETARY SYSTEM

The divergence among liberals (I use the term in the classical sense of stressing individual freedom as the ultimate goal, not in the modern corrupted sense) with respect to monetary arrangements arises, I believe, because of the difficulty of reconciling different objectives, of which two are central: first, freedom from government intervention in lending

* Adapted from a paper originally presented at the Mont Pelerin Society regional meeting in Viña del Mar, Chile, 19 November 1981.

and investing and from government manipulation of credit markets and of the quantity of money; second, a stable monetary framework that would provide a favorable environment for the operation of a free private market.

The problem is that these objectives have in practice proved incompatible. It is, indeed, relatively easy to develop hypothetical arrangements under which they would be complementary rather than competitive (e.g., a 100 percent gold standard plus a Marshallian tabular standard; or 100 percent reserve banking plus either a fixed rate of fiat money growth, or a stabilizing budget policy under which surpluses retire fiat money and deficits are financed by increases in fiat money)[1]. But what is attractive in principle has neither developed spontaneously in practice, when that was possible, nor appealed to legislators, when that was an option.

The reason for the incompatibility is not far to seek. A truly automatic system providing a reasonably stable monetary framework offers tempting opportunities for profit – financial and political – by introducing destabilizing and discretionary elements (for a fuller discussion, see Friedman, 1960, pp. 4–9). As a result, every actual system has been an uneasy compromise, even in predominantly liberal societies, and a compromise that has broken down from time to time at great social cost. That was as true during the supposedly halcyon days of the international gold standard as in the post-World War II period of fiat money inflation – any impression to the contrary derives from a "paradise lost" or "good old days" nostalgia in contemplating the past.

Similarly, those of us who have been concerned with policy have had to choose not among alternative ideal arrangements but among alternative realistic possibilities – realistic, I hasten to add, not in respect of *political* feasibility, which is precisely what we should seek to achieve and not rule out in advance, but in respect of the likely actual outcome of one or another set of arrangements. Liberals understand very well that the unintended (though often predictable) consequences of human action often overwhelm the intended results, for good and ill. There are not, and cannot be, clear and unambiguous guides in making such choices. Persons sharing the same basic objectives and the same economic analyses can nonetheless make very different choices – as the Mont Pelerin experience so fully documents.

---

[1] The stabilizing budget approach is recommended in my "A Monetary and Fiscal Framework for Economic Stability" (1948, pp. 245–64), and reprinted in my *Essays in Positive Economics* (1953, pp. 133–56). The fixed money growth approach is recommended as a "much simpler rule" that "would also produce highly satisfactory results" in my *A Program for Monetary Stability* (1960, pp. 90ff.).

2   THE APPROACH THROUGH GOLD

In concluding my 1961 Mont Pelerin paper on "Real and Pseudo Gold Standards," I wrote,

> Can we not all agree [on] ... the establishment of a thoroughly free market in gold, with no restrictions on the ownership, purchase, sale, import, or export of gold by private individuals? This means, in particular, no restrictions on the price at which gold can be bought or sold in terms of any other commodity or financial instrument, including national currencies. It means, therefore, an end to governmental price fixing of gold in terms of national currencies. (Reprinted in Friedman, 1968, pp. 247–65)

I went on to suggest the auctioning off of the US gold stocks, concluding, "Why should gold storage and the issuance of warehouse certificates be a nationalized industry?" (pp. 264, 265).

In a Mont Pelerin paper 4 years later on "The Political Economy of International Monetary Arrangements," I concluded:

> Return to a real gold standard might well be desirable but is currently impossible. It would require abandonment by all countries of the use of monetary policy as an instrument to affect domestic employment or price levels. ... The desirable liberal alternative is currently a system of freely floating exchange rates with gold having no special official role. All present restrictions on the ownership, transfer, or price of gold should be removed, and gold should become a truly free market commodity. As I argued in my earlier paper, paradoxically, this is more likely to foster a real gold standard than is clinging to the form of a gold standard while giving up its substance. Liberals least of all need to be told that what appears the long way round is often the short way home. (Friedman, 1968, pp. 278–9)

I quote these statements to stress the major change that has occurred with respect to gold since 1965. What I then described as "the desirable liberal alternative" is very nearly the actual current situation, at least so far as the United States and some other major countries are concerned: floating exchange rates (if not "freely" floating) and the elimination of all restrictions on private transactions in gold. Certainly, so far as the US is concerned, there is nothing to prevent a real gold standard from developing for private transactions. Individuals (or corporations) who choose to do so can write contracts with one another in terms of gold, can quote prices in terms of gold, can pay and receive gold in discharge of obligations. They can issue gold coins and warehouse receipts for gold. Indeed, I believe they could even issue currency denominated in gold, not only as warehouse receipts but even as unbacked promises to pay.

The one respect in which the situation differs from "the desirable liberal alternative" is that governments retain large gold stocks – though even here the US has disposed of more than half of the physical stock of gold it held at the time of the 1961 Mont Pelerin meeting.

At least one US financial institution currently provides gold-based banking, the Gold Standard Corporation in Kansas City, Missouri. It provides insured safekeeping in bullion, including deposit accounts on which checks can be written in ounces of gold and fractions thereof. It mints regular and proof editions of gold coins ranging from one-tenth of an ounce to one full ounce. There is nothing to prevent its coinage being used as hand-to-hand currency or its deposit accounts being used to transfer funds by check. If its services were to attract sufficient custom, there is nothing to prevent additional such institutions from being established and flourishing.

Some gold standard advocates regard the existence of legislation making government-issued currency "legal tender" as a serious obstacle to the development of a private gold standard. I believe that is a mistake. Historically, legal tender qualities have had a minor effect on the acceptability or value of a currency. They have never, for example, prevented an overissued currency from becoming worthless. A dramatic example of the irrelevance of legal tender quality occurred during the early stages of Communist Russia. The legal tender quality of the Soviet currency did not prevent it from generating a hyperinflation and becoming worthless. Simultaneously, Czarist-issued currency, which had no legal standing whatsoever, largely retained its value for internal transactions simply because the quantity was limited, there being no Czar to authorize or issue any more.

Another even more currently pertinent example is the experience of the US during the Civil War and post-Civil War greenback period. Two currencies circulated simultaneously: greenbacks and gold, the price of one in terms of the other being determined by the market. Banks offered two types of deposits: in gold or greenbacks. In most of the country, prices in stores etc. were commonly cited in greenbacks; in a few areas, notably the Far West, prices were cited in gold. Everywhere, however, payment could be made in either the one or the other at the free market exchange rate between them (for a discussion of this episode, see Friedman and Schwartz, 1963, pp. 25–9).

Nothing currently prevents a similar situation from developing, with the Federal Reserve Note as an official currency denominated in dollars and given legal tender qualities, and gold as an unofficial currency denominated in ounces or grams or any other convenient unit. Payments required by law to be made in "dollars" (taxes, purchases of government securities, discharges of obligations denominated in dollars) could be made either out of currency or deposits held in dollars or by converting gold coins or currency or deposits into dollars at the market rate of exchange.

If gold developed a wide use, the transactions costs involved in such conversions would become trivial. Moreover, gold would then effectively discipline government money issue, even though it had no legal tender quality. Any tendency to overissue would lead to a substitution of gold for dollars and a rise in the price of gold in terms of dollars. The effect would be to reduce both the length of the current lag between overissue and inflation of prices in terms of dollars and also the real yield to the government from inflation.

Is the widespread use of gold a likely outcome? My guess is that the answer is no, that it will not occur unless US monetary management becomes far worse than it has been and produces rates of inflation that are a substantial multiple of those that have been experienced. The advantage of a common medium of exchange, the resource costs of a real gold standard, and the transitional problems of overcoming habit and inertia will, I believe, be sufficient to prevent the emergence of a significant private gold standard.

However, I hasten to add, that is an empirical judgment, not a recommendation or an expression of opposition to private measures promoting the development of a private gold standard. If one did develop, I would welcome it.

What does concern me is something very different. If my judgment is right, and a private gold standard does not emerge, I fear that enthusiastic gold standard advocates will seek government assistance – repeating the mistake of so many persons who have paid lip-service to private enterprise, yet advocated government intervention at the first indication that the private market was not producing the results they preferred (whether those be private returns or public services). That process has already started. The result, at best, would be, as I wrote in 1965, "substitution of a pseudo gold standard," which would "involve political interventionism into international trade and payments, and occasional major crises, and would inhibit any real movement to freer trade" (Friedman, 1968, pp. 278–9).

3   THE APPROACH THROUGH COMPETITIVE MONEYS

The situation with respect to competitive money is in many ways similar to that of gold: there is every reason to permit complete freedom in the issuance of money; there has been a considerable degree of freedom which has only under very rare circumstances led to the emergence of widely used moneys as substitutes or alternatives to government-issued moneys. I conjecture that, as with a private gold standard, even greater freedom for the issuance of competitive moneys would not in fact lead to the emergence of any such a widely used money in the US (or other major countries) unless US monetary management becomes far worse than it has been.

As one example of the availability of a competitive money, there is nothing to prevent residents of the US from making contracts in terms of German marks, Japanese yen, Swiss francs, or any other national currency. There is nothing to prevent them from discharging obligations by transferring such a currency or claims on such a currency. Both German marks and Swiss francs have for many years maintained their purchasing power better, and with less fluctuation, than US dollars. Many residents of the US hold German marks and Swiss francs, or claims denominated in those currencies, as part of their portfolio of assets. But with perhaps rare exceptions, only those residents who engage in trade with Germany or Switzerland, or travel in those countries, use the currencies as a medium of circulation.

American Express traveler's checks are a private nonbank–issued currency that has attained wide use, but they are claims on a fixed number of US dollars strictly comparable to dollar deposits in a bank. They have remained free of regulation only through a quirk in the law.

A more far-reaching example of a potential competitive private monetary standard that has failed to develop is what Alfred Marshall called a "tabular" standard and what, in a reinvention of this approach, Ray White, then Governor of the Reserve Bank of New Zealand, called a "real dollar" standard. The essence of this approach is that contracts be indexed, that is, the terms be stated in nominal units of money adjusted by a stated price index. Marshall explicitly proposed that such indexation be voluntary. The only role he assigned to the government was to publish the price index that would be used to define *The Unit*, or the standard unit of purchasing power. Understandably, Governor White proposed that such indexation be legislated.

So far as I can see, at the time Marshall wrote (1887), there was nothing to prevent the widespread voluntary use of indexation, or the issuance of private currency or deposit claims denominated in terms of The Unit. There have, I believe, been only minor legal obstacles in the United States and perhaps other countries to a similar development. Partial indexation has occurred frequently and widely, particularly in labor contracts, long-term construction contracts, and government benefit programs. But anything even remotely approximating a tabular standard has arisen only under circumstances of very high and uncertain inflation rates, as in some South American countries where inflation has proceeded at rates in excess of 50 or 100 percent a year.

It seems reasonably clear that a voluntary tabular standard has failed the market test. One of Professor Hayek's expectations – or perhaps better hopes – was that competitive banking would lead to the emergence of private banks that would offer money denominated in purchasing-power units – Marshall's Unit or White's Real Dollar. That has always seemed to me highly unlikely because of the difficulty of securing purchasing-power assets to hedge such liabilities. I have been much impressed by the absence of any private issuance in the US of securities denominated in purchasing-power units, despite recent inflation that has been high and variable by historical standards, despite the spread of escalator clauses or indexation in other areas, and despite the extent of financial innovation that has occurred in recent years. The only actual example I know about is Irving Fisher's experiment with purchasing-power securities issued in the mid-twenties by his Kardex Corporation. But that reflected Fisher's economic theories, not market imperatives, and those securities were eliminated at the first opportunity when the corporation's financial structure was reorganized, on the occasion, I believe, of its merger with another corporation. If such securities were issued in any substantial amount, they would furnish the assets against which banks could offer purchasing-power deposits or currency.

The alternative is government purchasing-power securities. Many of us have for decades favored the US (and other) government's issuance of all longer-term debt securities in purchasing-power form – both to reduce the incentive for government to inflate as a way of redeeming (i.e., repudiating) its debt and to provide moderate-income citizens with a readily available and effective inflation hedge. We have so far been conspicuously unsuccessful in the US, though there has been a modest step in this direction in the UK, and much more extensive steps in such countries as Israel, Brazil, Argentina and Chile, where inflation has reached high double-digit and triple-digit levels.

If such government securities were ever issued on a large scale, they too would provide assets against which financial institutions could issue purchasing-power liabilities. But they would constitute in essence government, not private, money.

It may be that the failure of private institutions to issue purchasing-power securities reflects a situation in which there are widely separated multiple equilibrium positions, with no way to get from one to the other by small steps. A financial firm that experimented with such issues would have to bear the development costs; yet, if successful, it could rapidly be imitated by others, and thereby be prevented from reaping the benefits of its innovation. In that case, if the government broke the ice and issued purchasing-power securities, perhaps a flood of private issues would follow. However, I am highly skeptical of this, as of all similar, infant-industry arguments. Such considerations did not prevent the emergence of mutual funds, money market funds, or other innovations in financial intermediation.

In sum, there is every reason in the abstract to approve Professor Hayek's proposals for removing any legal obstacles to the development of private competitive money. There is little basis in experience for expecting any widely used private moneys to emerge in major countries unless governmental monetary management becomes far worse than it has been in the post-World War II period. And there is little basis in experience to expect any such extreme degeneration in monetary management except as the aftermath of a major military conflict.

4   THE APPROACH THROUGH CONSTITUTIONAL LIMITATION

The nineteenth-century gold standard represented an unwritten constitutional limitation on government monetary policy. So did the associated fiscal rule of balanced budgets. Both have disappeared. An alternative is to replace these unwritten limitations by enacting written constitutional limitations. The particular substitutes that I have favored are a fixed money-growth rule to replace the gold standard and a government spending limitation to replace the balanced-budget rule. I have presented the case for these particular substitutes at length in earlier publications and need not repeat that case here (see Friedman, 1960, ch. 4; Freidman and Freidman, 1980, ch. 9, ch. 10).

Let me only report recent US experience that suggests that such constitutional limitations may be realistic, though still long-odds, possibilities. With respect to the monetary rule, the Banking and Currency Committees in the House and Senate and the Joint Economic Committee have, since the mid-1970s, endorsed a policy, in the words of House Concurrent Resolution 133 passed in 1975, of maintaining "long run growth of the monetary and credit aggregates commensurate with the economy's long run potential to increase production, so as to promote effectively the goals of maximum employment, stable prices, and moderate long term interest rates." The identical wording was included in an amendment to the Federal Reserve Act that President Carter signed into law in November 1977. So a monetary growth rule is already embodied in legislation, though not yet into the Constitution – and there is, of course, a vast gulf between the two (on all this, see Weintraub, 1978, pp. 341–62).

With respect to fiscal policy, in 1981 the Judiciary Committee of the US Senate reported out by a substantial majority Senate Joint Resolution 58 proposing a "Balanced Budget-Tax Limitation Constitutional Amendment" (see US Congress, 1981). Despite early promise, both houses of Congress have not yet approved a balanced-budget/tax-limitation amendment by the necessary two-thirds vote, nor have a sufficient number of states requested that Congress call a convention to propose such an amendment. Nonetheless, such an amendment remains a staple in the debate over how to handle persistently large deficits.

Effective constitutional limitation is very far from being a reality. Yet I continue to believe that it is a promising approach, at least for the US, toward achieving the liberal objectives with respect to monetary and fiscal policy.

5   APPROACH THROUGH PEGGING TO A MAJOR COUNTRY

In 1972, I analyzed the problem of "Monetary Policy in Developing Countries" in a lecture that I gave in Israel. I summarized my "prescription for developing countries" as follows (Friedman, 1973, p. 59).

176 *The Political Economy of Monetary Policy*

For most countries, I believe the best policy would be to eschew the revenue from money creation, to unify its currency with the currency of a large, relatively stable developed country with which it has close economic relations, and to impose no barriers to the movement of money or prices, wages, or interest rates. Such a policy requires not having a central bank.

The second best policy, but one which has far greater political feasibility in the present climate of opinion, is to require a central bank to produce a steady and moderate rate of monetary growth, using the new money issued to finance part of government expenditures. The emphasis on a "moderate" rate of growth is partly to avoid so rapid an inflation that a large amount of real resources are wasted in efforts to hold down cash balances, partly to avoid creating pressures for government intervention to repress the inflation. The emphasis on a "steady" rate is to minimize the economic and social cost of erratic inflation, because if the inflation is erratic it is nearly impossible for people to anticipate and adjust to it.

It is a nice commentary on the economist's incompetence to judge political feasibility that what I described as the "best policy" has been adopted by at least one developing country – namely, Chile – while the "second best policy" which I claimed has "greater political feasibility" has been firmly adopted, so far as I know, by none.[2]

While, so far as I know, only Chile has in recent years effectively unified its currency with that of a major developed country, other countries, such as Panama and Guatemala, have done so for a long time and still continue to do so, and still other economies, such as Hong Kong and other British colonies, have done so in the past for long periods, though they no longer do. Hence, there is much experience on the basis of which it can be evaluated.

Experience since I gave the lecture in Israel has not led me to alter my views on the economics of the issue, though it has led me to become far more modest about judging political feasibility (in the sense of likelihood of adoption). Perhaps the example of Chile, if its policy continues to be as successful as it has been so far, will lead other developing countries to follow suit.

[Added in 1992. The preceding three paragraphs, correct when written in 1981, no longer are. Chile ended the pegging of its rate to the dollar in 1982, after the sharp appreciation of the US dollar plunged Chile into a disastrous recession. The Hong Kong dollar was unified with the US dollar in 1983 and remains unified in 1992. Israel unified its currency to the US dollar for a brief period in 1985. (For a full discussion of these episodes, see Friedman, 1992, ch. 9.)]

[2] I exclude Japan as a "developing country" in the sense in which I used the term. Japan has very successfully adopted the second policy since 1973.

6   CONCLUSION

This survey of alternative approaches to achieving liberal objectives in monetary policy suggests that while the relevant questions have not changed in the past two decades, some of the available answers appear to have done so. More important, while actual monetary stability has deteriorated, the likelihood of achieving monetary structures conducive to government nonintervention and stability have, I believe, improved greatly as part of the general turning of the tide away from collectivism and toward liberalism.

REFERENCES

Friedman, Milton (1948) "A Monetary and Fiscal Framework for Economic Stability" *American Economic Review*, vol. 38, no. 3, June, pp. 245–64.

Friedman, Milton (1953) *Essays in Positive Economics*, University of Chicago Press, Chicago, IL.

Friedman, Milton (1960) *A Program for Monetary Stability*, Fordham University Press, New York, NY.

Friedman, Milton (1968) *Dollars and Deficits*, Englewood Cliffs, Prentice-Hall, NJ.

Friedman, Milton (1973) *Money and Economic Development*, The Horowitz Lectures of 1972, Praeger, New York, NY.

Friedman, Milton (1992) *Money Mischief*, Harcourt Brace Jovanovich, New York, NY.

Friedman, Milton and Friedman, Rose (1980) *Free to Choose,* Harcourt Brace Jovanovich, New York, NY.

Friedman, Milton and Schwartz, Anna J. (1963) *A Monetary History of the United States, 1867–1960*, National Bureau of Economic Research Studies in Business Cycles, no. 12, Princeton University Press, Princeton, NJ.

US Congress, Senate, Committee on the Judiciary (1981) *Balanced Budget-Tax Limitation Constitutional Amendment*, Senate Report no. 97-151, 97th Congress, 1st session.

Weintraub, Robert E. (1978) "Congressional Supervision of Monetary Policy" *Journal of Monetary Economics*, vol. 4, no. 2, April, pp. 341–62.

12. On the Political Economy of Central Bank Independence

King Banaian, Richard C.K. Burdekin and
Thomas D. Willett*

1 INTRODUCTION

In recent years there has been growing acceptance of the view that the long-term costs of expansionary monetary policy can be quite high. This perspective, long associated with the Monetarist school, has focused attention on ways to restrain inflationary pressures. Thomas Mayer has been a leader in the movement to "increase substantially the weight given to achieving price stability in the formulation of monetary policy" (Mayer and Willett, 1988, p. 414). For example, in 1979 he proposed that the oaths of office required of Fed officials be expanded to include a promise to attach prime importance to price stability (see Mayer, 1979). Ten years later, Representative Neal tried (and failed) to impose a mandatory price stability objective on the US Federal Reserve System under House Joint Resolution 409. A price stability mandate was, however, enacted in New Zealand in 1989 – and has been accompanied by a sustained disinflation, with inflation averaging only 1.3 percent in the 12 months ending 30 June 1993. Other recent examples of this movement include the draft law specifying a price stability goal for the Bank of France that was approved by the French cabinet on 11 May 1993, and the Mexican constitutional amendment granting independence to the Bank of Mexico effective from 1 January 1994.

These developments have been accompanied by a substantial literature on institutional arrangements for central banks and the relationship between these arrangements and inflation performance (see the surveys provided by Burdekin and Willett, 1991, and Masciandaro and Spinelli,

* The authors thank participants in workshops at Budapest, Berkeley and Georgetown, where this paper was presented, and are especially grateful for helpful comments from Arthur Denzau, Michele Fratianni, Eduard Hochreiter, Thomas Mayer and Pierre Siklos.

1993). This literature generally focuses on "measuring" central bank independence, but, as Thomas Mayer has pointed out to us in private correspondence, it tends to confound several distinct issues. The problems here are highlighted by the question: Of what is the central bank supposed to be independent? In general, authors in this area have in mind independence from short-run political pressures for inflationary policies (cf. Willett, 1988, and Fratianni, von Hagen and Waller, 1993). The enactment of a binding commitment to a price stability goal would in this sense increase central bank "independence" in the United States, even though the Federal Reserve's discretion in setting monetary policy would be reduced. Furthermore, much of the literature has relied upon adding up scores on a number of facets of central bank institutional arrangements without carefully considering the interrelationships between them. As a consequence, there is a wide range of alternative rankings of central bank independence across the industrial countries.

Our primary objective in this paper is to take some initial steps towards the development of a more systematic analysis of how alternative institutional structures for central banks are likely to affect the control of inflationary pressures. We conclude that central bank freedom from government override, existence of an explicit mandate to promote price stability, and government power to dismiss (and appoint) central bank policy officials are likely to be of pre-eminent, although not exclusive, importance.[1] A major problem with "testing" such propositions, however, is the need to control for differences in underlying inflationary pressures across countries.

We know of no way to test for the deep causality issue that it is a society's inherent aversion to inflation that ultimately determines *both* the degree to which central banks are given the freedom to pursue price stability *and* the inflation record of that central bank. Given that this is less likely to be a problem when there is an actual *change* in the institutional arrangements over the period under investigation, New Zealand may provide a valuable case study for future research. In the meantime, one can at least attempt to control for some of the contemporaneous factors that might be expected to contribute to differences in inflationary pressures across countries. Somewhat surprisingly, many of the recent studies in this area have not included such controls. In section 3 we consider several control variables and

---

[1] These same factors are also stressed by Epstein and Schor (1986) and Bade and Parkin (1987).

present empirical evidence showing that distinguishing independent central banks solely on the basis of freedom from government override, as in Burdekin and Willett (1991), outperforms the multifaceted indices of Grilli, Masciandaro and Tabellini (1991) and Cukierman (1992) as a predictor of inflation performance for the industrial countries.[2]

2   ASPECTS OF INDEPENDENCE

Independence from Whom and for What Purpose?

In analyzing central bank independence, it is important to be clear about whether one is referring to independence from executive branch influence, independence from parliament, or independence from some other body (such as pressures from special interests and the general public). In Russia and several other former communist countries, the central bank is considered to be independent if it is free from influence by the executive branch of the government. The supposed independence of the Russian central bank has been widely reported in the Western press. This definition of executive branch independence is much too narrow, however, as witnessed by Russia's recent experience where a relatively anti-inflationary executive branch fought unsuccessfully for months to prod the central bank to restrict monetary growth – even after the inflation rate had risen above 1,000 percent per annum. The main opposition to the adoption of monetary tightening came from the industrial lobby in parliament – that is, from the very body to which the central bank is responsible. It is an open question whether on average pressures for excessively expansionary monetary policy will come more strongly from the executive or legislative branches of government.

Ultimately, advocates of central bank independence seek to insulate monetary policy from inflationary pressures. The relevant normative question for institutional design concerns the legal arrangements that can best bring about this result, and the related positive question for empirical research is how well the alternative institutional arrangements have functioned. Probably the most effective way of protecting monetary

---

[2] Grilli, Masciandaro and Tabellini (1991) add the scores for 15 different criteria, while Cukierman (1992) uses 17 criteria. Notably, however, Cukierman's ranking of legal independence gives the central bank's power to set monetary policy only one-fourth the weight

(continued on p. 181)

policy from pressures for excessive expansion is for such pressures to not exist in the first place. Thus, for example, the action most likely to convert Italy from a high- to a low-inflation country might be to import the inflation-hating population of Germany. This is hardly a realistic option, however.

The Bank of Japan has sometimes been classified as being relatively independent (cf. Bade and Parkin, 1987), even though, under Article 47 of the Bank of Japan Law, the central bank is directly subservient to the Finance Ministry (Aufricht, 1961, p. 435). While clearly having little or no formal independence from the government, monetary policy in Japan has, however, been relatively strongly insulated from pressures for inflationary monetary expansion. The Finance Ministry has enjoyed considerable independence within the Japanese government and the government has been dominated by a single political party (see also Cargill, 1989). It is unlikely, though, that another country wanting to fight inflationary pressures could import the Japanese political system. Nor, as political competition in Japan increases, will the past degree of monetary policy insulation necessarily be maintained without a revision of institutional arrangements.

One must also consider both the strength of the pressures that may emanate directly from the government and the pressures that may be generated from voters, interest groups, etc. As pointed out by Cukierman (1992, p. 349): "Obviously the degree of CB [Central Bank] independence plays a meaningful role only in the presence of differences in emphasis on alternative policy objectives between the political authorities and the CB." Thus, in reaching judgments on how effective institutional arrangements have been in restraining inflation, we need to consider how strong inflationary pressures have been, and not just look at relative inflation rates as has been done in most of the recent studies on this subject (see section 3).

Policy Independence and Mandated Objectives

In analyzing central bank independence, Tietmeyer (1991) has distinguished between institutional, functional and personal

---

attached to restrictions on the central bank's participation in the primary market for government securities. Grilli, Masciandaro and Tabellini's measure of "economic" independence also seems to place an excessive (5/7) weight on criteria describing the fiscal relationship between the central bank and the treasury.

independence.[3] Institutional independence refers to issues involving authority over monetary policy and coincides with what in earlier work (Burdekin and Willett, 1991; Burdekin, Wihlborg and Willett, 1992) we labeled "policy independence." This is the simplest classification and the one most commonly used in discussions of central bank independence. The key issues reduce to (1) whether the central bank or government has the authority to formulate monetary policy, (2) whether the government can issue directives to the central bank to pursue objectives other than price stability and (3) whether, in cases where the government can issue such directives, this is likely to cause the government to incur substantial costs. By the criterion that the central bank is able to set policy without provision for government override, the central banks of Austria, Germany, Switzerland and the United States are "independent." In Germany the government can delay the implementation of Bundesbank policy but cannot override it – while, in Austria, provisions for override apply only to situations where the Austrian National Bank violates the mandatory price stability objective or other legal provisions.

If one considers cases where the government has discretionary power to issue directives to the central bank, but only in a public manner that is likely to be politically costly, Canada, the Netherlands and post-1990 New Zealand are additional countries that would qualify as granting some degree of effective independence to their central banks. All three of these central banks have a statutory price stability goal. The Bank of Canada also has a potentially conflicting employment objective, however, and so does not possess the same unambiguous price stability mandate as that prevailing in the Netherlands and New Zealand. In most other countries it remains the case that, in the absence of limitations on government override, the central bank is left without any independent authority to determine monetary policy.

Masciandaro and Spinelli (1993) provide support for the importance of these considerations based on the results of interviews with central bank officials, who were asked to rate the relative importance of the various criteria laid out in Grilli, Masciandaro and Tabellini (1991). These interview results suggest that freedom from government override

[3] There is also the issue of the central bank's budgetary independence. Control of the central bank's budget could enable the government to influence or discipline an otherwise independent central bank. In practice, however, most of the central banks in industrial countries enjoy considerable budgetary autonomy – although exceptions are France and, to a lesser degree, New Zealand (Swinburne and Castello-Branco, 1991).

combined with a clear mandate for monetary stability are considered of pre-eminent importance by the central bankers themselves.[4] Less weight is given to the government's appointment power and to the participation of government representatives on the central bank policy board. These observations appear to be consistent with the German Bundesbank being consistently placed in the highest rank in studies of central bank independence despite the fact that government officials can participate in the deliberation of the policy board, and can even offer proposals, but have no vote and cannot issue directives.[5] Certainly, so long as the government cannot exercise veto power over the Bundesbank's policy decisions, any non-voting participation by the government representatives does seem justifiably relegated to a second order of importance.

The Fed and the Swiss National Bank also are free from any provision for government override. However, these central banks have a less clear mandate for price stability than does the Bundesbank. The only macroeconomic policy goal laid down in the Bundesbank Law is that the central bank safeguard the currency. In Switzerland and the United States the statutory central bank policy objectives are potentially conflicting, in the sense that both price stability *and* employment objectives are laid down. This has been less of a problem in Switzerland due both to the extremely low levels of unemployment and the government's ability to vary the number of "guest workers" so as to maintain, until now, near full-employment of Swiss citizens (see Burdekin, 1987). However, conflicts between the employment and price level objectives have been much more marked in the United States – which may help explain Federal Reserve Chairman Greenspan's support for the (ultimately unsuccessful) 1989 Neal proposal that would have mandated a zero inflation goal for the Fed. The recent advocacy of such a zero-inflation objective by Governor Crow of the Bank of Canada also is consistent with an apparent desire by central bankers to have a firm "bottom line."

Alesina and Summers (1993, p. 159) find that "the monetary discipline associated with central bank independence reduces the level and variability of inflation but does not have either large benefits or

---

[4] Among the criteria for "economic" independence, the central bank's ability to set the discount rate also receives a high rating, and falls only narrowly behind these other two factors.

[5] The Fed has greater formal institutional independence on this score, with no direct participation of government officials in the deliberation of the Federal Open Market Committee (FOMC) that makes the major decisions on monetary policy.

costs in terms of real macroeconomic performance."[6] Awareness of these longer-term relationships does not mean that short-term pressures will disappear overnight, however. The more explicit the commitment to price stability, the better. Thus, it is desirable that the central banks of Austria, the Netherlands and (since 1990) New Zealand each do have a clear mandate for price stability. While in Austria and the Netherlands this is combined with a requirement for exchange rate stability, no other objectives are laid down. All three do have some formal provision for government override. However, these provisions have never been used. The Austrian government's right to object to the Austrian National Bank's policy decisions applies only to a situation in which the central bank's policies are in conflict with the legislated objectives of maintaining the internal and external value of the currency.[7] Given that this provision appears to, if anything, reinforce these objectives, we have previously classified the Austrian National Bank as enjoying policy independence (see Burdekin and Willett, 1991).[8] The conditions for the exercising of government veto power in the Netherlands are also highly constrained (Hasse, 1990; Rood, 1990), but they are not formally tied to price and exchange rate objectives as in the Austrian case.[9]

The government's incentive to use the override provision in the Netherlands is nevertheless limited by the Governing Board's right to appeal against any directions from the Minster of Finance – with the

[6] For tests of the effects of central bank independence on sacrifice ratios and the slope of short-run Lucas supply curves, see Fratianni and Huang (1992) and Walsh (1994).

[7] Indeed, the central bank laws for both Austria and Germany include statements obliging the central bank to support the general economic policy directives of the government, as long as this does not conflict with the prime objective of supporting price or exchange rate stability. In the Austrian case, Article 4 of the National Bank Act actually states that "due regard shall be paid to the economic policy of the Federal Government." This article is, however, subordinate to Article 2, which requires the National Bank to "ensure with all the means at its disposal that the value of the Austrian currency is maintained with regard both to its domestic purchasing power and to its relationship with stable foreign currencies" (see Hochreiter, 1990).

[8] In contrast, Grilli, Masciandaro and Tabellini (1991) accord Austria only a low degree of political independence. This low ranking is influenced in part by the emphasis placed on the length of appointment for central bank officials (with points being awarded for appointments that exceed 5 years – so that the 5-year length of appointment at the Austrian National Bank falls just below this cutoff point). There is also an apparent misclassification in that the Austrian National Bank is stated to face mandatory participation of a government representative on the policy board. This is incorrect as the Governing Board *alone* is responsible for setting monetary policy.

[9] Article 26 of the Netherlands Bank Act 1948 (as quoted in Aufricht, 1967, p. 471) states: "In cases in which Our Minister deems it necessary for the purpose of coordinating the Government's monetary and financial policy and the policy of the Bank, he will give to the Governing Board, after the Bank Council has been heard, the directions required for the attaining of that object."

results of the dispute settlement, together with the Governing Board's objections, being published in the *Nederlandse Staatscourant* (see Aufricht, 1967, p. 471). In this respect, the Netherlands' institutional setting is somewhat analogous to that of New Zealand subsequent to the *Reserve Bank of New Zealand Act 1989*. While the New Zealand government has the authority to require the Reserve Bank to direct its policy towards some other objective besides the single price stability goal laid down in the Act, this can only be done through an Order in Council, which is, in effect, a cabinet decision that must be made public and is debatable in parliament (see *Reserve Bank of New Zealand Act 1989*, p. 9). These transparency requirements make an override likely to be quite costly politically in both the Netherlands and New Zealand. The single price level objective in New Zealand stands in sharp contrast to the previous requirement that the Reserve Bank also target production, trade and employment levels (Archer, 1992). Combined with the provisions for transparency with respect to any policy disputes or deviations from the price stability focus laid down in the Act, the Reserve Bank of New Zealand now appears to enjoy a high degree of effective independence.

Also of relevance is the ease or difficulty of changing central bank institutional structures. While developing countries such as Mexico have made constitutional provisions, central bank independence is typically granted by legislation in the industrialized countries.[10] It is possible for the status quo to acquire quasi-constitutional standing, however, as appears to be true of the German Bundesbank where "questioning its independence even seems to be a national taboo" (Tietmeyer, 1991, p. 182). Still, greater degrees of protection from institutional change serve to enhance policy independence. One benefit associated with the European System of Central Banks proposed under the Maastricht framework for European Monetary Union is that its independence would be protected by the treaty.

Personal Independence and Appointment Procedures

Neumann (1991) and Tietmeyer (1991) have used the term "personal independence" to describe the role played by mechanisms for appointment and dismissal of important central bank decision makers. In

---

[10] Switzerland is an exception in that provisions for central bank independence are included in the constitution.

particular, the less "political" the appointment process for central bank officials, the longer their term of office; and the more difficult it is for them to be dismissed, the greater is the likely effective independence of the central bank. While most heads of central banks and members of their policy boards are appointed directly by the government in power, there are some exceptions to this. For example, the Federal Reserve regional bank presidents are not appointed by the government and, as noted earlier, they appear to have been somewhat more likely to support monetary tightening than are the members of the Federal Reserve Board who are appointed by the US President.[11] Besides exhibiting more of an inflationary bias than the regional bank presidents, the voting patterns of the Board of Governors also appear to be influenced by the political affiliation of the president who made the appointment (see, e.g., Havrilesky, 1993, ch. 9).

A number of other central banks have members of their policy board who are not appointed directly by the national government. In Germany, a majority of the Bundesbank's policy board is comprised of the Land central bank presidents. The appointments of the Land central bank presidents are determined by the respective state governments, however, so that all of the Bundesbank Council members are political appointees in a broader sense. Indeed, the Council itself appears to have had reservations about some of the nominees for Land central bank president – during the 1960s and 1970s the Council put forward a number of objections to these nominations, even though it was unable to prevent the appointments from being made (Holtfrerich, 1988, p. 143). As in the United States, the relatively long, staggered terms of office are intended to limit the political influence that might be infused through the appointment process. The 8-year terms for the Council are twice as long as the 4-year interval between federal and state elections, while the "appointments were to take place at such intervals that during one legislative period only a portion of the seats in the Central Bank Council could be refilled" (Holtfrerich, 1988, p. 143).

Certainly, provision of a lengthy term of office with no dismissal except in highly circumscribed instances gives scope for greater independence. Ineligibility for reappointment removes a source of pressure from the government. On these criteria, the Federal Reserve

---

[11] The Fed's policy board is sometimes incorrectly classified as being entirely comprised of government appointees (cf. Bade and Parkin, 1987). Since the Board of Governors accounts for only seven votes out of twelve on the key monetary policy decision-making body, the FOMC, the percentage of government appointees is actually just 58 percent.

Board with its 14-year non-renewable terms would appear to score the highest among the industrial countries. By comparison, Switzerland is close to the middle of the industrial countries with 4-year terms. Yet, most recent analysis of the political economy of US monetary policy concludes that the executive branch usually succeeds in having a substantial influence on monetary policy (see Mayer, 1990).

No doubt some of the executive branch pressure in the United States comes from the power of moral suasion from the US President. To a large degree, however, this pressure may be exerted through the Federal Reserve Chairman, who has only a 4-year *renewable* term. No central bank head of an industrial country has a shorter term: the central bank heads in Greece and Spain are also given 4-year terms; Switzerland gives a 6-year term; Australia, Canada, Ireland and the Netherlands give 7-year terms; and Germany gives an 8-year term. It is true that costs to the US President from not reappointing a widely respected Federal Reserve Chairman could give the Chairman some leeway here. Nevertheless, concern about his reappointment may still give the Chairman considerable incentive to be responsive to the wishes of the government, especially as the end of the Chairman's term draws near. This provides the government with an important source of direct leverage, especially given the disproportionate power of the chairman in setting policy (Maisel, 1973, p. 110, attributes 45 percent of the power to the chairman and only 20 percent to the other governors).

Economic Independence and Fiscal Pressures

Another major category of central bank independence concerns the bank's ability to carry out anti-inflationary policies and bear the short-run costs that these policies may impose on interest rates, employment levels and so forth. Grilli, Masciandaro and Tabellini (1991, p. 366) refer to economic independence as "the capacity to choose *the instruments* with which to pursue these [monetary] goals" (emphasis in original). In a similar vein, Tietmeyer (1991, p. 180) discusses functional independence in terms of a bank's "sole and unrestricted authority to use the traditional instruments of monetary policy." Both Grilli, Masciandaro and Tabellini (1991) and Tietmeyer (1991) consider as an example the question of financing government budget deficits. What is at issue here is the effective ability of the central bank to determine monetary policy. It is generally agreed that the Fed's obligation to intervene to peg the market value of US government debt prior to the

1951 Fed-Treasury Accord left Fed policy almost entirely subordinate to fiscal policy actions. Even where no such formal requirements are in place, the central bank's ability to set an independent policy may still be threatened by the high short-run costs of forcing the government to rely on bond financing (see Burdekin and Langdana, 1992).

Since positive obligations with respect to financing government deficits may severely reduce the independence of monetary policy, prohibitions on financing government deficits would be a plus. We would, however, put less weight on this in countries with well-developed financial markets because concerns over the level of interest rates could still induce considerable indirect financing of government deficits. We suspect that far more important are pressures for monetary accommodation arising both from the overall magnitude of the budget deficit and from such other factors as the degree of wage and price flexibility and cost-push pressures. At the same time, if domestic financial markets are not well developed and there is little access to international capital markets, then even without any formal obligations to finance budget deficits, the emergence of huge budget deficits would make it difficult for the most independent of central bankers to maintain a low rate of monetary growth (see Leone, 1991). In the absence of a clear delineation of priorities, one can easily understand the following views expressed by Governor Guido Carli of the Banca d'Italia:

> Refusal [to finance the public sector's deficit] would make it impossible for the Government to pay the salaries of the armed forces, of the judiciary and of civil servants, and the pensions of most citizens. ... It would be a seditious act, which would be followed by a paralysis of the public administration. One must ensure that the public administration continues to function, even if the economy grinds to a halt.[12]

Thus, while we would not argue that provisions concerning financing of budget deficits are irrelevant – they may sometimes have important symbolic value – in terms of maintaining monetary stability they may be of less importance than the factors that determine the size of budget deficits. In this regard, the correspondence between the high degree of central bank independence in Germany and Switzerland and the extremely small, or negative, budget deficits in these countries (at least prior to the German reunification) may reflect an ability of independent central banks to discourage profligate fiscal policies. The German and Swiss governments are aware that they cannot count on money financing

[12] Quoted in Goodman (1992, p. 148).

but instead may have to resort to the more costly alternative of bond financing (see Burdekin and Laney, 1988).

A further major consideration is the role played by the exchange rate regime. While, on the one hand, requirements to support an undervalued exchange rate may force domestic monetary expansion, hard currency pegs to a low-inflation country like Germany can be an important source of monetary discipline (as in the Austrian case, for example, Hochreiter and Winckler, 1994). The evidence on the European Monetary System in this regard is quite mixed (see Burdekin, Westbrook and Willett, 1994). This is an important area for further research.

3   AGGREGATE INDICES AND EMPIRICAL ANALYSIS OF THE RELATIONSHIP BETWEEN CENTRAL BANK INDEPENDENCE AND INFLATION

As is clear from the many considerations raised in the discussion of institutional, personal and economic independence, difficult issues of weighting must be resolved in order to develop any overall judgment on the degree of central bank independence. Masciandaro (1993) provides one attempt to narrow the focus on central bank independence to the bank's capacity to control inflation and the procedures of accountability. We believe that, in the absence of either freedom from government override and/or a clear price stability mandate, such considerations as lengths of office for central bank officials and financial arrangements between central bank and treasury would be of little, if any, importance in influencing inflation performance. The pitfalls of just focusing on a linear sum of different attributes are reflected in our finding that – despite the many potentially important nuances of independence that have been raised in the recent literature – the simple criterion of whether or not the government has authority to override the central bank still appears to be a better predictor of inflation performance.

To investigate the relationship between the independence of central banks and inflation, we compiled data on 21 industrialized economies. In line with Burdekin and Willett (1991), Austria, Germany, Switzerland and the United States are coded as having independent central banks for the period of 1971–88 based on their statutory provisions against government override.[13] The first column of Table 12.1 shows the results of a regression analysis holding constant a number of factors that have been identified in the literature as causes of monetary expansion and inflation. The budget deficit, the openness of the economy, per capita GDP growth and the levels of income inequality and trade unionism are all entered in the regression alongside the central bank independence dummy. Four countries were removed from the sample because we lacked data on the level of income inequality in these economies. The results suggest that the four nations with independent central banks experienced average inflation rates that were approximately 3 percentage points below those of the other economies. The independence dummy is significant at the 10 percent level with the expected negative sign, but none of the coefficients is significant at the 5 percent level – likely due to the few degrees of freedom in the sample.

We offer a more parsimonious specification in column 2 of Table 12.1. The last three control variables – per capita GDP growth, the degree of unionization and the degree of income inequality – are removed from the regression. This allows us to reintroduce the four countries previously removed. The independence dummy is now easily significant at the 5 percent level; a result that is consistent with the earlier empirical support for this measure of central bank independence provided in Banaian, Laney and Willett (1983), Banaian et al. (1988), Burdekin and Laney (1988) and Havrilesky and Granato (1993). The remaining variables are also significant in the expected directions owing to lower standard errors.[14] Smaller deficits and greater openness of an economy are associated with lower inflation rates.

The independence dummy that we use is quite crude: it says that the Bundesbank is like the Federal Reserve and there is no distinction between the Bank of Italy and the Bank of Japan. Cukierman (1992) has developed a continuous index of central bank independence that ranges along a [0, 1] scale. In column 3 we use Cukierman's measure of legal independence based on his reading of the central bank laws and judgmental weighting of the different factors. Our independence dummy retains its significance while Cukierman's measure has the wrong sign and a *t*-statistic of less than 1. We likewise use his measure of turnover of central bank governors in the regression reported in column 4, and find it has no effect.

[13] The Penn World Tables Mark V end in 1988, and consistent series on the macroeconomic variables were not available to us after that time.
[14] Using the smaller sample of 17 countries, the *F*-statistic for the joint hypothesis that the omitted variables have zero coefficients was 1.31 (yielding a significance level of only 32.5 percent).

Table 12.1   Central bank independence as a deterrent to inflation

Independent variables	Regression number					
	1	2	3	4	5	6
Deficit/GDP	0.1342 (1.53)	0.1985 (2.86)	0.1989 (2.84)	0.2024 (2.57)	0.1460 (1.80)	0.1582 (2.15)
Trade volume/GDP	−0.0432 (1.68)	−0.0270 (2.24)	−0.0293 (2.35)	−0.0253 (1.71)	−0.0306 (1.93)	−0.0367 (2.48)
Independence dummy	2.761 (1.98)	3.164 (2.58)	4.317 (2.29)	3.034 (1.93)		1.916 (1.51)
Per capita GDP growth	−0.6133 (0.75)					
Percent of labor unionized	0.0346 (0.82)					
Inequality	0.39425 (0.81)					
Legal independence			3.789 (0.81)			
Turnover				2.232 (0.17)		
Political independence					−0.1684 (0.65)	
Economic independence					−0.7612 (2.64)	−0.5315 (1.72)
Adjusted R^2	0.53	0.58	0.57	0.52	0.62	0.69
Standard error	1.94	2.09	2.11	2.30	2.00	1.80
Number of observations	17	21	21	19	20	20

The *t*-ratios are in parentheses.

Sources: For macroeconomic conditions, World Bank, Penn World Tables Mark V; legal independence and turnover are from Cukierman (1992); and economic and political independence are from Grilli, Masciandaro and Tabellini (1991).

Cukierman's sample includes 49 developing countries excluded from our sample. This may help account for the fact that Cukierman's legal independence index has a significant effect on inflation performance in his empirical analysis but not in ours. Certainly, the turnover measure was found by Cukierman to work better for developing countries. We can, however, make two conjectures from these results. First, a simple reading of central bank laws on the financial relationship between central bank and government will not explain the pressures on central banks in their open market operations. Second, it is unclear whether the degree of turnover of central bank governors leads to more or less inflation in industrial countries. Few governors of the Fed serve out their full 14-year terms. Fed Chairmen usually do not remain on the Board after stepping down as chairs. Many find lucrative employment in the banking sector. This may register as high turnover yet reveals little information about *government* influence on the Fed. Moreover, a very accommodative governor is unlikely to be replaced, in which case low turnover may mean more rather than less inflation.

Grilli, Masciandaro and Tabellini (1991) offer two independence indices. The first index measures "political independence" and is dominated by the terms governing the selection, tenure and voting power of central bank governors. The second, measuring "economic independence," focuses primarily on the fiscal relationship between central bank and treasury. Both measures are included in regression reported in column 5 of Table 12.1. The economic independence measure adds a significant amount of explanatory power to the regression. Political independence has the right sign but enters the regression insignificantly. Column 6 shows, however, that if we substitute our independence dummy in place of the Grilli, Masciandaro and Tabellini political independence measure, neither the independence dummy nor the economic independence measure is statistically significant. Given that the overall goodness of fit is slightly higher than for the regression in column 2, where our independence dummy is entered alone, there may be some scope for additional reduction in inflationary bias in democracies by providing a central bank with institutional protection from fiscal pressures.[15]

---

[15] Other regressions tested whether the presence of an independent central bank reduces the inflationary effects of budget deficits, and whether relative inflation performance is influenced by the structure of wage bargaining. The former issue was tested by adding an interaction variable for central bank independence multiplied by the budget deficit, the latter by ranking the countries in terms of their corporatist structure. Neither variable contributed significant explanatory power to the regressions.

Table 12.2 "Corrected" average inflation rates for 21 economies, 1971–88

Country	Average inflation rate, adjusted for deficits and trade volume	Actual inflation rates
Japan	5.08	5.07
Germany	**5.77**	**4.22**
United States	**5.92**	**6.03**
Austria	**6.80**	**5.37**
Canada	7.38	7.04
Switzerland	**7.42**	**4.67**
Netherlands	7.47	5.31
Belgium	8.14	5.97
Sweden	9.81	8.73
France	10.03	8.96
Norway	10.20	7.68
Australia	10.32	9.90
United Kingdom	10.48	10.04
Denmark	10.50	8.30
Ireland	11.29	11.32
Finland	11.58	9.78
Luxembourg	11.72	5.81
New Zealand	11.92	12.14
Italy	12.03	13.45
Spain	13.06	12.94
Greece	15.53	15.97

The four countries classified as having independent central banks are marked in bold.
Source: World Bank, Penn World Tables Mark 5, and the authors' calculations.

One can approach the question a different way. Rather than assume the differences in inflation performance are due to variations in central bank structure, we can calculate the difference in inflationary experience for these countries while we hold openness of the economy and deficits constant. We do so by means of a pooled cross-section time-series regression for our 21 economies over the 19 years in question. Table 12.2 shows these results in the form of an average inflation rate "corrected" for differences in deficit and trade volume experience.[16] The

[16] The coefficients on deficits and openness were 0.124 and −0.028, respectively, similar to the results given in Table 12.1. The pooled regression had an adjusted R^2 of 0.41.

average "corrected" inflation rates are higher for the countries with dependent central banks: We can reject at the 1 percent significance level the null hypothesis that all 17 countries with dependent central banks had the same corrected rates as the United States.[17] While we cannot claim that the reason for the difference in these corrected inflation rates is necessarily the structure of their central banks, the results are not inconsistent with this view.

Two additional observations can be made from these adjusted inflation rates. First, in comparison to the actual rates of inflation shown alongside, the adjusted rates run over a far smaller range, suggesting that high deficits are associated with high inflation. Second, there are only two countries whose individual adjusted inflation rates are not higher than the rate for the set of four countries represented in our central bank independence dummy. In particular, Japan ranks ahead of all four countries with statutorily independent central banks. As argued in section 2, however, Japan's exceptionally good inflation performance may derive, at least in part, from the fact that the Bank of Japan and the Finance Ministry have enjoyed a high degree of functional independence from domestic political pressures. Canada ranks fifth, ahead of Switzerland but behind the other three countries with independent central banks. The Bank of Canada, while subject to government override, is subject to arrangements similar to those prevailing in the Netherlands (and now in New Zealand), in that any directive must be given in writing, published and laid before the legislature. Thus, like the Netherlands (which ranks seventh, just below Switzerland, in Table 12.2), Canada's effective degree of central bank independence is arguably higher than for the majority of the other countries classified as possessing dependent central banks.

4 CONCLUSIONS

We find evidence that statutory rules may provide a safeguard against inflationary bias relative to the average country with a central bank that is dependent on government. The corrected inflation rankings in Table 12.2 show that the four countries that we consider to possess the highest degree of central bank independence rank second, third, fourth and sixth

---

[17] We omitted the United States from the list of dummy variables employed. The F-statistic for the hypothesis that the coefficients on the 17 countries with dependent central banks are jointly zero was 6.73. The 1 percent critical value for the F-distribution is 2.11.

out of twenty-one. A more encompassing measure that included cases where government override was possible, but likely to be highly costly politically, would capture the countries ranked fifth and seventh – and likely only strengthen the empirical results reported in Table 12.1. This suggests that central bank independence deserves the serious consideration it has recently received as a means of offsetting inflationary biases. There are several routes to this independence, however, and further micro-analytic research is necessary to assess the relative importance of institutional arrangements such as restrictions on government override of central bank decisions, the existence of a clear price stability mandate, and the nature of the appointment process.[18]

REFERENCES

Alesina, Alberto and Summers, Lawrence H. (1993) "Central Bank Independence and Macroeconomic Performance: Some Comparative Evidence" *Journal of Money, Credit, and Banking,* vol. 25, no. 2, May, pp. 151–62.

Archer, David J. (1992) "Organizing a Central Bank to Control Inflation: The Case of New Zealand" presented at the 1992 meetings of the Western Economic Association, San Francisco, CA, July 9–13.

Aufricht, Hans (1961) *Central Banking Legislation: A Collection of Central Bank, Monetary and Banking Laws,* International Monetary Fund, Washington, DC.

Aufricht, Hans (1967) *Central Banking Legislation: A Collection of Central Bank, Monetary and Banking Laws; Volume II, Europe,* International Monetary Fund, Washington, DC.

Bade, Robin and Parkin, Michael (1987) "Central Bank Laws and Monetary Policy" (mimeo), Department of Economics, University of Western Ontario, June.

Banaian, King, Laney, Leroy O., McArthur, John and Willett, Thomas D. (1988) "Subordinating the Fed to Political Authorities Will Not Control Inflationary Tendencies" in Willett, Thomas D. (ed.), *Political Business Cycles: The Political Economy of Money, Inflation, and Unemployment,* Duke University Press, Durham, NC.

Banaian, King, Laney, Leroy O. and Willett, Thomas D. (1983) "Central Bank Independence: An International Comparison" *Economic Review,* Federal Reserve Bank of Dallas, March, pp. 1–13.

Burdekin, Richard C.K. (1987) "Swiss Monetary Policy: Central Bank Independence and Stabilization Goals" *Kredit und Kapital,* vol. 20, no. 4, pp. 454–66.

Burdekin, Richard C.K. and Laney, Leroy O. (1988) "Fiscal Policymaking and the Central Bank Institutional Constraint" *Kyklos,* vol. 41, no. 4, pp. 647–62.

Burdekin, Richard C.K. and Langdana, Farrokh K. (1992) *Budget Deficits and Economic Performance,* Routledge, London.

---

[18] One promising line of research involves the study of optimal incentive contracts for monetary policy decision makers (see Walsh, 1992, and Fratianni, von Hagen and Waller, 1993).

Burdekin, Richard C.K., Westbrook, Jilleen R. and Willett, Thomas D. (1994) "Exchange Rate Pegging as a Disinflation Strategy: Evidence from the European Monetary System" in Siklos, Pierre L. (ed.), *Varieties of Monetary Reform: Lessons and Experiences on the Road to Monetary Union*, Kluwer Academic Publishers, Boston, MA.

Burdekin, Richard C.K., Wihlborg, Clas and Willett, Thomas D. (1992) "A Monetary Constitution Case for an Independent European Central Bank" *World Economy*, vol. 15, no. 2, March, pp. 231–49.

Burdekin, Richard C.K. and Willett, Thomas D. (1991) "Central Bank Reform: The Federal Reserve in International Perspective" *Public Budgeting and Financial Management*, vol. 3, no. 3, pp. 619–49.

Cargill, Thomas F. (1989) *Central Bank Independence and Regulatory Responsibilities: The Bank of Japan and the Federal Reserve*, Monograph 1989-2, Salomon Brothers Center for the Study of Financial Institutions, New York University, NY.

Cukierman, Alex (1992) *Central Bank Strategy, Credibility, and Independence: Theory and Evidence*, MIT Press, Cambridge, MA.

Epstein, Gerald A. and Schor, Juliet B. (1986) "The Political Economy of Central Banking" Discussion Paper No. 1281, Harvard Institute of Economic Research, July .

Fratianni, Michele and Huang, Haizhou (1992) "Central Bank Independence and Optimal Conservativeness" (mimeo), Indiana University, Bloomington, IN, December.

Fratianni, Michele, von Hagen, Jürgen and Waller, Christopher (1993) "Central Banking as a Political Principal-Agent Problem" (mimeo), Indiana University, Bloomington, IN, October.

Goodman, John B. (1992) *Monetary Sovereignty: The Politics of Central Banking in Western Europe*, Cornell University Press, Ithaca, NY.

Grilli, Vittorio, Masciandaro, Donato and Tabellini, Guido (1991) "Political and Monetary Institutions and Public Financial Policies in the Industrial Countries" *Economic Policy*, 13, October, pp. 341–92.

Hasse, Rolf H. et al. (1990) *The European Central Bank: Perspectives for a Further Development of the European Monetary System*, Bertelsmann Foundation, Gütersloh, Germany.

Havrilesky, Thomas (1993) *The Pressures on American Monetary Policy*, Kluwer Academic Publishers, Boston, MA.

Havrilesky, Thomas and Granato, James (1993) "Determinants of Inflationary Performance: Corporatist Structures vs. Central Bank Autonomy" *Public Choice*, vol. 76, no. 3, July, pp. 249–61.

Hochreiter, Eduard (1990) "The Austrian National Bank Act: What Does It Say About Monetary Policy?" *Konjunkturpolitik*, vol. 36, no. 4, pp. 245–56.

Hochreiter, Eduard and Winckler, Georg (1994) "Signaling a Hard Currency Strategy: The Case of Austria" *Kredit und Kapital*, 27, in press.

Holtfrerich, Carl-Ludwig (1988) "Relations between Monetary Authorities and Governmental Institutions: The Case of Germany from the 19th Century to the Present" in Toniolo, Gianni (ed.), *Central Banks' Independence in Historical Perspective*, Walter de Gruyter, New York, NY.

Leone, Alfredo (1991) "Effectiveness and Implications of Limits on Central Bank Credit to the Government" in Downes, Patrick and Vaez-Zadeh, Reza (eds), *The Evolving Role of Central Banks*, International Monetary Fund, Washington, DC.

Maisel, Sherman J. (1973) *Managing the Dollar*, W.W. Norton, New York, NY.

Masciandaro, Donato (1993) "Policymaking Hazards, Monetary Policy and Central Bank Design" (mimeo), Centre for Monetary and Financial Economics, Universita Commerciale Luigi Bocconi, Milan, Italy, April.

Masciandaro, Donato and Spinelli, Franco (1993) "Monetary Constitutionalism Once Again: Theory, Institutions and Central Banks' View" (mimeo), Centre for Monetary and Financial Economics, Universita Commerciale Luigi Bocconi, Milan, Italy, February.

Mayer, Thomas (1979) "Using the Constitution to Fight Inflation" *American Banker*, November 29, pp. 11–12.

Mayer, Thomas (1990) (ed.) *The Political Economy of American Monetary Policy*, Cambridge University Press, New York, NY.

Mayer, Thomas and Willett, Thomas D. (1988) "Evaluating Proposals for Fundamental Monetary Reform" in Willett, Thomas D. (ed.), *Political Business Cycles: The Political Economy of Money, Inflation, and Unemployment*, Duke University Press, Durham, NC.

Neumann, Manfred J.M. (1991) "Precommitment by Central Bank Independence" *Open Economies Review*, vol. 2, no. 2, pp. 95–112.

Reserve Bank of New Zealand Act 1989 (1990) Government Printer, Wellington, New Zealand.

Rood, Jan Q. Th. (1990) "The Position of the Netherlands: A Lesson in Monetary Union" in Sherman, Heidemarie (ed.), *Monetary Implications of the 1992 Process*, St Martin's Press, New York, NY.

Swinburne, Mark and Castello-Branco, Marta (1991) "Central Bank Independence and Central Bank Functions" in Downes, Patrick and Vaez-Zadeh, Reza (eds), *The Evolving Role of Central Banks*, International Monetary Fund, Washington, DC.

Tietmeyer, Hans (1991) "The Role of an Independent Central Bank in Europe" in Downes, Patrick and Vaez-Zadeh, Reza (eds), *The Evolving Role of Central Banks*, International Monetary Fund, Washington, DC.

Walsh, Carl E. (1992) "Optimal Contracts for Central Bankers" Working Paper No. 92-07, Federal Reserve Bank of San Francisco, November.

Walsh, Carl E. (1994) "Central Bank Independence and the Costs of Disinflation in the EC" (mimeo), University of California, Santa Cruz, April.

Willett, Thomas D. (1988) (ed.) *Political Business Cycles: The Political Economy of Money, Inflation, and Unemployment*, Duke University Press, Durham, NC.

13. The Bank of Japan and Federal Reserve: An Essay on Central Bank Independence

Thomas F. Cargill*

INTRODUCTION

The relaxation of binding constraints on portfolio flexibility referred to as "deregulation" or "financial liberalization" has fundamentally altered the structure of domestic financial systems, increased world economic integration, and raised familiar issues about central bank policy. The financial transition in particular has focused attention on the question of whether the institutional relationship between the central bank and the government influences central bank policy outcomes, especially the ability to control inflation.

The traditional view that emphasizes the importance of formal independence has found recent support from a small but growing number of studies (e.g., Alesina, 1988; Alesina and Summers, 1993; Bade and Parkin, 1988; Burdekin and Willett, 1991; Cukierman, Webb and Neyapti, 1992; and Grilli, Masciandaro and Tabellini, 1991) that offer evidence consistent with the hypothesis that formally independent central banks have better records of price stability than less independent banks. While these studies focus on inflation performance, the results logically extend to other related activities of the central bank. One might argue, for example, that for the same reasons independent central banks have better inflation records they would also have better records at regulating and supervising the financial system.

These findings are interesting and suggestive. At the same time there are troubling issues not adequately dealt with by the empirical literature.

* I am grateful to King Banaian and Thomas Mayer for comments on an earlier draft; however, I remain responsible for all errors.

The objective of this paper is to raise some of these issues in the context of the experiences of Japan and the United States. The policy outcomes of the Bank of Japan and the Federal Reserve, two different institutionally organized central banks, suggest that the relationship between outcomes and independence from government is complex to say the least. Leaving aside technical problems with the empirical literature, the relative performances of the Bank of Japan and the Federal Reserve contradict the prediction that formally independent central banks generate lower inflation rates. This paper concludes that at least from the experiences of the Bank of Japan and the Federal Reserve, formal independence is no guarantee of a stable monetary environment. There may be reasons why a legally independent central bank is preferable to a dependent bank; however, to draw the conclusion that independence is needed for the ongoing responsibilities of the central bank is simplistic.

The remainder of the paper consists of four sections. In the second section recent developments that define the context of the independence question are reviewed. The third section summarizes the empirical literature. The Bank of Japan and the Federal Reserve along with their inflation records are compared in the fourth section. The fifth section explores the implications of the two records for the independence question. A concluding section ends the paper.

CONTEXT OF THE INDEPENDENCE QUESTION

Four developments during the past two decades have significantly changed the context of the independence question: financial transition; consensus on the role of monetary policy as a stabilization instrument; link between macroeconomic performance and political institutions; and the public-choice theory of regulatory policy.

First, the financial transition toward more open and competitive markets has highlighted the critical role of the central bank in the process. The US experience illustrates how the failure to maintain price stability generated serious disruptions in the financial system in the 1970s and 1980s, weakened depository institutions by exposing them to new and unexpected risk, and generated a disruptive financial reform process. In contrast, countries such as Japan that maintained price stability during the financial transition avoided many of the problems experienced in the United States. Their transition has been smoother, more gradual, and frequently more successful (Cargill and Royama, 1988).

The transition itself has raised other issues for central bank policy. Increased competition, enhanced opportunities to manage risk, and market-sensitive loan and deposit rates raise the probability that any one depository institution will fail and thus, increase the importance of the central bank's role as the lender of last resort. In addition, the changing context of monetary policy has required central banks to reevaluate their operating procedures, intermediate targets, role in financial regulation, and their overall relationship to government.

Second, research has established that monetary policy is *the* instrument of stabilization; at the same time, research has shown that monetary policy cannot effectively manage short-run demand in the tradition of the Keynesian model. At least among academic economists and many central bankers, there is a consensus that monetary policy should focus primarily on achieving a low and steady inflation rate in the long run.

Third, research has established a theoretical link between macroeconomic performance and political institutions that cannot be rejected by the empirical literature (Mayer, 1990; Willett, 1988). The central bank forms the link between macroeconomic performance and political institutions in these political business cycle models, and the evidence further suggests that even formally independent central banks such as the Federal Reserve contribute to the political business cycle.

Fourth, the record of monetary and financial policies rejects the market failure view of government regulation. The evolution of financial and monetary regulation is more consistent with the public-choice view. The public-choice view regards regulation as the outcome of a complex set of economic and political incentives that may or may not coincide with the general welfare. Regulators are agents while the general public, along with a large set of affected sectors, are the principals. The regulatory utility function contains two parameters: the general welfare and the maintenance/enhancement of its own regulatory power. As a result the outcome of regulation is not always in the public interest. The regulator may conclude that response to specific agents rather than the general public will more likely maintain and enhance its regulatory power. In this regard, central banks are motivated by self-interest in a complex setting of economic and political institutions that may lead to outcomes adverse to the general public, such as inflationary monetary policy. In the context of the public-choice approach it is not clear why a formally independent central bank would be more likely to achieve a better inflation record. In fact models such as the one suggested by Kane (1990) show that formally independent central banks are just as capable of non-optimal monetary policy as dependent central banks.

ASSESSMENT OF PREVIOUS EMPIRICAL RESEARCH

Empirical work on the relationship between independence and inflation performance fall into two categories. Studies such as Willett et al. (1988) fit single-equation regressions to cross sections of time-series data. An index of central bank independence along with other variables are used to explain the inflation rate. Other studies such as Burdekin and Willett (1991) compare in a less rigorous statistical manner the ranking of central banks according to degree of independence and their inflation records.

Despite the variety of countries investigated and methods employed, the studies suggest that a formally independent central bank is more likely to achieve a low inflation rate. Burdekin and Willett, for example, conclude

> the inflation statistics ... lend further support to the conclusion that more independent central banks have, on average, delivered lower inflation rates. This observation holds true both for the 1960–89 period examined as a whole and also on the basis of a decade-by-decade breakdown, thus adding to the impression that such central bank institutional structures really do make a difference. (Burdekin and Willett, 1991, p. 13)

These results are suggestive. However, three considerations raise doubts about the statistical association: econometric problems; the index of independence; and the failure of the results to account for the comparative performances of the Bank of Japan and the Federal Reserve in the postwar period.

The regression results are based on cross sections of time-series data with coefficients constrained to be constant over time. At a minimum this type of data presents difficult technical problems. The large number of factors influencing the inflation rate make it difficult to summarize the relationship between independence and inflation for so many countries over long periods of time. In addition, recent structural changes taking place in the domestic financial systems of most countries, in the context of globalization of finance, make it difficult for reduced-form equations with time-invariant coefficient estimates to capture the relationship between independence and inflation.

A more serious problem with this type of research, however, resides in the need to construct a country-invariant and time-invariant index of independence from government. The rankings rely on formal rules that define the relationship between the central bank and government. Formal rules, however, can at best only approximate the relationship and at worst, provide misleading information (Mayer, 1976). Eijffinger and Schaling (1993) illustrate some of the problems of constructing indexes of independence.

Assuming the formal rules provide a reasonable basis for indexing central bank independence, they are not capable of distinguishing between a large number of cases because no one rule or small number of rules can uniquely separate central banks from each other in terms of independence. Rankings may force an ordinal measure of independence when in fact none exists in practice. There is no doubt that formal rules allow one to distinguish between say, the Bank of Japan or the Bank of Korea and the Federal Reserve or the Bundesbank, but it may be too much to ask formal rules to distinguish between the large number of central banks of the industrialized or developing countries.

A serious problem arises from the more likely possibility that formal rules provide a misleading view of central bank independence. Reliance on formal rules implicitly assumes that formal independence renders a central bank less sensitive to government pressure. This is an oversimplified view. Central banks are agents responding to a variety of principals and, like any government agent, are concerned with maintaining and enhancing power within government. Formal independence is a valued sign of power in any government and as such, an independent central bank may be willing to accommodate agents other than the general public that can more effectively maintain or enhance that power. This point was succinctly summed up by Samuelson: "The Fed is a prisoner of its independence" (cited in Mayer, 1990, p. 6).

A more serious matter, however, is the failure of the empirical studies to account for the contrasting inflation records of the two largest economies in the world. The Bank of Japan, a formally dependent central bank, has clearly achieved a better inflation record than the Federal Reserve, a formally independent central bank (Cargill, 1993). In fact, the Bank of Japan has one of the best inflation records among the industrialized countries. When Japan is recognized as a low-inflation country, it is often regarded as a special case to the general rule that formally independent central banks are likely to generate better policy outcomes (Parry, 1992). There are at least three problems with this approach. First, to eliminate Japan from the 15 or so major industrialized countries of the world without weighting is to eliminate from consideration about 7 percent of the sample; second, to eliminate Japan from the list of industrialized countries weighted by economic importance is to eliminate one of the more important inflation records from the analysis; and third, there is a heavy burden of proof on these studies to show why Japan should be regarded as an exception, given the high degree of formal dependence of the Bank of Japan on the government relative to other central banks. None of the studies have attempted to provide a strong argument to explain why Japan should be regarded as an exception.

JAPAN AND THE UNITED STATES

Friedman and Schwartz (1963) stressed the need to complement statistical relationships between money and output with historical studies of major monetary events. Only in this manner could the causation from money to economic activity be verified. The same argument applies to the issue of central bank independence. The problems associated with measuring the relationship between central bank independence from government and macroeconomic performance require a closer examination of specific inflation records and the central bank's institutional framework.

Do the actual experiences and institutional settings agree with the predictions from the statistical studies?

The Bank of Japan and the Federal Reserve provide an interesting comparison for this issue. They are among the most important central banks in the world; they differ in their formal relationship to government; they conducted monetary policy during the 1970s and early 1980s in the context of large central government deficits; they conduct monetary policy in the context of major structural changes in the financial system; and most important, their inflation records contradict the prediction that independent central banks generate lower inflation rates. The Bank of Japan since 1975 has generated a lower inflation rate than the United States and yet, the Federal Reserve is one of the most formally independent central banks in the world while the Bank of Japan would rank considerably lower in the degree of formal independence. In fact some economists regard the Bank of Japan as a model central bank (Hutchison and Judd, 1989) in terms of its commitment to price stability. Few have considered the Federal Reserve to be a similar role model.

A clearer picture of the two central banks can be obtained by considering their structure, their relationship to government, their operating procedure, and most important, their inflation record.

Structure

The industrialization of Japan commenced with the establishment of the Meiji Government in 1868. The Meiji Restoration was intended to replace the feudal regime maintained by the Tokugawa Shogunate and to begin a process of modernization to attain and ultimately surpass the level of industrialization of the West. The Bank of Japan was established in 1882 in response to the failure of a national banking system established in 1872 which had been modeled on the US national banking system. The Ministry of Finance established the Bank of Japan in response to the over-issuance of currency and resulting inflation. The Bank of Japan was thus established by the Ministry with a mandate to control inflation.

The Bank of Japan was reorganized for wartime activity in 1942 by the Bank of Japan Law which remains in force. The Bank of Japan at the end of the war advocated changes in the law to reduce its formal dependence on the Ministry. The Committee on Financial System Research in 1956 discussed the issue of independence but could not decide on "what should be the most rational form of relationship between the Government and the Bank of Japan" (Shionoya, 1962, p. vi). In recent years the Bank of Japan has renewed its efforts to have the matter reconsidered (Suzuki, 1987), but without success.

The Bank of Japan is organized as a special corporation of the government with 55 percent of its shares held by the government. The remaining 45 percent are held by private individuals, private institutions and local governments. Trading is permitted. The Bank of Japan is structurally centralized; that is, all major decisions are made by the Tokyo headquarters.

The Federal Reserve was organized in 1913 at a much later stage of economic development. The incentives to establish the Federal Reserve were also related to the failure of a national banking system responsible for issuing the national currency; however, it took the US longer to respond to these problems.

The Federal Reserve differs from the Bank of Japan in two important respects: regionalism and decision-making units within the central bank. The Federal Reserve was originally organized as a decentralized central bank reflecting the dual system of finance in the United States. While power has gradually shifted to the center, regional components of the Federal Reserve continue to play an important role in the formulation and execution of monetary policy through the formal participation of regional presidents on the Federal Open Market Committee and the role of regional banks in administering the discount window and, to a lesser extent, in setting the discount rate. Regionalism plays no significant role in the decision making of the Bank of Japan.

The Board of Governors of the Federal Reserve and the Policy Board of the Bank of Japan are often regarded as comparable in terms of decision making. Both are at the top of the administrative structure; however, they differ considerably in their policy formulation roles. The Board of Governors dominates the formulation and execution of monetary policy because it constitutes seven of the twelve-member Federal Open Market Committee and the Chair of the Board of Governors serves as chair of the Federal Open Market Committee. The Board solicits input from its staff and the regional banks, but ultimately sets the tone of monetary policy with little commitment to follow their advice.

The Policy Board is less independent of the other components of the central bank. In fact, the Policy Board usually adopts policies recommended by the Executive Board, which consists of the Governor, Vice-Governor and several executive directors representing various functions within the Bank of Japan. The Executive Board is the major decision-making entity within the Bank of Japan. In addition, the executive directors representing the various components of the Bank rely heavily on the recommendations of their staff. One could say the Board of Governors combines the functions of the Policy Board and the Executive Board and formulates policy with less reliance on lower-level components. In terms of current concepts in comparing Japan and the United States, monetary policy in the United States adopts a "top-down" management style; in Japan, the "bottom-up" style is the rule. As a manifestation of this different management style, Bank of Japan policy is not normally identified with any one individual – a situation much different than in the United States, where monetary policy is frequently influenced by and identified with the Chair of the Board of Governors.

Relationship to Government

In almost every respect the Bank of Japan is formally more dependent on government than the Federal Reserve. This is most clearly expressed by the Bank of Japan Law which intends the Bank of Japan to be dependent on government (Suzuki, 1987). This principle is reflected in many aspects of Bank of Japan operations. The Ministry of Finance is represented on the Policy Board and more important, appointments to the Policy and Executive Boards require Ministry approval. Traditionally the Governor of the Bank of Japan has alternated between a Bank of Japan and a Ministry of Finance individual. Finally, it is difficult to imagine any major Bank of Japan action that is not first discussed with the Ministry. The Bank of Japan has in recent years advocated more formal independence; however, there is little support for such a change.

In sharp contrast, the Federal Reserve is formally independent of the government. The Federal Reserve Act clearly adopts the principle of formal independence, and in fact formal independence was increased in 1935, when the Federal Reserve Board was reorganized to its current structure.

Monetary Policy Operations

There were differences between the operating procedures of the Bank of Japan and the Federal Reserve prior to the start of financial reform in the mid-1970s; however, the differences were not as significant as one might expect. The Federal Reserve operated in a more open and competitive environment with deep and wide money-market instruments. It adopted an "interest-rate focused" policy targeting short-term rates as key operating variables, which in turn influenced the cost and availability of credit. This transmission process was explicitly expressed in the Federal Reserve's econometric model first developed in the late 1960s. In contrast, the Bank of Japan operated in an internationally isolated financial environment subject to extensive regulatory and administrative control; however, the Bank of Japan also adopted an "interest-rate focused" policy since the interbank rate was the key operating variable, which in turn influenced the availability of credit. The cost of credit was not a major intermediate target of Bank of Japan policy because of the rigidly controlled interest-rate structure in Japan prior to the start of financial reform (Suzuki, 1980).

The financial liberalization in Japan changed the operating environment of the Bank of Japan and has brought the two central banks much closer in terms of operating procedures. Dotsey (1986) compared the operating procedures of the Federal Reserve and the Bank of Japan and found few significant differences. Hutchison (1986) also found that the Bank of Japan had an "interest-rate focused" policy similar to the Federal Reserve.

Inflation Performance

Table 13.1 lists the inflation records of Japan and the United States. In the case of Japan there are three identifiable periods: the High Growth Period from 1955 to the late 1960s; the late 1960s to 1975; and the post-1975 period.

During the High Growth Period of the Japanese economy from 1955 through the late 1960s, the inflation rate exceeded the US rate; however, this was also accompanied by a 10 percent annual growth of output. In addition, maintaining the fixed exchange rate at ¥360 took precedence over price stability.

In the late 1960s policy makers became increasingly concerned about the ability of the Japanese economy to continue the rapid growth of the High Growth Period. Pressure was brought on the Bank of Japan to ensure continued high growth. This policy found its most explicit expression in the Tanaka plan of 1972, designed to maintain 10 percent growth in real output for the coming decade. The result was an acceleration in the inflation rate that reached 30 percent in 1973. While some of the inflation was due to higher oil prices, the major factor was inflationary monetary policy.

In 1973 the Bank of Japan initiated tight monetary policy with the concurrence of the Ministry of Finance. The anti-inflation policy sharply reduced inflation by 1975 and eventually achieved price stability for all practical purposes in the 1980s. The Bank of Japan's commitment to price stability and the willingness of the Ministry of Finance to permit a price stabilization policy were not deterred by the first and second oil price shocks.

Table 13.1 Inflation rates in Japan and the United States (GNP deflator)

Year	Japan	United States
1956	4.7	3.4
1957	6.7	3.5
1958	−0.6	2.2
1959	4.6	2.6
1960	7.1	1.6
1961	7.7	1.0
1962	4.5	2.1
1963	5.4	1.6
1964	5.5	1.5
1965	5.3	2.7
1966	4.8	3.6
1967	5.5	2.8
1968	4.9	5.0
1969	4.4	5.4
1970	6.6	5.6
1971	5.6	5.7
1972	5.5	4.7
1973	12.8	6.6
1974	20.8	9.0
1975	7.9	9.8
1976	7.1	6.3
1977	5.9	6.7
1978	4.8	7.3
1979	3.1	8.8
1980	3.7	9.1
1981	3.3	9.6
1982	1.9	6.5
1983	0.8	3.8
1984	1.2	3.8
1985	1.4	3.0
1986	1.9	2.6
1987	−0.3	3.1
1988	0.6	3.3
1989	1.5	4.1
Average 1956–67	5.1	2.4
Average 1968–75	8.6	6.5
Average 1976–89	2.6	5.6

In addition, the shift to flexible exchange rates after 1973 combined with financial liberalization provided the Bank of Japan with more flexibility to pursue price stability. The Bank of Japan directed this new flexibility toward the goal of price stability despite its formal dependence on the Ministry of Finance and the emergence of large central government deficits after 1973. The adverse experience of the early 1970s convinced Bank of Japan and Ministry officials that monetary policy should focus on long-run price stabilization. The Ministry of Finance did not interfere with the Bank of Japan's policies since it did not want to be held responsible for the type of adverse effects easy monetary policy had generated in the early 1970s.

Japan's macroeconomic performance from the mid-1970s through the mid-1980s has few equals among the industrialized countries, with the exception of West Germany and Switzerland. Declining inflation rates, sustained real GNP growth in the range of 3 to 5 percent, and limited business cycle activity characterized Japan's macroeconomic performance during this period. There is a general consensus among Japan observers that this outcome owes much to the successful price stabilization policies of the Bank of Japan. This is an impressive performance considering the various shocks experienced by Japan during the past two decades.

In the case of the United States, there are also three identifiable periods: 1950s through mid-1960s; mid-1960s to early 1980s; and early 1980s to the present. The first period represents low inflation while the second period witnessed an acceleration of the inflation rate that eventually reached 20 percent in early 1980. The inflation rate during the 1970s imposed severe problems on the US economy, especially on the financial sector. Inflation generated gaps between unregulated interest rates and Regulation Q ceilings on time and saving deposits. Depository institutions experienced new and difficult-to-manage disintermediation and interest-rate risk. Market innovations emerged to take advantage of the gap; however, these innovations were not available to all market participants and exposed depository institutions to additional risk. In particular, savings and loan associations found it difficult to operate in this environment. The collapse of the savings and loan industry in the late 1980s originated in the disruptive financial environment of the 1970s caused by inflationary monetary policy. The situation reached a crisis in 1979 and 1980, and along with major financial legislation the Federal Reserve adopted an aggressive anti-inflation policy stance much as the Bank of Japan did in 1973.

The third period starting in the early 1980s is one of price stability, as the Federal Reserve sought to reestablish its credibility as a price-stabilizing central bank, though Japan continued to have a better inflation record in the 1980s.

INFLATION AND CENTRAL BANK INDEPENDENCE

The first period in Japan and the United States ends in the second half of the 1960s when the inflation rates in both countries began to accelerate. The inflation records during this period appear consistent with the empirical finding that countries with formally independent banks have lower inflation rates. Japan's inflation rate from 1956 to 1967 averaged 5.1 percent with a standard deviation of 2.0, compared to an average US inflation rate of 2.4 percent with a standard deviation of 0.8 over the same period. During this period the Bank of Japan responded to directions from the Ministry of Finance and was regarded as less than an equal, whereas the Federal Reserve maintained a formal independence from government. US inflation was indeed lower than Japanese inflation; however, by the end of the 1960s the two inflation rates converged. The special features of the Japanese economy during this period, however, reduce the information content of the period for the independence issue. The Japanese economy in the 1950s and 1960s was rapidly trying to reindustrialize after the devastating effects of war.

Each country's inflation rate departed from the earlier period starting in the late 1960s. US inflation started a gradual upward movement that was not reversed until the early 1980s. The Japanese inflation rate accelerated more rapidly; however, the Bank of Japan initiated a tight monetary policy that significantly reduced the inflation rate by 1975 (Pigott, 1980). There is little disagreement that the Bank of Japan's inflationary monetary policy in the late 1960s and early 1970s was a response to Ministry of Finance policy. This period clearly shows how an expansionist government can easily take advantage of its institutional arrangement with the central bank to obtain accommodating monetary policy. The line of influence from the Ministry of Finance to the Bank of Japan was clear and obvious to all observers. The expansionary policy was a failure. Rather than high real output growth, the policy generated an inflation rate that reached 30 percent and produced significant disruptions in both the real and financial sectors of the economy. The Bank of Japan then initiated a tight monetary policy with concurrence by the Ministry of Finance. The Bank of Japan continued its tight monetary policy despite the first oil-price shock of 1973.

US inflation in the 1970s did not reach the levels of Japanese inflation; however, the gradually increasing inflation rate had serious effects on the economy, especially the financial sector.

The reasons for Federal Reserve expansionary monetary policy during this approximate 15-year period are varied. They include technical deficiencies in operating procedures, failure to appreciate the relationship between money and inflation, and both implicit and explicit political considerations. The important point is that the Federal Reserve's formal independence offered no protection to the economy from Federal Reserve policy failures.

Why has the Bank of Japan achieved a more stable macroeconomic environment than the Federal Reserve? The answer is not to be found in the formal relationship each central bank has to its respective government. The two inflation records suggest that the degree of formal independence is overshadowed by other factors.

Cargill and Hutchison (1990) suggest a number of economic and institutional differences between Japan and the United States account in general for a smaller interaction between macroeconomic performance and political institutions. Some of these factors include the following: political party domination; composition of the population and income distribution; unionization; magnitude of the short-run trade-off between inflation and output; housing policy; dependence on exports and international trade; and the structure of regulation and degree to which regulatory authorities are held accountable for policy failures.

In most instances Japan's political and economic institutions are more compatible with price stability and hence, irrespective of the formal relationship to the government, the Bank of Japan finds it easier to achieve price stability because of a widespread consensus for this objective. The government is also aware of the consensus and because of the institutional relationship with the Bank of Japan cannot blame an "independent" Bank of Japan for failures to achieve price stability. Government agencies in Japan, viewed in their entirety, take responsibility for policy outcomes. There are fewer degrees of freedom for shiftability of blame for poor policy outcomes than in the United States.

In the case of the United States, the Federal Reserve's failure to maintain price stability occurred despite its formal independence. The failure to achieve price stability during the 1970s was due to the combined factors of poor leadership and the lack of a consensus for price stability. Just as the formal dependence of the Bank of Japan in Japan actually made it less likely that government would pressure the central bank for expansionary monetary policy, the independence of the Federal Reserve actually increased the likelihood that the central bank would be more susceptible to those pressures. There is significant political gain in the United States to pressure the Federal Reserve and simultaneously blame the "independent" central bank for adverse outcomes from inflation. The Federal Reserve's desire to maintain formal independence could very well account for a willingness to accommodate those agents that perceive benefits from inflationary monetary policy.

These comments do not imply that the Bank of Japan lacks political pressure. Cargill and Hutchison (1991a, 1991b), for example, find that the political business cycle hypothesis in general cannot be rejected for Japan and, in particular, find evidence consistent with the hypothesis that Bank of Japan operations are influenced by elections. The comments only suggest that the set of political and economic institutions in Japan during the past two decades have produced better central bank policy outcomes than in the United States. The formal relationship between each country's central bank and the government is one of the least important elements of the differing macroeconomic performance of the two countries.

CONCLUDING COMMENTS

There are two lasting contributions central banks can offer because of their ability to control liquidity: long-run price stability and the services of the lender of last resort. What is the optimal institutional arrangement for the central bank that will provide it with the best opportunity to achieve these responsibilities? Economists and central bankers argue that central banks should be independent, and recent empirical work appears to support this view. The issue, however, is far more complex. These empirical results lack a firm statistical and theoretical foundation, and good arguments have not yet been offered to explain why Japan should be regarded as a special case. If anything, Japan should be regarded as a troublesome issue and should caution against generalized statistical relationships between central bank policy outcomes and formal rules of organization. Central bank policy outcomes depend on a multitude of economic and political aspects of the operating environment. Formal independence is only one of these elements and may ultimately be far less important than the current research suggests.

REFERENCES

Alesina, Alberto (1988) "Macroeconomics and Politics" *NBER Macroeconomic Annual, 1988*, The MIT Press, Cambridge, MA.

Alesina, Alberto and Summers, Lawrence H. (1993) "Central Bank Independence and Macroeconomic Performance" *Journal of Money, Credit and Banking*, 25, May, pp. 151–62.

Bade, Robin and Parkin, Michael (1988) "Central Bank Laws and Monetary Policy" Department of Economics, University of Western Ontario, London, Ontario, Canada, unpublished.

Burdekin, Richard C. and Willett, Thomas D. (1991) "Central Bank Reform: The Federal Reserve in International Perspective" *Public Budgeting and Financial Management*, 3, pp. 619–49.

Cargill, Thomas F. (1993) "The Bank of Japan: A Dependent But Price Stabilizing Central Bank" *Public Budgeting and Financial Management*, 5, pp. 131–9.

Cargill, Thomas F. and Hutchison, Michael M. (1990) "Monetary Policy and Political Economy: the Federal Reserve and the Bank of Japan" in Mayer, Thomas (ed.), *The Political Economy of American Monetary Policy,* Cambridge University Press, Cambridge.

Cargill, Thomas F. and Hutchison, Michael M. (1991a) "Political Business Cycles With Endogenous Election Timing: Evidence from Japan" *Review of Economics and Statistics*, 73, November, pp. 733–9.

Cargill, Thomas F. and Hutchison, Michael M. (1991b) "The Bank of Japan's Response to Elections" *Journal of the Japanese and International Economies*, 5, pp. 120–39.

Cargill, Thomas F. and Royama, Shoichi (1988) *The Transition of Finance in Japan and the United States: A Comparative Perspective,* Hoover Institution Press, Stanford, CA.

Cukierman, Alex, Webb, Steven B. and Neyapti, Bilin (1992) "Measuring the Independence of Central Banks and Its Effect on Policy Outcomes" *World Bank Economic Review*, 6, pp. 353–98.

Dotsey, Michael (1986) "Japanese Monetary Policy: A Comparative Analysis" *Monetary and Economic Studies,* The Bank of Japan, 4, pp. 105–27.

Eijffinger, Sylvester and Schaling, Eric (1993) "Central Bank Independence in Twelve Industrial Countries" *Banca Nazionale Del Lavoro: Quarterly Review*, 184, March, pp. 49–89.

Friedman, Milton and Schwartz, Anna J. (1963) *A Monetary History of the United States, 1867–1960*, Princeton University Press, Princeton, NJ.

Grilli, Vittorio, Masciandaro, Donato and Tabellini, Guido (1991) "Political and Monetary Institutions and the Public Finance Policies in the Industrial Countries" *Economic Policy,* 13, October, pp. 341–92.

Hutchison, Michael M. (1986) "Japan's 'Money Focused' Monetary Policy" *Economic Review,* Federal Reserve Bank of San Francisco, Summer, pp. 33–46.

Hutchison, Michael M. and Judd, John P. (1989) "What Makes a Central Bank Credible?" *Weekly Letter,* Federal Reserve Bank of San Francisco, July 7 and 14.

Kane, Edward J. (1990) "Bureaucratic Self-Interest as an Obstacle to Monetary Reform" in Mayer, Thomas (ed.), *The Political Economy of American Monetary Policy*, Cambridge University Press, Cambridge.

Mayer, Thomas (1976) "Structure and Operations of the Federal Reserve System" in *Compendium of Papers Prepared for the Financial Institutions and the Nation's Economy Study*, pp. 669–725, Committee on Banking, Currency and Housing, 94th Congress, Second Session, GPO, Washington, DC.

Mayer, Thomas (ed.) (1990) *The Political Economy of American Monetary Policy*, Cambridge University Press, Cambridge.

Parry, Robert T. (1992) "Low Inflation and Central Bank Independence" *Weekly Letter*, Federal Reserve Bank of San Francisco, July 17.

Pigott, Charles (1980) "Wringing Out Inflation: Japan's Experience" *Economic Review*, Federal Reserve Bank of San Francisco, Summer, pp. 21–42.

Shionoya, Tsukumo (1962) *Problems Surrounding the Revision of the Bank of Japan Law*, The Beckhard Foundation, Nagoya, Japan.

Suzuki, Yoshio (1980) *Money and Banking in Contemporary Japan*, Yale University Press, New Haven, CT.

Suzuki, Yoshio (ed.) (1987) *The Japanese Financial System*, Clarendon Press, Oxford.

Willett, Thomas D. (ed.) (1988) *Political Business Cycles: The Political Economy of Money, Inflation, and Unemployment*, Duke University Press, Durham, NC.

Willett, Thomas D., Banaian, King, Laney, Leroy O., Merzkani, Mohand and Warga, Arthur D. (1988) "Inflation Hypotheses and Monetary Accommodation: Postwar Evidence from the Industrial Countries" in Willett, Thomas D. (ed.), *Political Business Cycles: The Political Economy of Money, Inflation, and Unemployment*, Duke University Press, Durham, NC.

PART V

The Methodology of Empirical Macroeconomics

14. John Stuart Mill and the Problem of Induction

Abraham Hirsch

It has been argued (Blaug, 1980; Boland, 1982) that the problem of induction, first recognized by Hume in the eighteenth century and made the center of attention in philosophy by Karl Popper in recent times, has had a profound effect on economic methodology. No one, however, has presented evidence to show directly how, when explicitly considering the problem of induction, methodologists have responded. What they have done instead is to argue that given the kinds of results that methodologists (and economists) have derived, they must have implicitly held views about the problem of induction attributed to them. That this approach is the preferred one is perhaps not surprising given the fact that economic methodologists have not as a rule concerned themselves with the problem of induction even when, as in the case of J.N. Keynes, they were trained logicians. But there is one economic methodologist, distinguished logician as well as economist, who did directly concern himself with the problem of induction. John Stuart Mill, in his role of logician, dealt directly with the problem of induction and even talked about white swans and black crows. In this paper I will try to show that from the modern point of view Mill's solution of the induction problem is unsatisfactory and to indicate how this affected Mill's logic of science generally and his logic of economic science more specifically.

To begin with we need to consider what is meant by the "problem of induction" since there are different versions of it. In accord with the version formulated by David Hume, as interpreted by Karl Popper, the induction problem arises when we ask, and find that we must answer in the negative, the following question: "Are we rationally justified in reasoning from repeated instances of which we have had experience to instances of which we have had no experience?" (Popper, 1974, p. 1018). This takes in, for example, the well-known example of white swans: no matter how many white swans one has seen in the past and even though one has never seen swans of another color, this cannot yield the grounds for rationally defending the proposition that any swans that will be seen will be white. Popper recommends the revision of this version of the induction problem both because "[r]egularities or laws are proposed by Hume's own term 'instance'; for an instance is an instance of something – of a regularity or of a law." And "we must widen the scope of reasoning from instances to laws so that we can take heed also of counter-instances." In accord with this revision the induction problem comes about because the following question can only be answered in the negative: "Are we rationally justified in reasoning from instances ... of which we have had experience to the truth or falsity of corresponding laws, or to instances of which we have had no experience?" (Popper, 1974, p. 1020).

This revision serves Popper well but it leaves what is for our purposes a serious ambiguity. We could interpret the problem of induction to mean that instances *alone* cannot rationally support corresponding laws or generalizations, or we can take it to mean that instances no matter how supplemented cannot give the required support. The former (narrower) version rules out *directly* deriving defensible generalizations from specific instances but does not rule out the possibility of doing so via a more roundabout process, such as appealing to higher generalizations. The latter (broader) one, which is the one we tend to think of as the problem of induction today, rules out this possibility as well. It tells us that no empirical generalization can be rationally supported (or "proved") by empirical evidence in no matter what shape or form. In effect it rests upon the belief that uncertainty is unavoidable; it shows up the problem which the American philosopher Charles Peirce had encountered at the end of the last century and that his pragmatist followers like John Dewey have continued to be concerned with in our own time.[1]

The problem of induction presented less of a challenge to Mill than to Pierce and his followers because Mill interpreted it narrowly. He was concerned with finding a better basis for knowledge claims than the adding up of observations of instances. He felt that something more was needed. But contrary to what pragmatists believed,[2] he felt that a better basis *could* be found. Since by his time black swans had already been observed in Australia, Mill could not but agree that "[m]ankind were

[1] For example, John Dewey wrote a whole book called *The Quest For Certainty* (1929) with the purpose of showing the confusion that results when philosophers argue as if certainty were attainable. In many of his works Dewey touches on this problem (e.g., Dewey, 1938, pp. 157–8 and Dewey, 1950/1920, pp. 41–2).

[2] The philosopher Karl Popper falls in between. He feels, like the pragmatists, that empirical generalizations cannot be proved to be true. But like Mill, and unlike the pragmatists, he feels that they could be proved to be false.

wrong, it seems, in concluding that all swans were white," but he went on to ask, "are we also wrong when we conclude that all men's heads grow above their shoulders and never below, in spite of the conflicting testimony of the naturalist Pliny?" Since Mill felt that we were not, the central question for him was why there was a difference between the two cases. More generally Mill asked, "Why is a single instance, in some cases, sufficient for a complete induction, while, in others, myriads of concurring instances, without a single exception known or presumed, go such a very little way toward establishing a universal proposition?" (1973, 3.3.3).[3] *That* was the problem of induction as Mill saw it.

Mill's answer was very straightforward. The reason we should not accept the assertion that all swans are white (or all crows are black) but should accept that there were no men wearing their heads underneath their shoulders is "because there is less constancy in the colors of animals than in the general structure of their anatomy" (1973, 3.4.2). From this kind of consideration Mill derives the basic heuristic of his general theory of induction. It is the following: "This mode of correcting one generalization by means of another, a narrower generalization by a wider, which common sense suggests and adopts in practice, is the real type of scientific induction" (1973, 3.4.2). This, of course, is a generally accepted view in everyday life, in our time no less than Mill's. It is why we are suspicious of unexplained correlations and was the reason why Mill considered what he called the "practical man" the antithesis of the scientist.

What I have tried to show so far is that in some respects at least Mill *did* solve the problem of induction as *he* conceived it. First, he gives us the rule that unexplained correlations cannot be held with confidence (or accepted as scientific propositions), whereas statements which can be supported by wider generalizations can. Second, in Mill's view theories have to be "proved" to be accepted. Theories are proved by showing that the laws of the causes embodied in their premises are supported by one or more of the four methods of experimental inquiry,[4] or introspection in the social sciences (1973, 6.4.1), and that deductions from these premises obey the laws of deductive logic, that is, so far as sciences are *inexact*.[5] For sciences which are *exact*, we must also prove by verification that the implications accord with what actually happens

---

[3] The three numbers in the references to Mill's *Logic* (1973) refer to book, chapter and section.

[4] The purpose of the famous four methods is that of "singling out from among the circumstances which precede or follow a phenomenon those which it is really connected by an invariable law ..." (3.8.1).

[5] For the meaning of this term see p. 221 below.

(1973, 6.3.1, 6.3.2 and 3.11.3).[6] In both cases we have a fail-safe tool, according to Mill, for judging whether theories are acceptable to science; they are acceptable if they can be "proved," otherwise not. If we interpret the term "proved" to refer merely to a process which gives a more solid basis for belief, *ceteris paribus*, than we would have without it, Mill's position can be defended,[7] but this is not what Mill meant. Mill felt that proof showed that the statements (or theories) were true and therefore certain.

Mill's formulation, of course, is not a solution to the problem of induction which we could accept today because it does not come to grips with the uncertainty which is a characteristic not only of unexplained correlations or unproved generalizations but of *all* generalizations. When we "correct a narrower generalization by a wider one" we still do not have a rational basis for arguing that our results are "true," given the traditional logician's conception that one possible false instance makes a whole theory false. The same uncertainty that attaches to generalizations resulting from instances derived from specific experience attaches as well to the broader ones on which Mill would rely. The truth of the generalizations about the constancy of colors and of the general nature of the anatomical structure of animals themselves can no more be rationally defended than can those about white swans and men carrying their heads above their shoulders.

One of the effects of Mill's belief that certainty is attained when theories or causal laws are proved before being admitted into science led him to express more confidence in some of his beliefs than was in fact warranted. Though not usually given to overstatement, Mill occasionally made some remarkably wide claims,[8] such as the much-publicized one about value theory in economics, and about the social sciences generally, that for "many of those effects which it is of most importance to render amenable to human foresight and control" it is possible "to make predictions which will *almost*[9] always be verified and general propositions which are almost always true" (1973, 6.3.1). This was possible because the laws of human nature embedded in the premises of the theories had been proved to be true. The bit of uncertainty that remained was the result of not knowing whether all of the pertinent causal laws had been included, not doubts about the truth of the causal laws themselves.

---

[6] In a forthcoming article I deal with the differences between Mill's logic of the (advanced) physical sciences, of the social sciences generally, and of economics in particular.

[7] E.g., Hausman (1992).

[8] "Happily, there is nothing in the laws of value which remains for the present or any future writer to clear up; the theory of the subject is complete: the only difficulty to be overcome is that of so stating it as to solve by anticipation the chief perplexities which occur in applying it ... " (Mill, 1909, 3.1.1, p. 436).

[9] The "almost" derives from the fact that the social sciences are not "exact."

Mill's belief that scientific formulations had been demonstrated to be true had an even more direct effect on his notions about how knowledge in science grows. This is so because if the laws of the causes had been proved to be true, as Mill believed had been the case, they never need be revised or changed and the only way for knowledge to grow would be to add newly discovered causal laws to our theories. This led Mill to the dichotomy between sciences which were exact and those which were not exact. Thus Mill argues (1973, 6.3.1) about astronomy:

> It has become an exact science because its phenomena have been brought under laws comprehending the whole of the causes by which the phenomena are influenced, whether in a great or only in a trifling degree, whether in all or only in some cases, and assigning to each of these causes the share of effect which really belongs to them.

In contrast, for the inexact science of tidology "the only laws as yet accurately ascertained are those of the causes which affect the phenomenon in all cases and in a considerable degree ... " (1973, 6.3.1). Even in these sciences no room is left for improving the causal laws themselves.

Mill's belief that the only way to derive knowledge which is true is to make certain that the formulations are proved made him rather contemptuous even of recognized authorities when they put forth notions about science which did not include proof. Thus Mill's contemporary, William Whewell, the distinguished historian of science, after an extensive study of the history of the physical sciences, had concluded that certain empirical generalizations about inquiry in science could be safely accepted. He had argued, for example, that if a theory not only gives reliable predictions but in addition predicts unexpected results and these predictions are borne out, such a theory should be accepted as part of science even if the laws of the causes on which the theory rests had not been proved. Mill treated this suggestion with contempt. He argued (1973, 3.14.6):

> it seems to be thought that an hypothesis of the sort in question [which rests on a law or laws which have not been proved] is entitled to a more favorable reception if, besides accounting for all the facts previously known, it has led to the anticipation and prediction of others which experience afterward verified ... Such predictions and their fulfillment are, indeed, well calculated to impress the uninformed, whose faith in science rests solely on similar coincidences between its prophecies and what comes to pass. But it is strange that any considerable stress should be laid upon such coincidence by persons [like Whewell] of scientific attainments.[10]

[10] Mill does not cite Whewell by name in this instance but it is quite clear that he had Whewell in mind (cf. 1973, 2.14.4).

What this shows, I think, is that Mill had run together his more restricted induction problem with the broader one, so that when the criteria he had established were met, he felt that *certainty* had been attained. There would then be no exceptions; the laws involved would be not only sufficient but necessary as well and the causes not only the invariant antecedents but the *unconditional* invariant antecedents. But this would be true only if when we had "proof" we had thereby solved the broader induction problem.[11] One of the driving forces in Mill's methodology is the belief that "proof" achieves this end. From this it followed that given a choice between a theory whose premises are "true"[12] but which does not predict or retrodict at all well and one which predicts and retrodicts very well but whose premises (or laws of the causes embedded in the premises)[13] have not been shown to be "true," the first theory is without question superior to the second because while the knowledge which it contains may be small, it does contain knowledge, whereas the second theory does not contain any knowledge at all.[14] But once one gets rid of Mill's questionable notion that proof of empirical generalizations is possible, it becomes apparent that though theories are preferable to empirical generalizations *ceteris paribus*, it is possible that one might be able to learn more about the world from good empirical generalizations than from imperfect theories.

I have so far considered the effect of the problem of induction on Mill's conception of science generally; since economics in Mill's view *was* a science, this applied to economics as well. But Mill's view of the problem of induction affected his view of economics in important additional ways. This came about because for Mill "in any tolerably advanced science [which included economics] there is properly no such thing as an exception" (1967, p. 337). And since in economics the implications of the theory often did not accord with what actually happens – where the divergences were in fact the rule – from the

---

[11] Otherwise there could not be any "unconditional invariant antecedents," as indeed there cannot be, though there can be generalizations that are warranted on the basis of the best evidence available. Warranted assertions are not "proved."

[12] Mill felt that introspection yielded "true" results in the philosopher's sense. For example, in the Introduction to the *Logic* (1973) Mill tells us: "Whatever is known to us by consciousness is known beyond possibility of question."

[13] In Mill's view the laws of the causes embedded in the premises of theory constitute the substance of science; for example, "The really scientific truths, then, are not these empirical laws but the causal laws which explain them" (1973, 6.5.1).

[14] This is shown, for example, in Mill's views about the "practical man." He did not deny that the practical man might in many instances be able better to account for what happens in the world than the "scientist," and for the purpose of applying economic theory he suggested that the practical man be used as part of the team. But so far as science was concerned the practical man was out completely (Mill, 1967, pp. 324–9; 333–5).

standpoint of science the laws of economics could not be taken to
encompass the implications and predictions of the theory.[15] Economics
was a science of "tendencies"[16] or causal laws whose truth had been
established for each one acting separately; while as a science it included
combinations of these causes into implications, the implications were
only hypothetical; they could not be considered true because they could
not be proved. Or to put it in Mill's terms, the laws of the effects were
missing from this science.

There followed from this point of view important implications for
economic science. One was that economic *science* and *applied*
economics were distinct domains. Economic science included only part
of the whole. Applied economics, where one tried for practical reasons
to derive useful predictions, and in the process used procedures which
were non-scientific, was in Mill's view like the advice of the "practical
man," non-scientific. In this scheme of things "verification" fell outside
the realm of science. As Mill put it: "To verify the hypothesis itself ... is
no part of the science at all, but of the application of science" (1967,
p. 325). Mill does talk about verifying hypotheses, but these are
hypotheses about how best to deal with practical problems at particular
times and particular places and that incorporate the advice of the
sociologist and the "practical man" and fall into the area of applied
economics.[17]

Mill was very practical minded and his great wish was to contribute to
an economics that would help solve pressing social problems. But he
was also a logician and as logician he had the burden of formulating
criteria for judging the validity of what was claimed to be "scientific."
Here the problem of induction got in the way and led Mill to develop an
economic methodology which to some extent at least was subversive of
his objectives as economist because it made him posit a barrier between
economic science and applied economics. Once such a barrier is
established it is only too tempting for economic science, so conceived,
to go off on its own to develop intricate structures, to pay little attention
to observation and verification, and to make the criterion for the
acceptance of theoretical argument logical coherence above all else. And

---

[15] Hausman (1992) disagrees with this interpretation. I discuss Hausman's position in a
forthcoming article.

[16] The term "tendency" is used by Mill (1973, 3.10.5) to make clear that one cannot
expect to get good predictions or retrodictions from only a knowledge of causal laws acting
separately. When Mill therefore speaks of a *science* of tendencies he implies that we have
certain knowledge only of the separate causal laws, not in how they combine, and not all of
the pertinent ones. An inexact science thus, in Mill's view, is a science of tendencies.

[17] I have dealt with this matter in Hirsch (1992).

even when the need for verification or falsification in economic science is recognized, within the context of Mill's methodology one faces the almost irresistible temptation to downplay the importance of observation and make it a relatively minor element in the process of inquiry. The *serious* business of economic science involves formulating coherent structures. That this Millian tendency is today stronger than ever is shown by Thomas Mayer (1993).

It should be evident from what was said in this section that Mill's methodology needs revision in light of the problem of induction. But can Millian methodology be made acceptable even if such revision is done? And if so, what kind of revision needs to be made? I will deal with these questions in a forthcoming article. I will also there show why, though I agree with Blaug (1980) and with Boland (1982) that the way the problem of induction has been handled by economic methodologists has had effects on economic methodology, both broad and deep, I disagree with them about what these effects have been.

REFERENCES

Blaug, Mark (1980) *The Methodology of Economics or How Economists Explain*, Cambridge University Press, Cambridge.

Boland, Lawrence A. (1982) *The Foundations of Economic Method*, George Allen and Unwin, London.

Dewey, John (1929) *The Quest for Certainty*, Milton, Balch and Co., New York, NY.

Dewey, John (1938) *Logic: The Theory of Inquiry*, Henry Holt, New York, NY.

Dewey, John (1950/1920) *Reconstruction in Philosophy*, enlarged edn, New American Library, New York, NY.

Hausman, Daniel M. (1992) *The Inexact and Separate Science of Economics*, Cambridge University Press, Cambridge.

Hirsch, Abraham (1992) "John Stuart Mill and the Business of Science" *History of Political Economy*, Winter.

Hirsch, Abraham (forthcoming) "John Stuart Mill on the Methodology of Economics and Other Sciences."

Mayer, Thomas (1993) *Truth versus Precision in Economics*, Edward Elgar, Aldershot, England.

Mill, J.S. (1909) *Principles of Political Economy*, book III, ch. 1, p. 436, Longmans, Green and Co., New York, NY.

Mill, J.S. (1967) *Essays on Economy and Society* in Robson, J.M. (ed.), *The Collected Works*, vol. 4, University of Toronto Press, Toronto.

Mill, J.S. (1973 [1843]) *A System of Logic Ratiocinative and Inductive*, in Robson, J.M. (ed.), *The Collected Works*, University of Toronto Press, Toronto.

Popper, Karl (1974) *The Philosophy of Karl Popper* in Schlipp, P.A. (ed.), *The Library of Living Philosophers*, Open Court, La Salle, IL.

15. The Methodology of Empirical Science Economics: A Closer Look

D. Wade Hands*

---

1 INTRODUCTION

Thomas Mayer is known primarily for his work on monetary economics, but during the last few years he has also written extensively on the topic of economic methodology. Many of his recent papers (1980, 1990, 1991 and 1993b) have emphasized methodological issues, and his most recent book, *Truth versus Precision in Economics* (1993a), is a full-length study in economic methodology. This book provides a coherent and well-articulated statement of his position on the methodological evaluation of economic theories. Although Mayer's methodological work has clearly been motivated by a desire to understand and to appraise certain developments in contemporary macroeconomic theory, the methodological arguments are themselves quite general and can be discussed independently of this particular application.

The purpose of this paper is to expand upon Mayer's methodological position in a way that provides us with additional insights into the methodological preferences that have influenced modern economic theory. In particular, I will take Mayer's basic distinction between "formalist theory" and "empirical science theory" (defined below) as my starting point, but then go beyond Mayer's dichotomy to expand his category of "empirical science" into two separate poles of methodological attraction. I argue that these two methodological poles, or more specifically the tension between these two poles, can be used to clarify a number of issues in the history of modern economics: issues that remain subtly concealed from Mayer's methodological discussion. I specifically discuss Chicago economics and how this additional tension

* Bruce Caldwell provided helpful comments on an earlier draft of this paper.

within Mayer's category of "empirical science economics" has manifested itself in various ways during the history of the Chicago research program. Although my discussion is intended to be an extension of Mayer's basic methodological ideas, the argument actually carries us quite a long way from Mayer's original position (particularly regarding the Chicago School). The conclusion briefly relates the argument in this paper to recent work in economic methodology.

2   MAYER'S DICHOTOMY

Mayer's methodological analysis hinges fundamentally on his distinction between two different types of economic theorizing: "formalist" economics and "empirical science" economics. As he states in *Truth versus Precision in Economics*:

> This book argues that we should draw a much sharper distinction than is usually done between two types of economic theory. One, formalist theory, is abstract theory that is concerned with high-level generalizations, and looks towards axiomization. The other, empirical science theory, focuses on explaining past observations and predicting future ones. (1993a, p. 7)

While Mayer admits that he may have exaggerated the distinction between these two types of economic theory, the distinction is nonetheless one that captures "the essence of a central methodological division amongst mainstream economists" (Mayer, 1993a, p. 27).

Mayer clearly prefers empirical science economics to formalist economics, even though he does not advocate the complete elimination of formalist theorizing. For Mayer both types of economic theory are justified; the problem is simply to get the right mix. There is, according to Mayer, a trade-off between these two approaches, and the economics profession is currently consuming far more formalist theory and far less empirical theory than would be the case if it were consuming the socially optimal allocation of these two different approaches.

According to Mayer's reading of the history of economic thought, there was an earlier time – a time that roughly corresponded with the rise and development of monetarism – when the professional mix was more properly balanced. Formal theory existed even in this earlier period, and some economists concerned themselves exclusively with mathematical theorems, but there were also several economists, in fact a majority, who were more concerned with testing and empirical economics. This changed during the last few decades, when the economics profession adopted a "new methodology."

In the 1970s and 1980s the methodological preferences of economists shifted. Skill at deriving subtle implications of rational utility maximization became the measure of an economist's proficiency. The new methodology insists, not only that all statements about the behavior of agents be consistent with utility or profit maximization, but also requires that this consistency be spelled out explicitly in mathematical models. Formalism is praised, and 'intuitive' is a term of derogation. Ad hocery is now the most serious of sins. ... Shortcuts that facilitate empirical work, such as Marshallian partial equilibrium, are avoided in favor of more formal general equilibrium. (Mayer, 1991, p. 231)

What is new about the "new methodology" is not the existence of formal methods, but the dominance of formal methods; "the 'new methodology' is new in the sense that what had previously been the methodological preferences of a few economists now became the methodology that dominates economics, at least in the 'right circles' " (Mayer, 1991, p. 232).

Mayer provides a microeconomic explanation for the current hegemony of formalist economics. The explanation is basically one of market failure; economists write primarily for other economists, creating a kind of "producer's sovereignty." As Mayer explains:

The reason for this market failure is that the market is dominated by producers, predominantly academic economists, so that the usual market discipline does not exist. Unlike academic researchers in fields such as medicine or law who work for a large market of practitioners, academic economists, by and large, write for each other. Hence their tastes, not the consumers', determine what is produced. (1993a, p. 10)

Even those who do not accept Mayer's "market failure" explanation for *why* formalist theory has come to dominate the discipline, should agree with his empirical claim that such methods have in fact become dominant.[1]

Given Mayer's work on monetarism and monetary economics, it is not surprising that he has been particularly interested in applying the "formalist versus empiricist" dichotomy to the rise of new classical macroeconomics. For Mayer, monetarism was a shining example of how good empirical science economics should be done; "the exemplar of good methodological practice is Milton Friedman" (1993a, p. 5). The problem is that the new methodology and the increased influence of formal economics has not been kind to monetarism. "The monetarists' slogan: 'Just look at these facts and you will see that the money supply determines nominal GNP,' now gathers few recruits" (Mayer, 1991,

[1] Mayer's use of economic theory to explain (and to criticize) the methodological practice of economists is similar to earlier work by Tullock (1966) and more recent work by Wible (1991). I discuss this "economic approach" to questions of economic methodology, as well as some of its potential pitfalls, in Hands (1994).

p. 233). The macroeconomics of the new methodology is the new classical macroeconomics; "The war cry of the new classicals: 'look at my sophisticated techniques' is more exciting to those who have been trained in these techniques" (Mayer, 1991, p. 233). For Mayer the replacement of Milton Friedman's brand of monetarism by the new classical macroeconomics of Lucas, Sargent, Wallace et al. constitutes the paradigm case of the victory of formalist over empirical methodology. "The new classical coup d'état is a striking attempt to impose a formalist regime on what was previously largely an empirical science domain" (Mayer, 1993a, p. 80).[2]

The formalist/empirical dichotomy is clearly quite important to Mayer's overall methodological position. For him there has been a drastic and undesirable change in macroeconomic theory, a change in its basic emphasis. This change in emphasis, Mayer believes, is the product of a fundamental change in the profession's methodological values: a change from empirical science economics to formalist economics. While Mayer can explain this change (using microeconomics), and while he argues that formalist economics is not entirely without virtue, he nonetheless feels, and feels rather strongly, that this change in methodological values has been bad for economics.

3   TWO POLES WITHIN EMPIRICAL SCIENCE ECONOMICS

Recall Mayer's own characterization of empirical science theory: "empirical science theory, focuses on explaining past observations and predicting future ones" (Mayer, 1993a, p. 7). Notice that in Mayer's portrayal of empirical science, successful science involves two separate goals: *prediction* and *explanation*. These two goals – unlike the goals that serve to differentiate formalist from empirical science – are both internal to empirical science, and Mayer characterizes them as perfectly consistent and compatible. As Mayer views empirical science, good

---

[2] Mayer's 1990s criticism of the new classical macroeconomists is reminiscent of Friedman's criticism of Oscar Lange and the formalist neoclassical/Keynesian synthesis of the 1940s.

> His [Lange's] emphasis is on the formal structure of the theory, the logical interrelations of the parts. He considers it largely unnecessary to test the validity of his theoretical structure except for conformity to the canons of formal logic. His categories are selected primarily to facilitate logical analysis, not empirical application or test. ...The theory provides formal models of imaginary worlds, not generalizations about the real world. (Friedman, 1946, p. 618)

theories (in economics or in any other science) should *both predict and explain*; there is not, and should not be, a trade-off between these two scientific goals.

Mayer is certainly not alone in characterizing empirical science by these two consistent and fundamental goals. The argument that good scientific theories are theories which both predict future phenomena and explain that which has already been observed is a well-established position within the philosophy of natural science. This position is called the *symmetry thesis*, since it contends that empirical prediction and scientific explanation are essentially two (symmetric) ways of viewing the same deductive argument.

Although variants of the symmetry thesis date back to antiquity, the origin of the modern version of the thesis is usually attributed to Hempel and Oppenheim's famous paper on the logic of scientific explanation in 1948. The model of scientific explanation presented by Hempel and Oppenheim, the so-called D-N (for "deductive nomological") model of scientific explanation, characterizes scientific explanation as deduction from general laws. This D-N model, although repeatedly subjected to philosophical criticism, has nevertheless remained the standard view against which other models of scientific explanation are judged.[3]

In their 1948 paper on scientific explanation Hempel and Oppenheim presented the following rather explicit statement of what later came to be called the "symmetry thesis":

> It may be said, therefore, that an explanation of a particular event is not fully adequate unless its explanans, if taken account of in time, could have served as a basis for predicting the event in question. Consequently, whatever will be said in this article concerning the logical characteristics of explanation or prediction will be applicable to either, even if only one of them should be mentioned. (Hempel, 1965, p. 249)

This original (strong) statement by Hempel and Oppenheim remains the classic statement of the symmetry thesis, even though Hempel later weakened it to say that while all D-N explanations are also scientific predictions, not all D-N predictions are necessarily scientific explanations (Hempel, 1965, p. 366).

---

[3] This paper is certainly not the place to attempt a detailed discussion of the D-N model of scientific explanation. The original Hempel and Oppenheim (1948) paper is reprinted in Hempel (1965) along with Hempel's other papers on scientific explanation. An excellent survey of the literature on scientific explanation from Hempel and Oppenheim to the present is provided by Salmon (1989). The D-N model is also discussed in most surveys of economic methodology such as Blaug (1992), Caldwell (1982) or Hausman (1992). I discuss the D-N model and relate it to rational action explanations in Hands (1991).

The symmetry thesis was important enough to Hempel and Oppenheim that they called an explanation "incomplete" when it explained but did not predict. An "incomplete explanation may at best be considered as indicating some positive correlation between the antecedent conditions adduced and the type of phenomenon to be explained" (Hempel, 1965, p. 250). They argued that while it was clearly possible for explanations in fields like history or the social sciences to be bona fide (symmetric) scientific explanations, they often were not; the explanations provided by a social science like economics were often "incomplete." One of Hempel and Oppenheim's examples of an incomplete explanation was the supply and demand explanation of a fall in the market price of cotton. They argued that such explanations must rely on "certain regularities in the behavior of individuals who are trying to preserve or improve their economic position," and since such laws "cannot be formulated at present with satisfactory precision and generality, and therefore, the suggested explanation is surely incomplete" (Hempel, 1965, p. 252).

The symmetry thesis has often been viewed as a weak point in the entire D-N program; those seeking to attack the general D-N approach to scientific explanation often do so by directing their assault at the symmetry thesis. Perhaps even worse for the symmetry thesis is the fact that it has continued to be a perennial bone of contention even among those philosophers of science who generally accept the D-N model of scientific explanation. During the years preceding the publication of the original Hempel and Oppenheim paper, a number of philosophers offered counterexamples to the symmetry thesis, cases of perfectly acceptable scientific explanations that could not be used to generate accurate predictions. Some of these counterexamples were aimed at the D-N model of explanation in general while others were only directed at the symmetry thesis in isolation. One case of this latter type of criticism was the extended debate between Hempel and Michael Scriven, while one case of the former type of criticism was the famous debate between Hempel and William Dray on the function of general laws in history.[4]

The extended debate over the symmetry thesis clearly demonstrates that many philosophers of science would not accept Mayer's

[4] See Hempel (1965, pp. 364–76) for his response to the first round of such criticisms and Salmon (1989) for a more general discussion of the literature. Suppes (1985) discusses a number of such counterexamples including a spoon balanced on a knife edge, a "birdie" in golf achieved by bouncing the golf ball off a tree limb at just the right angle, and, perhaps more relevant to the philosophy of science, deterministic systems driven by chaotic dynamics.

characterization of empirical science. The matter is simply more complex than saying that empirical science both predicts and explains. It is clear that even within the narrow context of logical empiricist philosophy of science where the D-N model is accepted as *the* model of scientific explanation, there are still many philosophers of science who would not agree that such D-N explanations necessarily provide grounds for prediction. If one is to leave this narrow logical empiricist realm and consider alternative models of explanation – for instance pragmatic or unification-based notions of explanation – then the lack of symmetry becomes even more pronounced.[5] If, in addition to these alternative characterizations of explanation within the philosophy of natural science, we add the possibility that economic explanations are fundamentally different (in form) from the type of explanations provided by natural science – a view endorsed by many Austrians and institutionalist economists, among others – then the distance between explanation and prediction becomes truly enormous.

I have no intention of trying to settle the controversy over the symmetry thesis in philosophy of science, or of trying to settle the question of the proper model for explanation in a social science such as economics, but what I would like to suggest is that the goals of prediction and explanation represent two possible poles within the empirical science of economics. This is not to say that they can never coexist. It is simply to suggest that certain economists and certain research traditions within economics have leaned more toward one of these poles, while other economists and other research traditions have leaned more toward the other pole. For example, the Coase theorem and the related literature on transactions cost economics is primarily concerned with explanation; it attempts to explain how various organizations and social structures emerge as a result of minimizing, or at least economizing on, transactions costs. A similar "primarily explanation" argument could be made for public choice theory where the goal is often to explain observed political institutions on the basis of the maximizing behavior of individual agents. On the other hand, there are many areas within economics where the focus is almost exclusively on prediction. For example, economists engaged in the construction of macroeconomic (or even microeconomic) forecasting models are primarily concerned with predicting the behavior of economic variables and are almost never concerned with explanation. These examples come

---

[5] Salmon (1989) also discusses many of these alternatives to the D-N model of explanation.

from "mainstream" economics; if one adds the work of many Austrian and Institutionalist economists to the explanatory side, and many business and financial forecasters to the predictive side, the number of polar cases will multiply still further.

Again, the point is not that all "empirical science economics" is purely explanatory or purely predictive; in fact I would say that most economics has elements of both. The argument is rather that these two poles represent the two end points of a continuum – like monopoly and perfect competition represent the end points of a continuum based on the number of firms in the industry – and that we can use this continuum, and the tension between the two poles, to help us understand the theoretical choices that have been made in economics. Just like Mayer's dichotomy between formalist and empirical science economics represents two different poles for our methodological values, prediction and explanation represent two different methodological poles *within* the category of empirical economics.

This tension between the explanatory and predictive poles in empirical science economics has certainly been recognized by other economists. Consider the following remarks by James Buchanan, for example.

> It seems to me that rather early in the game a conflict emerges between the use and abuse of economic theory in a *predictive scientific* sense, and its use in what we may call an *explanatory* sense. If I may speak loosely here, we may think of a tradition stemming from the classical economists and running through Marshall to Friedman and the other modern positivists, a tradition that is essentially predictive. On the other hand, and by comparison and contrast, we can think of a tradition with some classical roots also but extending directly from the Austrians, and notably through Wicksteed, Knight, Hayek, and Mises, in which tradition the role of economic theory is largely if not wholly *explanatory*. (1979, p. 74, italics in original)

While not every reader will agree with Buchanan's placement of individual economists, it is difficult to deny the basic argument; certain economists – all within the general category of empirical science economics – have emphasized explanation while others have emphasized prediction. These represent significantly different *poles of methodological value* and they have clearly influenced the choices that economists have made about the theories they endorse and the theories they pursue. The presence of these two poles within empirical science economics does not deny Mayer's basic distinction between formalist and empirical economics. There can be a trade-off between formalist and empirical economics just as Mayer argues, and yet there can also be a trade-off between prediction and explanation within the more general category of empirical economics.

Figure 15.1 provides a nice schematic of the argument. Mayer's categories of formalist and empirical economics represent two different sets of methodological values, and yet, within the category of empirical science, there is a further tension between prediction and explanation.

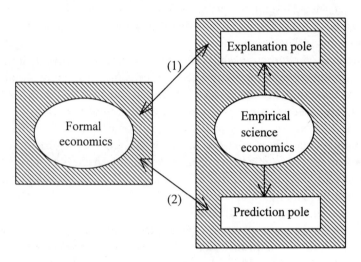

Figure 15.1   Methodological poles in economics

Various research programs in economics can be "located" in this diagram. For example, if we focus exclusively on neoclassical economics then the "explanation pole" of empirical science economics would really mean "explanation on the basis of the intended or unintended consequences of individually rational action by economic agents."[6] Given this characterization of the explanatory pole, one could view the methodological preferences of the new classical economics as a combination of "formal economics" and the "explanation pole" of empirical science economics [indicated by (1) in Figure 15.1], rather than a pure case of formalist economics. This is particularly clear for a theoretical issue like the time inconsistency of monetary policy – an issue that Mayer calls "a typical example of modern methodology" (1991, p. 250). The time inconsistency literature is certainly formalist, but it also is explanatory; it explains the time inconsistency of monetary

[6] Focusing exclusively on neoclassical economics obviously begs the interesting, but more difficult, question of "locating" economic theorists and theories whose concern is primarily "explanation" but do not desire "neoclassical" explanations. Since this discussion, like most of Mayer's methodological discussion, focuses exclusively on neoclassical economic theory (broadly defined) these more general considerations, however interesting, will simply be neglected.

policy on the basis of the rational action of individual economic agents (including the monetary authority). Similar arguments could be made for other aspects of the new classical macroeconomics. It is not that such macroeconomic theorizing does not share any of the methodological values of (neoclassical) empirical science economics, it is simply that their only connection with such values is with the explanatory pole within empirical science.

Now consider the case where the only connection between formalist economics and empirical science economics comes at the prediction pole [indicated by (2) in Figure 15.1]. I would suggest that much of the Keynesian-based big-macroeconometric modeling of the 1960s could be characterized in this way. The big Keynesian macro models contained a lot of mathematical formalism, and they shared the empirical science goal of prediction – what they lacked was the desire to "explain." Such models started with Keynesian ideas about certain relationships among aggregated economic variables, empirically estimated these relationships, and then used them for prediction.

For Mayer the right way to do economics – and the monetarist way of doing economics – is in the middle of the empirical science category: a balance between (neoclassical) explanation and prediction. What was wrong with 1960s Keynesian economists was that their methodological preferences drifted (clockwise) toward formalism while retaining the preference for prediction. On the other hand, what is wrong with the new classical economists is that their methodological preferences have drifted (counter-clockwise) toward formalism while still retaining the preference for (neoclassical) explanation. It could actually be argued that Mayer's own methodological preferences are not quite in the middle of the empirical science category – they are (like the preferences of Milton Friedman) closer to the prediction than the explanatory end of the continuum – but that issue carries us into the next section.

4   METHODOLOGICAL TENSION AND THE CHICAGO SCHOOL

In his 1982 study of the Chicago School of economics, Melvin Reder discussed one issue that has, over the years, "seriously divided the Chicago School" (1982, p. 25), Milton Friedman and George Stigler in particular. The issue is the proper role of economists, more specifically Chicago School economists, in governmental policy advising.

Milton Friedman's view on this matter is rather conventional; the proper role of the economist is to be a scientifically informed policy advisor. As Reder states, "Soon after coming to Chicago, Friedman began to combine economic research with advocacy of specific proposals for socioeconomic reform (negative income tax, substitution of publicly subsidized private schools for public schools, making participation in social security voluntary, abolishing licensure for doctors, volunteer army in lieu of the draft)" (1982, p. 25). This view, the economist as informed policy advisor, is consistent with the earlier Chicago view reflected in Henry Simons' *A Positive Program for Laissez Faire* (1934); the economist can and should use the best available economic theory and empirical data to make informed policy recommendations to governmental and monetary authorities. Both sides of the Keynesian versus monetarist policy debate in the 1970s shared this common view of the role of the economist. They disagreed about the content of the advice, but agreed that it was in fact the proper role of the economist to give it.

Stigler's view was quite different and perhaps more subtle. If the basic neoclassical view of human behavior is correct, and all individuals act in their own rational self-interest, then shouldn't those in government act in their own rational self-interest as well? If those in government do act in their own self-interest then why should their behavior reflect the social interest or public good any more than the behavior of any other individual in the economy? In addition – and here is the main disparity with the (more common) Friedman view – why should those in government or the monetary authority care about the advice of an economist proposing policies that are presented in the social interest? The goal from Stigler's point of view is the goal that came to characterize much of public choice theory: to explain, on the basis of the rational self-interest of the individual agents involved, how the government's policy came to be what it is. Economists should not recommend policy, they should explain policy. As Reder characterized Stigler's position:

> Stigler has come to think of political decision makers as endogenous participants in a political-economic process. ... So viewed, politicians are incapable of acting on advice as to the promotion of the general welfare, and unlikely to be much interested in receiving such advice. Their concerns, indeed their only possible concerns, are getting reelected or otherwise retaining office, and advancing in political influence. (1982, p. 26)

As Reder presents this rift within the Chicago School, it is solely as a disagreement about political economy and the role of the economist; it is not as a disagreement about "economic methodology." While it *certainly is* a disagreement about political economy, I would also argue that it reflects a fundamental difference in *methodological values*. In terms of Figure 15.1, the tension between Friedman's view of the role of the economist and Stigler's view of the role of the economist mirrors the tension between a methodological preference for a predictive science of economics and a methodological preference for an explanatory science of economics.

First consider Friedman's position. Friedman desires an economic science that is capable of providing reliable policy advice. Such reliable policy advice is based on empirical prediction and control; one can only use policy to control the behavior of economic variables if one has an economic science capable of providing reliable predictions about the behavior of those variables. Prediction is the focus of Friedman's well-known essay on the methodology of positive economics (1953). This methodological emphasis on prediction seems to be entirely consistent with his view of the role of the economist as policy advisor.[7]

Stigler's view is quite different. Stigler is more concerned with explanation – for example explaining why regulatory agencies tend to be captured by those they regulate, or why the federal government tends to run a deficit. Prediction and control is not the main issue for this type of

---

[7] It is probably more appropriate to refer to this as Friedman's "traditional" view of the role of the economist. Recent work, such as Friedman (1986), suggests that Friedman may have changed his position on this issue and may now be closer to Stigler.

Hirsch and de Marchi (1990) find an inconsistency between Friedman's positive methodology and his political economy. On their reading, Friedman's methodology is a version of John Dewey's pragmatism and his political economy follows Frank Knight; the result is that "Friedman's way of doing political economy differs radically in some ways from his way of doing positive economics" (1990, p. 280). Such an inconsistency is *not* present in the above reading of Friedman's scientific methodology or his "method" of political economy. On the above reading of Friedman the main goal of economics is to produce scientific theories that are capable of reliably predicting economic phenomena – explanation is not totally unimportant, but it is not the main methodological value. The reason why we want a predictive science of economics is because we want to make reliable policy recommendations about how to control certain economic phenomena. These policy recommendations may sometimes be the same recommendations that have been offered by others (such as Frank Knight) but that does not mean that Friedman's methodology or his view of the proper role of the economist is the same as Knight's. Of course none of this implies that Friedman's policy recommendations are beyond reproach. It could be that the microeconomic theory on which Friedman bases many of his policy recommendations is not as predictively successful as he believes it is (a suggestion made by Hirsch and de Marchi, 1990, and a main theme in Rosenberg, 1992). My point is that even if Friedman were wrong about the success of the economic theory that he uses, it does not make him inconsistent with respect to his methodological view of what good economic science should do (predict) and what the proper method of doing political economy should be (to make scientifically sound policy recommendations).

economic inquiry. Why predict the behavior of economic variables if there is no desire to control the behavior of those variables through policy? Stigler's project is not concerned with empirical prediction for public control; it is concerned with explaining the observed behavior of public officials on the basis of individual rational action.

Arguing that Friedman and Stigler exhibit a particular methodological commitment to one of these two goals does not mean that they are totally unconcerned with the other goal – the issue is simply one of identifying their primary methodological focus. In the case of both of these economists there appears to be one primary methodological value and that value is also consistent with their views on political economy and the role of the economist.

The tension between prediction and explanation becomes even more clear if we look back one generation to two important precursors of the modern Chicago School: Wesley Clair Mitchell and Frank Knight. Mitchell was a student at Chicago and a founder of the National Bureau of Economic Research (NBER); he influenced Stigler through the NBER-Columbia connection and he influenced Friedman as a teacher and senior colleague at the NBER (as well as indirectly through Arthur Burns).[8] Knight had a direct influence on both Friedman and Stigler as an influential member of the Chicago economics department from 1927 until 1958, and he even served as Stigler's thesis advisor. Despite their Chicago common ground, Mitchell and Knight had profoundly different views of both economic methodology and political economy.

Mitchell had been influenced by the institutionalist economics of Thorstein Veblen very early, and his political economy reflected this institutionalist influence throughout his career. Mitchell, like most of the second generation of institutionalist economists, sought rational and social-democratic control over the excesses and uncertainties of a free market economy. Convinced that such rational control required reliable and objective information about the economy, Mitchell became "convinced that statistics provided a royal road to economic science and social control" (Ross, 1991, p. 325).[9] The rational choice perspective of neoclassical economics was rejected and a new economics was to be

[8] Sources for the relationship among the four economists (Mitchell, Knight, Friedman and Stigler) and their relationship to the Chicago school more generally, include Hirsch and de Marchi (1990), Hirsch and Hirsch (1980), Reder (1982) and Ross (1991).

[9] Dorothy Ross (1991, particularly ch. 9) provides an excellent discussion of how the anxiety and disillusionment of World War I and the failure of progressivism initiated a turn toward prediction and control in American intellectual life. Ross documents how this desire for control contributed to the scientism that came to dominate American social science after the 1940s. According to Ross, "Mitchell is the best example of the confident turn to science" (1991, p. 324).

founded on behaviorism at the micro level and objective statistical analysis of economic phenomenon at the macro level: "behavior, unlike motive, could be studied by objective methods" and "the most important method for the study of economic behavior was statistics" (Ross, 1991, p. 385). This new economics abandoned the neoclassical explanatory framework and turned to statistics and empirical prediction as a source for the desired control. "Institutionalists, such as Wesley Clair Mitchell, ... wrote off economic theory as mostly a misguided enterprise, and opted for an economic theory that was truly predictive" (Hirsch and Hirsch, 1980, p. 133).

Knight's view is diametrically opposed to Mitchell's on both political economy and methodology. For Knight the free market should be given a very wide reign and collective control should be kept at a minimum; on methodology Knight was an antipositivist, totally rejecting the idea that economics should be, or could be, a predictive science. Knight's antipositivism is clearly consistent with his free market political economy – one does not need an economic science that provides reliable predictions if one does not desire to control the economy – but there is much more to his methodological position than simply the argument that prediction is not "needed." For Knight the physical sciences *are* actually based on prediction and control: "From the standpoint of knowledge, the problem of control is a problem of *prediction*" and science is merely "the *technique of prediction*" (Knight, 1935, p. 109, italics in original). The problem is that the knowledge we have of individuals is not of this type, it is intentional knowledge based on the beliefs, desires and purposes of individuals. We as economists and other social scientists have direct experiences with such intentional states and thus we have access to a type of knowledge, but it is not the predictive knowledge of physical science.[10] "In short: The formal principles of economic theory can never carry anyone very far toward the prediction or technical control of the corresponding economic behavior" (Knight, 1940, p. 30). For Knight economics is incapable of doing that which Mitchell wanted economics to do; "The kind of science the institutionalists wanted, an empirical science of actual economic behavior, a science not of formal economic rationality but of substantive choices, was impossible" (Ross, 1991, p. 426).

---

[10] Hammond (1991) provides a careful discussion of Knight's methodology and relates it to some of the recent literature on the "rhetoric of economics." There is some very interesting work to be done relating Knight's methodological position to the controversy over "folk psychology" in the philosophy of psychology. This literature is seldom connected with economics (Rosenberg, 1992, and elsewhere, is an exception), but Knight clearly seems to be considering the same issues (in the 1930s and 1940s). I briefly discuss folk psychology and its relationship to economics in chapter 11 of Hands (1993).

The "two poles" distinction within empirical science thus helps us to understand the differences between Mitchell and Knight; Mitchell clearly emphasized the predictive pole, while Knight, although he would not call it "empirical science economics" because that term was reserved for physical science, clearly emphasized the explanatory pole. This mirrors – but in an exaggerated and more aggressive way – the methodological tension between Friedman and Stigler.[11] Even within the Chicago School of economics there exists a tension between those who, for many different reasons, emphasize prediction, and those who, again for many different reasons, emphasize explanation. Recognition of this tension helps us understand the various positions that have been taken by various members of the Chicago School over the years.

5 CONCLUSION

The argument has been made that Mayer's categories can be expanded, and that by expanding empirical science economics into the two separate poles of prediction and explanation we can better understand the theoretical preferences of various economists, including those in the Chicago School. Thus we have a better understanding of some of the theoretical decisions made by the profession, but is that all that we have learned, or is there an additional moral to the story?

Actually there is another moral to the story, and it is a moral about the *importance of methodological preferences*. Even if one suspends judgment on the traditional methodological question of which methodological preference is the "right" or "best" methodological preference, and focuses exclusively on the actual behavior of the individual economists, then the above discussion emphasizes that *methodology still matters*. That is, even if one follows recent trends in economic methodology (and philosophy of science more generally), trends that downplay or even deny the possibility of ever finding the one right methodology of science, then there is still a role for the study of methodology. The above discussion points out that economic scientists

---

[11] Hirsch and Hirsch (1980) discuss the differences between Friedman and Knight in terms that are related to the terms used above; they argue that Friedman viewed economics as a "predictor" science, while Knight viewed it as an "assumer" science. While their use of "predictor" maps squarely into my "predictive pole," the same cannot be said for the relationship between their "assumer" and my "explanatory pole." Without trying to explore this difference in any detail, let me just note that for Hirsch and Hirsch the difference between "predictor" and "assumer" is roughly the difference between "good science" and "bad science" respectively; I am making no such normative distinction.

have methodological preferences and that these methodological preferences are *operative* in their professional decisions. The beliefs and desires of scientists include epistemic beliefs and desires, preferences for certain methodological approaches over others, and these influence their scientific behavior. Not only are there such methodological preferences and not only do they influence professional behavior, they are also – as the Friedman/Stigler and Mitchell/Knight cases point out – inexorably intertwined with other values such as political and ideological preferences.

Philosophical discussion about economics has, over the last decade or so, become less and less concerned with the traditional questions of economic methodology, and more and more concerned with issues such as the social construction of scientific knowledge and the rhetoric of professional discourse. The above exercise in exposing methodological preferences and tracing their impact on the profession's theoretical discourse should demonstrate that traditional methodological considerations – issues such as the relationship between prediction and explanation – can still have an important role to play even in the context of this recent philosophical turn. Mayer's methodological categories can serve as a useful first step in such an inquiry, but they are only a first step.

REFERENCES

Blaug, M. (1992) *The Methodology of Economics*, 2nd edn, Cambridge University Press, Cambridge.

Buchanan, J.M. (1979) "Professor Alchian on Economic Method" in *What Should Economists Do?*, pp. 65–79, Liberty Press, Indianapolis, IN.

Caldwell, B.J. (1982) *Beyond Positivism: Economic Methodology in the Twentieth Century*, George Allen & Unwin, London.

Friedman, M. (1946) "Lange on Price Flexibility and Employment: A Methodological Criticism" *American Economic Review*, 36, pp. 613–31.

Friedman, M. (1953) "The Methodology of Positive Economics" in *Essays in Positive Economics*, pp. 3–43, University of Chicago Press, Chicago, IL.

Friedman, M. (1986) "Economists and Economic Policy" *Economic Inquiry*, 24, pp. 1–10.

Hammond, J.D. (1991) "Frank Knight's Antipositivism" *History of Political Economy*, 23, pp. 359–81.

Hands, D.W. (1991) "Popper, the Rationality Principle and Economic Explanation" in Shaw, G.K. (ed.), *Economics, Culture and Education: Essays in Honour of Mark Blaug*, pp. 108–19, Edward Elgar, Aldershot, England.

Hands, D.W. (1993) *Testing, Rationality, and Progress: Essays on the Popperian Tradition in Economic Methodology*, Rowman and Littlefield, Lanham, MD.

Hands, D.W. (1994) "The Sociology of Scientific Knowledge and Economics" in

Backhouse, R. (ed.), *Contemporary Issues in Economic Methodology*, pp. 75–106, Routledge, London.

Hausman, D.M. (1992) *The Inexact and Separate Science of Economics*, Cambridge University Press, Cambridge.

Hempel, C.G. (1965) *Aspects of Scientific Explanation*, The Free Press, New York, NY.

Hempel, C.G. and Oppenheim, P. (1948) "Studies in the Logic of Explanation" *Philosophy of Science*, 15, pp. 135–75.

Hirsch, A. and de Marchi, N. (1990) *Milton Friedman: Economics in Theory and Practice,* University of Michigan Press, Ann Arbor, MI.

Hirsch, A. and Hirsch, E. (1980) "The Heterodox Methodology of Two Chicago Economists" in Samuels, W.J. (ed.), *The Methodology of Economic Thought*, pp. 131–50, Transactions Books, New Brunswick, NJ.

Knight, F.H. (1935) "The Limitations of Scientific Method in Economics" in *The Ethics of Competition and Other Essays*, pp. 105–47, Harper & Brothers, New York, NY.

Knight, F.H. (1940) " 'What is Truth' in Economics?" *Journal of Political Economy*, 48, pp. 1–32.

Mayer, T. (1980) "Economics as a Hard Science: Realistic Goal or Wishful Thinking?" *Economic Inquiry*, 18, pp. 165–78.

Mayer, T. (1990) "The Twilight of the Monetarist Debate" in Mayer, T. (ed.), *Monetarism and Macroeconomic Policy*, pp. 61–90, Edward Elgar, Aldershot, England.

Mayer, T. (1991) "The Monetarist Debate and the New Methodology" in Mayer, T. and Spinelli, F. (eds), *Macroeconomics and Macroeconomic Policy Issues*, pp. 229–60, Edward Elgar, Aldershot, England.

Mayer, T. (1993a) *Truth versus Precision in Economics*, Edward Elgar, Aldershot, England.

Mayer, T. (1993b) "Friedman's Methodology of Positive Economics: A Soft Reading" *Economic Inquiry*, 31, pp. 213–23.

Reder, M.W. (1982) "Chicago Economics: Permanence and Change" *Journal of Economic Literature*, 20, pp. 1–38.

Rosenberg, A. (1992) *Economics – Mathematical Politics of Science of Diminishing Returns?* University of Chicago Press, Chicago, IL.

Ross, D. (1991) *The Origins of American Social Science*, Cambridge University Press, Cambridge.

Salmon, W.C. (1989) "Four Decades of Scientific Explanation" in Kitcher, P. and Salmon, W.C. (eds.), *Scientific Explanation*, pp. 3–219, University of Minnesota Press, Minneapolis, MN.

Simons, H. (1934) *A Positive Program for Laissez Faire; Some Proposals for a Liberal Economic Policy*, University of Chicago Press, Chicago, IL.

Suppes, P. (1985) "Explaining the Unpredictable" *Erkenntnis*, 22, pp. 187–95.

Tullock, G. (1966) *The Organization of Inquiry*, Duke University Press, Durham, NC.

Wible, J.R. (1991) "Maximization, Replication, and the Economic Rationality of Positive Economic Science" *Review of Political Economy*, 3, pp. 164–86.

16. In Defense of Data Mining: Some Preliminary Thoughts

Kevin D. Hoover*

... it may turn out to be true – reversing Quetelet's expression – that "*La nature que nous interrogeons c'est une urne.*" (John Maynard Keynes, 1921/1973, p. 468)

Data mining, like many other vices, is at once generally condemned and widely practiced. Economists routinely condemn data mining with loaded terms such as "fishing," "grubbing" and "number crunching," as well as the now shop-worn witticism: "if you torture the data long enough it will confess" (Leamer, 1978, p. 1, surveys the aspersions of economists on data mining). The viciousness of data mining is nonetheless so much embedded in the mores of the economics profession that textbooks rarely find it necessary to discuss the practice. Few have attempted to explain the exact nature of the sin. Michael Lovell (1983) is an honorable exception. He approaches data mining as a moralist, attempting both to understand the human fallibility and to propose appropriate penalties. Thomas Mayer (1980, 1993) is more the pragmatic social reformer, taking it as given that data mining is bad and proposing various remedial actions to mitigate its ill effects. Edward Leamer (1978, 1983) is more world weary: to live is to sin, to apply econometrics is to mine data; the problem is to find ways to make data mining informative. Leamer's view is in the same spirit as those who would legalize prostitution or drug use in the hope that, once legalized, they could be more effectively regulated for health and safety.

One result of the prejudice against data mining is that many economists distrust econometrics in much the same way that the public distrusts statistics: "one can prove anything with statistics"; "there are lies, damned lies, and statistics."[1] Given the mostly unanalyzed nature of

---

* I am grateful to Thomas Mayer, Steven Sheffrin and James Hartley for comments on an earlier draft.
[1] See Mayer (1992b) for a survey of economists' generally sceptical attitudes toward econometric results.

the prejudice against data mining, it is somewhat surprising that remedies are widely available. Mayer (1992a; cf. 1993, ch. 10) proposes a folk remedy: to publish all the regressions one has run, not just the good ones. Leamer (1978, 1983) proposes a sweeping social reform: econometrics should become Bayesian in substance if not in form. Lovell (1983) proposes strict enforcement of the existing codes: *t*-statistics should be penalized in proportion to the degree of data mining. In this paper, I will take the role of the bleeding-heart liberal: data mining is misunderstood, and once it is properly understood, it is seen to be no sin at all.

To understand data mining, it is useful to determine at the start just what it is. Its forms turn out to be varied. All have the property, however, that the econometrician seeks a "better" result (e.g., higher R^2 or higher *t*-statistics or the significance of a particular variable) through a search over possible regressors or their lagged values or transformations (differences, logarithms, etc.) or over possible functional forms or subsets of the observations (different time periods with time-series data or different ranges with cross-section data). The objections to data mining all spring from the feeling that there is something disreputable about regarding a statistical result that was adapted to a desired outcome as evidence in favor of that outcome being a property of the world. Textbooks typically teach that theory suggests a hypothesis that can be tested statistically. The test is then run. If the data favor the test, perhaps another test is run; if the data reject the test, the theory is falsified, and the process stops with a rejected theory. That such a nonadaptive strategy is not actually practiced does not prevent it from being the accepted ideal. The question of the legitimacy of data mining is related to another, larger, long-standing question in the history of the philosophy of science: does a theory gain more support from predicting unknown results than from merely accommodating the known data? I will consider some aspects of this question in relation to data mining.

A paradox arises with either the narrower question of statistical practice among economists or the larger question of the choice of theories. Following a version discussed by Peter Lipton (1991, ch. 8), we will call this the *twin paradox*. Suppose that one twin derives a result from an economic theory that suggests particular variables will be important in a particular functional form. He then runs the corresponding regression and finds that the theory is confirmed. Even on an unremittingly falsificationist account (Popper, 1959; Blaug, 1992) this is a favorable outcome for the theory. Now suppose that the other twin forgoes all theory, and simply searches through the data until he finds a functional form and a set of regressors that yield a high R^2 and significant t-statistics on all the regressors: he "mines" the data. Suppose that he comes up with precisely the same regression as his twin. We have two conflicting intuitions about this situation. On the one hand, the first twin's evidence would appear to lend strong support to the theory. In general, a procedure such as he followed seems convincing, whereas an atheoretical fishing expedition seems likely to produce good results only by chance. On the other hand, since the regressions are identical, if the first twin's results describe features of the world, the second twin's results must also describe exactly those same features. One might take a more subjectivist or Bayesian view and argue that the first twin has better rational grounds for believing his results than does the second twin. But suppose that they have a sister, who has not involved herself in the investigation, but looks to their results to form her beliefs. Is she to believe that the theory is well supported because of the first twin's results or less well supported because of the second twin's method? An adequate account of data mining should resolve the paradox.

1   WHY DOES DATA MINING WORK?

It is helpful to begin by trying to understand why data mining works at all. Why does it appear that, through extensive search, data can be made to appear to support widely different hypotheses? Data mining can achieve "better" results by exploiting correlations in the data that do not reflect those properties of the underlying processes that generate the data that are of immediate interest. In short samples, data are full of adventitious correlations. If two coins are flipped 10 times each, there may be a high correlation between the pattern of heads and tails of each coin; yet, if the coins are independent, this correlation would not persist for another 10, 20 or 30 flips. Relatively short runs of time-series data are subject to the same possibility: given thousands of macroeconomics series, there are bound to be a few that are very well correlated with, say, GNP for 30 years of data, even though there is no real connection between them and GNP, and even though the correlation is unlikely to persist for another year, much less 30 more years.

Another source of data mining success is not in the adventitious properties of data, but in its genuine properties taken out of context.

Despite typically being written as equations, regressions are directional – the dependent and independent variables are treated asymmetrically. They are often used as if their asymmetry recapitulated the causal asymmetry of the world, but they do not always succeed. Thus, suppose that in fact A, B and C cause D, which in turn causes E. It can easily happen that a regression of D on E fits far better than one of D on A, B and C, even though the latter regression is the one that recapitulates the causal structure of the world. Similarly, because of the way in which they are in fact generated, A, B and C may be collinear, and this may present opportunities for data mining. The recent literature on cointegration (and the earlier literature on spurious regressions) presents another case: causally unrelated variables may be highly correlated simply because they are growing. Cumulative rainfall in California is no doubt correlated with the number of AIDS cases in New York City (cf. Hendry, 1980).

2   THE CASE AGAINST DATA MINING

To describe why data mining works appears to condemn it. That, however, is partly because I have omitted to discuss one possibility, namely that data mining may work simply because it uncovers the truth, in the sense of the regression that truly recapitulates the causal structure of the world. Such an argument is, of course, based on the prejudice that the whole issue should be formulated in terms of causal structure. Given my previous work (Hoover, 1990, 1991, 1993; Hoover and Sheffrin, 1992) this prejudice is perhaps understandable. Still, data mining has only rarely been discussed in explicitly causal terms.

Lovell (1983) argues that data mining distorts conventional test statistics. Thus in a regression of an independent random variable on another independent random variable, there is in population only a 1 in 20 chance of obtaining a t-statistic greater than 2 in absolute value. But suppose that there is a set of independent random variables, try each in turn as a regressor until the set is exhausted or until a t-statistic greater than 2 is obtained, then the chances of obtaining a t-statistic significant at the conventional 5 percent level are considerably greater than 1 in 20. Inferences based on conventional 5 percent tests are likely to be misleading. Lovell suggests formulae to correct the size of statistical tests to account for the effects of data mining. Leamer (1978) also sees the failure of test statistics calculated in the conventional ways to conform to canons of classical statistics as a cost of data mining. But Leamer does not share Lovell's hope that amelioration is possible. Rather he sees the practice of econometrics as so far divorced from classical statistics that only a Bayesian approach can possibly rationalize and guide what econometricians actually must do in practice.

In considering the higher level problem of theory choice, Lipton (1991, ch. 8) distinguishes between *prediction*, when a result can be deduced (logically, not necessarily temporally) prior to its observation, and *accommodation*, when the only known observations are used in the formulation of the theory. Philosophers of science have found it difficult to explain precisely why a theory is better supported by prediction than by accommodation. Lipton begins by observing that theories are typically many steps removed from observational consequences. To deduce such consequences, a scientist must appeal to numerous auxiliary assumptions and facts. A careful choice of auxiliaries may assure that the theory implies the known observed facts, whereas other reasonable selections of auxiliaries would result in the theory not implying the observed facts. Since these auxiliaries are not of the essence of the theory, they do not bear directly on the truth or falsity of the theory. Lipton calls the selection of a set of auxiliaries for the purpose of securing a desired result *fudging*. A predicted result cannot be fudged, as it is not known; whereas an accommodated result can be easily fudged. The best explanation of the observational success of the theory is its truthlikeness in the case of prediction and its having been fudged in the case of accommodation.

Leamer's (1983) analysis of the fragility of econometric results appears to be related to Lipton's analysis. Data may be divided into *free variables*, which theory dictates should be in a regression; *focus variables*, a subset of the free variables which are of immediate interest; and *doubtful variables*, which competing theories suggest might be important.[2] Relative to the theory under scrutiny, the doubtful variables are the analogues of Lipton's auxiliaries. Leamer argues that a theory is not well supported if the focus or other free variables are sensitive to the choice of doubtful variables. Data mining on Leamer's interpretation is almost always fudging.

The reported support of a theory for Lipton and the reported regression for Leamer may be what they are either because of the way the world is or because of the wishes and desires (perhaps only implicit)

---

2 These terms are due to McAleer, Pagan and Volker (1983) and are clearer than Leamer's original nomenclature.

of the investigator. Conclusions that arise from properties of the investigator must be discounted. Woodward (forthcoming) is more explicit on this point. For him, a successful theory articulates the causal structure of the world, and a successful regression recapitulates that causal structure. Thus, if a regression "succeeds" because it uses regressors that lack any rationale based on causal capacities, it does not then support the theory. Data mining ("peeking at the data" as he puts it) in Woodward's view is undesirable because it encourages (or, at least, permits) this practice.

Different diagnoses of the undesirability of data mining suggest different remedies. Woodward's analysis almost immediately suggests the classic advice of the econometric textbook: theory proposes, data disposes. Mayer's (1992a) suggestion that every regression run by an investigator should be reported, so that the robustness of a coefficient of interest or lack thereof will be obvious to any reader is formalized in Leamer's (1983) proposal for *extreme bounds analysis*. To implement extreme bounds analysis, Leamer suggests estimating a set of regressions. The regressors in each regression include all of the free variables, but each includes a different linear combination of the doubtful variables. The extreme bounds of the set of estimated coefficients for the focus variables then provide a measure of the robustness of the focus variable to data mining. Lovell (1983) computes critical values for t-statistics that are higher in proportion to the amount of search that was needed to find the final specification.

3   THE DEFENSE

Both Leamer's and Lovell's views treat the regression as a means of calculating the degree to which data supports or compels belief: the regression connects the thing investigated with the investigator. Thus the analogy between the econometric problem of specification search and the larger problem of theory choice seems a close one. In Leamer's Bayesian framework different people with different priors will be led rationally to different conclusions. On the one hand, Leamer (1983, p. 38) embraces the subjectivity of this feature of Bayesianism by arguing that the "mapping is the message": ideally, what should be reported is the function that transforms priors into posteriors; then each person can calculate what, given the data, they ought rationally to believe. On the other hand, respect for the views of others, the needs of public policy and a feeling that science needs consensus argue that just providing mappings is not enough.[3] Extreme bounds analysis can be seen in a Bayesian framework as a way of discriminating between instances in which consensus emerges despite disparate priors and instances in which no consensus is possible.

Lovell's classical approach does not admit heterogeneous rational beliefs. But this raises a problem. Particular regressions may be suggested by theories or may test theories; but theories themselves are not suggested without some prior empirical support. Suppose, for example, in the twin paradox that the twin's sister first saw the data-mined regression and then formulated a theory that was, in ignorance of its provenance, tested by the other twin apparently without data mining at all. What degree of rational belief should attach to this theory for the second twin or, for that matter, for the sister or the other twin? The degree of data mining already involved in any theory under serious discussion is literally incalculable, which calls into question the usefulness of Lovell's penalty formulae.

My defense of data mining starts with breaking the link between theory and statistical calculations, such as regressions. We speak of regressors explaining regressands; of hypotheses or theories being tested when we run regressions; of predictions from regressions; of the significance of regression coefficients. To the degree that we mean there to be a close connection between regressions and theories, these terms are misleading equivocations. Regressions are not theories and they do not explain phenomena; they are calculations, ways of representing the data, that may or may not be revealing of features of the world. Regressions should not be thought of as measures of the import of data for rational belief, but as filters, analogous to filters that might be placed on telescopes or microscopes, in order to make data more revealing.[4] Some filters are helpful, some are useless or worse. On this view, regressions results are themselves the observations that theory must account for and not part of the theoretical apparatus themselves. The attack on data mining is grounded in the view that regressions test hypotheses and that data mining compromises these tests. In the view

[3] Thomas Mayer has argued (private communication) that respect for the views of others suggests precisely that we just provide the mappings and let them make their own minds up. I do not believe that this really is "respect;" for it says not only that I do not wish to impose my interpretation on you, but also that I have no need to pay heed to your interpretation. To truly respect the opinions of others is to entertain them seriously and to consider carefully whether they may not in fact be right. There is something solipsistic about the fundamental notions of Bayesianism.

[4] What is said of regressions is generally true of other statistical calculations as well.

being argued for here, regressions do not test anything directly, although they may be an input into a test.

The model for statistical hypothesis testing are experimental setups such as ones involving drawing balls from urns or rolling dice that are found in any elementary statistics text. A typical problem in this context might be that we know an urn might have either one half or one third white balls and the rest red balls; we draw three red and two white balls from the urn; we conjecture and want to test the hypothesis that our urn is the one with one third white balls. Standard tests are available that use the Neyman-Pearson framework of balancing the possibility of making type I against type II error using a loss function.[5]

Interpreted on the analogy with urns, regressions represent quite complicated experimental setups. In probabilistic terms, a regression is a conditioning relationship. Thus on the urn analogy, whenever conditioning variables change, the urns or sequence of urns one was drawing from would be different. The question "Does this urn contain one third white balls?" is not really the same question in regressions with different conditioning variables or, for that matter, with different estimated coefficients for nonfocus variables. To be accurate, the question must be posed: Does the urn in this experimental setup contain one third white balls? When the regression is different, even if it has the same dependent variable, the experimental setup is different: it is not "this" but some other setup. It is hardly surprising then that data mining "works." If we can change the setup until we get the number we like, almost any number can be had. But the result does not constitute a test of the original setup. We are either not answering the question that we set out to answer, or we did not ask a well-posed question to start with. Once we have a stable setup, we can ask well-posed questions about it, but these are questions about the setup, not about the world directly. How they reflect on the world depends on the relationship of the setup to the world, which must be established on other grounds.

The urn analogy is applied to econometrics because regressions were originally conceptualized in the context of randomized, controlled experiments as might, for example, be found in studies of the response of crop yields to fertilizers. Here the textbook assumptions that regressors are fixed in repeated samples are nearly literally true.[6] These

---

[5] This approach is difficult to apply in practice because loss functions are rarely fully articulated and alternative hypotheses are rarely finite.

[6] Leamer (1983, pp. 31–3) argues that one can never be assured that this assumption is fulfilled even in this "classic" case. He concludes that there really is no difference in kind between "natural" and "random" experiments.

conditions are not fulfilled in typical econometric applications. For some, this calls the whole use of regressions into question.

However, there is another way of looking at it. Reconsider the logic of regressions.

The elementary textbooks tell us that given certain assumptions (e.g., the errors are mean zero, with constant variance, zero covariance and the regressors are fixed in repeated samples), an ordinary least-squares regression is the best linear unbiased estimator.[7] If the initial assumptions are fulfilled, the estimated error terms from such a regression have desirable properties of randomness: they are not serially correlated, they have constant variance, approximate normality and so forth. In fact, when most arbitrary regressions are run, the estimated error terms do not have these properties. This, of course, calls into question the validity of the assumptions in this case as well as the validity of inferential procedures or statistical tests that rely on these assumptions. In general the urn analogy does not apply. But if the regressions actually recapitulated the causal structure of the world, the assumptions would in fact be fulfilled and the urn analogy would apply.

Thus the failure of the estimated errors to be random is evidence that the particular regression does not belong to the class of possible recapitulations of the causal structure of the world. It is a minimal necessary condition, but certainly not a sufficient condition, to belong to this class that estimated errors be random. Through data mining it is often possible to construct members of this class. In other words, data mining can amount to a search for a regression that acts as if a suitable experimental setup generated the data, that is, as if the urn analogy were perfect.

Having searched for such a regression, the *t*-statistics on the regressors do not constitute an independent test of their importance. What they tell us is that we have succeeded in searching out a regression in the desirable class, i.e., that we have found a filter that defines the estimated errors in a certain way. The only useful tests to be based on such a regression are tests of the errors so estimated against errors estimated using some other (possibly data-mined regression) as a filter. We can, for example, fit such a regression over one period, and then ask whether it fits equally well over another − i.e., ask whether there has been a change in the structure generating the data. This is a well-formulated question about the properties of random data for which the

---

[7] Related results can be derived *mutatis mutandis* for other estimation methods.

urn analogy and standard test statistics apply as well as they do anywhere.[8]

To have created by data mining a regression with certain properties is not in itself to have discovered anything of significance about the world. But it may be a necessary first step. The subsequent steps involve comparing the properties of the data-mined regression to other candidates or using them as tools to establish causal orders.

This way of looking at data mining suggests that the emphasis given in econometrics textbooks to estimation is misplaced. The desirable properties of estimators (e.g., the BLUEness of the ordinary least-squares regression or the implicit probability maximization of the maximum likelihood estimator) are derivable only if narrow initial assumptions are fulfilled. In general, they will not be fulfilled. Specification search may give the estimated errors the same properties as if they had been fulfilled; these properties, however, are not properties of the world, but of the estimators themselves. Theories do not dictate, for example, t-statistics. The t-statistic is a joint result of the correlation between the dependent and independent variables in the world, the sample variation of the independent variable, and the number of observations. An insignificant t-statistic may mean that a variable has no economic effect or it may mean that there has not been enough sample variation to make that effect observable; a significant t-statistic may mean that a variable has an economic effect or it may mean that the sample is too small to control for adventitious correlation. Such statistics cannot themselves test a theory.

Estimation is in the end merely a convenient way to quantify a particular statistical filter; but it is not the only way. Suppose that one of our twin econometricians obtained estimates in a regression and recorded the coefficient values, but was killed in a duel before he recorded the estimation method, the standard errors or any other indication of the provenance of the regression. We might call this the dead twin paradox or Fermat's last regression (after the famous theorem left without its proof). The errors estimated by this regression are easily computed, although the t-statistics are unknown. However this regression was computed (even if it was not really a regression, but an inspired guess of the coefficient values), it can be evaluated. Are the estimated errors white noise innovations of zero mean and constant variance? Is it stable? That is, if we use the same coefficient values in

---

[8] The question of how to set thresholds in Neyman-Pearson inference are beyond this paper.

another sample, do the estimated errors have the same properties as the original estimated errors? Does it encompass or is it encompassed by a competing regression? These and similar questions are all independent of the particular method of obtaining coefficient values.

The statistical framework in which these questions can be properly asked and answered is the one suggested by the urn analogy. Arbitrary regressions do not, however, conform to the urn analogy. And data mining may be the only way to obtain regressions that do conform. But when we mine the data it is not the test statistics that are descriptive of the properties of the estimator that matter, but tests on the estimated errors – that is, tests on the contents of the urn that the regression defines. Indeed this is true whether or not we mine the data. So the resolution to the twin paradox in its statistical formulation is that the paradox arises only because we focus on the wrong features of the regressions. Both twin's regressions define precisely the same estimated errors, and therefore can be used in precisely the same way. Whichever regressions generated the t-statistics, the t-statistics are the wrong things to look at to judge the support that data give to a theory. The paradox is felt only because we slide between the statistical question and the larger question about the relationship between observations and the support of theories. The burden of this paper is that this question, despite its superficial similarity, is really a different one from the one about statistical practice. The failure to note this difference leads us to focus on the wrong features of the regression, and confuses matters generally.

4   REMEDIES RECONSIDERED

As was noted in section 2, various solutions to the "problem" of data mining have been mooted. It will clarify the nature of the defense suggested in this paper to reexamine those remedies in light of the considerations raised in the last section.

A frequently proposed solution to the data mining problem is that only robust results should be believed. Mayer's proposal to report all regressions, not just the favorable ones, is an argument for robustness. But what would one do with all the regressions? What criteria would allow one to choose among them? Full information is all well and good, but without discrimination it is useless.

Leamer's extreme bounds analysis aims to provide the discrimination criterion. A coefficient on a focus variable is robust if the extreme bounds of its values under all alternative linear combinations of the doubtful variables is narrow. The notion of robustness here is an odd one. Suppose that variable D is in fact determined by a linear combination of mutually orthogonal variables A, B and C and a residual error term. Suppose that the coefficient on C relative to its variance is small compared to the coefficients on A and B compared to their variances, and that the variance of C is relatively small compared to the variance of the error term. Now suppose that a regression is run of D on A, B and C and that the *t*-statistic on C is significant at a little over the 5 percent level. The regression of D on A, B and C recapitulates the true structure of the world. Of course, we do not know in practice how D is generated. But what happens if C is the focus variable and A and B are taken as doubtful? In regressions that omit A, B or both, the standard error on C will rise so that the coefficient value is not well determined. The extreme bounds may be large, and we would conclude that no consensus on the value of the coefficient on C is possible.

The problem is actually worse than that; here we have restricted the universe of regressors to A, B and C, all mutually orthogonal, but what if the possible regressors are A through Z (excluding D of course) and they are collinear to varying degrees? One answer might be the following: So much the worse for us; there is perhaps a truth of the matter, but the data simply will not reveal it. Our defense of data mining suggests a different analysis. The problem is that *t*-statistics or the variability of coefficient estimates in the face of alternative sets of regressors are measures not of the influence of a particular regressor alone, but of the ability of the regression to extract a signal. When regressors A and B are dropped, C becomes insignificant, not because it is not a determinant of D in fact, but because so weak a determinant either requires lots of data or good controls on other sources of variation (which is what A and B provide) in order to stand out. Similarly, in the face of collinear but not really causal regressors, the influence of C may be hidden. There is no reason at all to believe that a true regressor, merely by virtue of being true, should be robust to changes in specification. Data mining at its best provides the necessary controls to allow the signal to be extracted effectively.

The open issue, however, is where to stop. Since we have no direct window on the truth, how do we know that a data-mined regression actually recapitulates the causal structure of the world? Lovell's (1983) Monte Carlo experiments indicate that data mining may systematically pick out the wrong regression. Leamer (1983) argues that we should give up the goal of correspondence with truth as chimerical; consensus is all that is possible. The defense of data mining suggests, however, that it is not consensus that matters, but resolution. Thus, if two regressions (perhaps both data mined) describe the same dependent variable, and both fulfill the necessary conditions to apply the urn analogy, we require a means of choosing between them. The properties of their estimated errors (R^2, t-statistics, etc.) alone are not enough. It is true, and this is the basis for the theory of encompassing (see Hendry, 1988; Hendry and Richard, 1987), that in large samples the true regression must have the lowest sample variance. This is of course a necessary, not a sufficient, condition. There can be no sufficient conditions; for that would mean that we had warrant of the truth. We must seek other marks of correspondence between truth and the regressions. Although no such mark will allow us to certify the truth, they may allow us to discriminate between seriously held competing regressions. For example, consider two apparently well-specified regressions I and II. If II has a lower variance than I, and when reestimated on a new set of data (e.g., on additional years of data not used in the original estimation) it appears to have stable coefficients whereas I does not, then we can rule I out.[9] We cannot of course know that II is true. There may be omitted orthogonal determinants that would further lower the variance or there may be determinants that do not have enough variability relative to their importance to rise above the background noise or some of the explanatory power of the regressors may arise from adventitious collinearity. Such issues need not concern the investigator until there is a seriously offered alternative regression. Then the process of resolution must be pursued.

Adventitious collinearity may still confound the interpretation of regressions. But where extreme bounds analysis and the penalty approach take the collinearity as given, and seek only to determine how large a barrier it poses to a consensus, the defense of data mining suggests that we should seek to understand its sources. Here we appeal to Reichenbach's (1956, p. 157) "common cause principle." This states

---

[9] Note that Lovell's Monte Carlo experiments concentrate on pairwise comparisons of alternative regressors. It does not, therefore, effectively mimic the general-to-specific modeling approach (McAleer et al., 1983; Hendry and Mizon, 1990), which relies on the methodology of encompassing (Hendry, 1988; Hendry and Richard, 1987). The general-to-specific approach can be thought of, in part, as combining the virtues of maximization of R^2 and maximization of t-statistics. Lovell considers each of these as independent stopping criteria for specification searches, but he does not consider them as a joint criterion. In work-in-progress, Stephen Perez and I are using methods similar to Lovell's to evaluate the general-to-specific approach.

that a correlation between two variables arises because one is the cause of the other or because both have a common cause. It implies that it will rarely be sufficient to stop with a regression. We must instead understand the causal structure that generates collinearity. To the extent that economic theory is a reflection of established, empirical causal knowledge, this explains Woodward's (forthcoming) and most economists' preference for regressions that are first derived from a priori theory. But what we must recognize is that such theories may not be sufficiently complete to confront the world or that they may not reflect established, empirical knowledge, especially when there are competing theories seriously maintained by informed economists. In these cases, empirical methods of resolution must be tried. Some suggestions for the discovery of causal structure are found in Hoover (1990, 1991; Hoover and Sheffrin, 1992) and in Glymour et al. (1987).

Reichenbach's common-cause principle makes sense only in populations, not in small samples. The only solution to adventitious collinearity is to extend the data set. Suppose, for instance, that a coin shows heads on 10 flips. We are apt to conclude that the coin is unfair. This is particularly likely if there is other information suggesting that the coin is not balanced. Nevertheless, there is no way to be sure that we have not observed a low probability realization of a fair coin-flipping process. If we extend the data set by flipping the coin many more times and heads shows an approximately equal number of times as tails, then we are justified in rejecting the belief that the coin is unfair. Had the coin been destroyed after the first 10 flips, the matter would be perpetually open to question.

Despite having separated the questions, it turns out that the statistical issue of data mining sheds some light on the larger question of the relation of theory to evidence. Just as we wish to discriminate between the hypotheses that the coin is fair and that the coin is biased, we should seek to discriminate between theories, not to question whether they are supported or not individually. For theories, the issue is whether accommodated data or successful predictions give more support to a theory. Any theory, however, accommodates *some* data, otherwise it would not be seriously entertained. Whether a theory predicts or not is partly a matter of its form and partly a matter of the data itself. A theory may be particular to a singular event (e.g., a theory of why a particular airplane crashed) or may rely on auxiliaries that can be filled in only after a result is known, in which case the theory may be explanatory but not predictive. If there is no feasible way of obtaining more data (as with the coin that is destroyed after 10 flips), then no predictions are possible.

It is not, however, the lack of predictions but the exhaustion of the data set that prevents us from discriminating between two theories that both accommodate the same data. Many historical or literary controversies are insoluble because of the exhaustion of data. Economic controversies might be as well. If economic institutions change rapidly enough in ways that change the causal structure connecting economic variables, there may never be sufficient data to isolate the causal structures and discriminate between alternative theories. We have no choice but to live with the limitations of the data. Nonetheless, when data sets are not exhausted, data mining may be an essential part of constructing observations that permit the isolation of the causal structure of economic data and the discrimination between economic theories.

REFERENCES

Blaug, Mark (1992) *The Methodology of Economics: Or How Economists Explain*, 2nd edn, Cambridge University Press, Cambridge.

Glymour, Clark, Scheines, Richard, Spirtes, Peter and Kelly, Kevin (1987) *Discovering Causal Structure: Artificial Intelligence, Philosophy of Science and Statistical Modeling*, Academic Press, Orlando, FL.

Hendry, David F. (1980) "Econometrics: Alchemy or Science?" *Economica*, vol. 47, no. 188, November, pp. 387–406.

Hendry, David F. (1988) "Encompassing" *National Institute Economic Review*, August, pp. 88–92.

Hendry, David F. and Mizon, Grayham E. (1990) "Procrustean Econometrics: or Stretching and Squeezing Data" in Granger, C.W.J. (ed.), *Modelling Economic Series: Readings in Econometric Methodology*, Oxford University Press, Oxford.

Hendry, David F. and Richard, Jean-François (1987) "Recent Developments in the Theory of Encompassing" in Cornet, Bernard and Tulkens, Henry (eds), *Contributions to Operations Research and Economics: The Twentieth Anniversary of Core*, MIT Press, Cambridge, MA.

Hoover, Kevin D. (1990) "The Logic of Causal Inference: Econometrics and the Conditional Analysis of Causation" *Economics and Philosophy*, vol. 6, no. 2, October, pp. 207–34.

Hoover, Kevin D. (1991) "The Causal Direction Between Money and Prices: An Alternative Approach" *Journal of Monetary Economics*, vol. 27, no. 3, May, pp. 381–423.

Hoover, Kevin D. (1993) "Causality and Temporal Order in Macroeconomics or Why Even Economists Don't Know How to Get Causes from Probabilities" *British Journal for the Philosophy of Science*, vol. 44, no. 4, December, pp. 693–710.

Hoover, Kevin D. and Sheffrin, Steven M. (1992) "Causation, Spending and Taxes: Sand in the Sandbox or Tax Collector for the Welfare State?" *American Economic Review*, vol. 82, no. 1, March, pp. 225–48.

Keynes, John Maynard (1921/1973) *Treatise on Probability* in *The Collected Writings of John Maynard Keynes*, vol. 8, Macmillan, London.

Leamer, Edward (1978) *Specification Searches: Ad Hoc Inference with Nonexperimental Data*, John Wiley, Boston, MA.

Leamer, Edward (1983) "Let's Take the Con Out of Econometrics" *American Economic Review*, vol. 73, no. 1, March, pp. 31–43.

Lipton, Peter (1991) *Inference to the Best Explanation*, Routledge, London.

Lovell, Michael C. (1983) "Data Mining" *The Review of Economics and Statistics*, vol. 65, no. 1, February, pp. 1–12.

Mayer, Thomas (1980) "Economics as a Hard Science: Realistic Goal or Wishful Thinking" *Economic Inquiry*, vol. 18, no. 2, April, pp. 165–78.

Mayer, Thomas (1992a) "What Do Significance Tests Signify?" Department of Economics, University of California, Davis, Working Paper No. 397, May.

Mayer, Thomas (1992b) "What Economists Think of Their Econometrics" University of California, Department of Economics, Working Paper No. 406, September.

Mayer, Thomas (1993) *Truth versus Precision in Economics*, Edward Elgar, Aldershot.

McAleer, Michael, Pagan, Adrian R. and Volker, Paul A. (1983) "What Will Take the Con Out of Econometrics" *American Economic Review*, vol. 75, no. 3, June, pp. 293–307.

Popper, Karl R. (1959) *The Logic of Scientific Discovery*, Hutchinson, London.

Reichenbach, Hans (1956) *The Direction of Time*, University of California Press, Berkeley and Los Angeles, CA.

Woodward, James (forthcoming) "Causation and Explanation in Linear Models" in Little, Daniel (ed.), *On the Reliability of Economic Models*, Kluwer, Dordrecht.

The Economic Works of Thomas Mayer: A Bibliography

BOOKS AND MONOGRAPHS

Monetary Policy in the United States (1968) Random House, New York, NY. Abridged paperback version: *Elements of Monetary Policy* (1968), Random House, New York, NY. Chapter 6, pp. 407–19, reprinted in Chrystal, A. (ed.), *Monetarism* (1990) (Series: Schools of Thought in Economics), Edward Elgar, Aldershot, Hants, England; Brookfield, VT, USA.

Intermediate Macroeconomics: Output, Inflation, and Growth (1972) W.W. Norton, New York, NY (with D.C. Rowan).

Permanent Income, Wealth and Consumption: A Critique of the Permanent Income Theory, the Life-Cycle Hypothesis, and Related Theories (1972) University of California Press, Berkeley, CA.

The Structure of Monetarism (1978) W.W. Norton, New York, NY (with contributions by M. Bronfenbrenner, K. Brunner, P. Cagan, B. Friedman, H. Frisch, H. Johnson, D. Laidler and A. Meltzer). Previously published in *Kredit und Kapital* (1975) vol. 13. German translation, 1978.

Money, Banking and the Economy (1981, 1984, 1987, 1990, 1993) W.W. Norton, New York, NY (with J. Duesenberry and R. Aliber). Also published in Chinese, Estonian, Romanian and Portuguese editions.

Disclosing Monetary Policy (1987) Salomon Brothers Center for the Study of Financial Institutions, Monograph #1987-1, New York University, New York, NY.

Monetarism and Macroeconomic Policy (1990) (Series: Economists of the Twentieth Century), Edward Elgar, Aldershot, Hants, England; Brookfield, Vermont, USA.

Truth versus Precision in Economics (1993) (Series: Advances in Economic Methodology), Edward Elgar, Aldershot, Hants, England; Brookfield, Vermont, USA.

Doing Economics: Essays on the Applied Methodology of Economics (in press) Edward Elgar, Aldershot, Hants, England; Brookfield, VT, USA.

Edited or Coedited

The Political Economy of American Monetary Policy (1990) Cambridge University Press, Cambridge. Paperback edition, 1993.

Monetary Theory (1990) (Series: International Library of Critical Writings in Economics, #7), Edward Elgar, Aldershot, Hants, England; Brookfield, Vermont, USA.

Macroeconomics and Macroeconomic Policy Issues (1991) Avebury Academic Publishing Group, Aldershot, Hants, England; Gower Publishing Company, Brookfield, Vermont, USA (with Franco Spinelli). Italian edition published by Banca di Trento e Bolzano, 1991.

Fiscal and Monetary Policy (in press) (International Library of Critical Writings in Economics), Edward Elgar, Aldershot, Hants, England; Brookfield, Vermont, USA (with S. Sheffrin).

PAPERS IN PROFESSIONAL JOURNALS

"How Freely Can Income Flows be Changed Under Socialism? The Limits of Redirection of Income Flows in a Centrally Controlled Economy" (1950) *American Journal of Economics and Sociology,* vol. 9, no. 2, April, pp. 307–14.

"The Effects of a Wage Change Upon Prices, Profits and Employment" (1951) *Economic Journal,* vol. 61, no. 243, September, pp. 518–30.

"Mr. Colin Clark on the Limits of Taxation" (1952) *Review of Economics and Statistics,* vol. 34, no. 3, August, pp. 232–42 (with J. Pechman).

"Comment" (on Liu, T. and Chang, C. "U.S. Consumption and Investment Propensities: Prewar and Postwar") (1953) *American Economic Review,* vol. 43, no. 1, March, p. 145.

"Lead Times for Fixed Investment" (1955) *Review of Economics and Statistics,* vol. 37, no. 3, August, pp. 300–4 (with S. Sonenblum).

"The Inflexibility of Monetary Policy" (1958) *Review of Economics and Statistics,* vol. 40, no. 4, November, pp. 358–74. Reprinted in Thorn, R. (ed.), *Monetary Theory and Policy: Major Contributions to Contemporary Thought* (1966), 1st edn, Random House, New York, NY.

"The Empirical Significance of the Real Balance Effect" (1959) *Quarterly Journal of Economics,* vol. 73, no. 2, May, pp. 275–91.

Reprinted in Shaw, G. (ed.), *The Keynesian Heritage* (1988) (Series: Schools of Thought in Economics), Edward Elgar, Aldershot, Hants, England; Gower Publishing Company, Brookfield, Vermont, USA.

"Plant and Equipment Lead Times" (1960) *Journal of Business,* vol. 33, no. 2, April, pp. 127–32.

"The Distribution of Ability and Earnings" (1960) *Review of Economics and Statistics,* vol. 42, no. 2, May, pp. 189–95. Reprinted in Atkinson, A.B. (ed.), *Wealth, Income and Inequality* (1973) (Series: Penguin Modern Economics Readings), Penguin Education, Harmondsworth; (1980) Oxford University Press, Oxford.

"Liquidity Functions in the American Economy" (1960) *Econometrica* vol. 28, no. 4, October, pp. 810–34 (with M. Bronfenbrenner). Reprinted in Mueller, M. (ed.), *Readings in Macroeconomics* (1966) Holt, Rinehart and Winston, New York, NY. Reprinted in Chrystal, A. (ed.), *Monetarism* (1990) (Series: Schools of Thought in Economics), Edward Elgar, Aldershot, Hants, England; Brookfield, VT, USA.

"The Quantity Theory and the Balanced Budget Theorem" (1961) *Review of Economics and Statistics,* vol. 43, no. 1, February, pp. 88–90.

"Monetary Theory: New and Old Looks: Discussion" (1961) *American Economic Review,* vol. 51, no. 2, May, pp. 57–9.

"Is the Portfolio Control of Financial Institutions Justified?" (1962) *Journal of Finance,* vol. 17, no. 2, May, pp. 311–17. Reprinted in Ritter, L. (ed.), *Money and Economic Activity: A Selection of Readings in the Field of Money and Banking* (1967), 3rd edn, Houghton Mifflin, Boston, MA.

"An Extension of Sidgwick's Equity Principle" (1962) *Quarterly Journal of Economics,* vol. 76, no. 3, August, pp. 454–63 (with S. Johnson).

"The Permanent Income Theory and Occupational Groups" (1963) *Review of Economics and Statistics,* vol. 45, no. 1, February, pp. 16–22.

"Dr. White on the Inflexibility of Monetary Policy" (1963) *Review of Economics and Statistics,* vol. 45, no. 2, May, pp. 209–11.

"Rejoinder to Professor Eisner" (1963) *Econometrica,* vol. 31, no. 3, July, pp. 539–44.

"Compensatory Balances: A Suggested Interpretation" (1963) *National Banking Review,* vol. 1, no. 2, December, pp. 157–66 (with I. Scott).

"Reply to Dr. White" (1964) *Review of Economics and Statistics,* vol. 46, no. 3, August, p. 324.

"Some Characteristics of Union Members in the 1880s and 1890s" (1964) *Labor History,* vol. 5, no. 1, Winter, pp. 57–66.

"Multiplier and Velocity Analysis: An Evaluation" (1964) *Journal of Political Economy,* vol. 72, no. 6, December, pp. 563–74.

"A Graduated Deposit Insurance Plan" (1965) *Review of Economics and Statistics,* vol. 47, no. 1, February, pp. 114–16. Reprinted in Jessup, P. (ed.), *Innovations in Bank Management* (1969) Holt, Rinehart and Winston, New York, NY.

"Tests of the Relative Importance of Autonomous Expenditures and Money" (1965) *American Economic Review,* vol. 55, no. 4, September, pp. 729–52 (with M. DePrano). Reprinted in Wood, J. and Woods, R. (eds), *Milton Friedman: Critical Assessments* (1990) vol. I (Series: Critical Assessments of Contemporary Economists), Routledge, London and New York.

"Rejoinder" (to Friedman and Meiselman) (1965) *American Economic Review,* vol. 55, no. 4, September, pp. 791–2 (with M. DePrano). Reprinted in Wood, J. and Woods, R. (eds), *Milton Friedman: Critical Assessments* (1990) vol. I (Series: Critical Assessments of Contemporary Economists), Routledge, London and New York, NY.

"Interest Payments on Required Reserve Balances" (1966) *Journal of Finance,* vol. 21, no. 1, March , pp. 116–18.

"Trade Credit and the Discriminatory Effects of Tight Money" (1966) *National Banking Review,* vol. 3, no. 4, June, pp. 543–6.

"The Propensity to Consume Permanent Income" *American Economic Review* (1966) vol. 56, no. 2, December, pp. 1158–77. Summary: "Reddito e propensione al risparmio" (1967) *Mercurio,* October, pp. 8–10.

"The Lag in the Effect of Monetary Policy: Some Criticisms" (1967) *Western Economic Journal,* vol. 5, no. 3, September, pp. 324–42. Reprinted in Mittra, S. (ed.), *Money and Banking: Theory, Analysis and Policy; A Textbook of Readings* (1970) Random House, New York, NY. Reprinted in part in Prager, J. (ed.), *Monetary Economics: Controversies in Theory and Policy* (1971) Random House, New York, NY.

"Advance Sales of Government Securities" (1969) *Journal of Finance,* vol. 24, no. 3, June, p. 592.

"Scadding and Mitchell on Monetary Controls: Some Comments" (1971) *Journal of Money, Credit and Banking,* vol. 3, no. 2, pt. 2, May, pp. 412–14.

"Our Financial Institutions: What Needs Changing?" (1971) *Journal of Money, Credit and Banking,* vol. 3, no. 1, February, pp. 13–20.

"Risk and Regulation in Banking: Some Proposals for Federal Deposit Insurance Reform" (1971) *Stanford Law Review*, vol. 23, May, pp. 857–902 (with K. Scott).

"The Federal Reserve's Policy Procedures: A Review of a Federal Reserve Study and an Ensuing Conference" (1972) *Journal of Money, Credit and Banking*, vol. 4, no. 3, August, pp. 529–50.

"Efficiency of Monetary Policy in Industrialized and Less-Developed Countries: An Interchange" (1972) *Economic Journal*, vol. 82, no. 328, December, pp. 1368–73 (with E. Eshag).

"Financial Guidelines and Credit Controls" (1972) *Journal of Money, Credit and Banking*, vol. 4, no. 2, May, pp. 360–74.

"Tests of the Permanent Income Theory with Continuous Budgets" (1972) *Journal of Money, Credit and Banking*, vol. 4, no. 4, November, pp. 757–78.

"The Distribution of the Tax Burden and Permanent Income" (1974) *National Tax Journal*, vol. 27, no. 1, March, pp. 141–6.

"Personal Savings in the Postwar World: Implications for the Theory of Household Behavior: Discussion" (1975) *American Economic Review* vol. 65, no. 2, May, pp. 22–4.

"Selecting Economic Hypotheses by Goodness of Fit" (1975) *Economic Journal*, vol. 85, no. 340, December, pp. 877–83.

"The Interest Rate Snap-Back and its Implications for the Keynesian-Quantity Theory Dispute" (1976) *Banca Nazionale del Lavoro – Quarterly Review*, no. 118, September, pp. 203–21.

"Professor Pesek's Criticism of Monetary Theory: A Comment" *Journal of Economic Literature* (1977) vol. 15, no. 3, September, pp. 908–14.

"Some Reflections on the Current State of the Monetarist Debate" *Zeitscrift für Nationalökonomie* (1978), vol. 38, nos 1–2, pp. 61–84. Reprinted in Teigen, R. (ed.), *Readings in Money, National Income, and Stabilization Policy* (1978), 4th edn, R.D. Irwin, Homewood, IL.

"Consumption in the Great Depression" (1978) *Journal of Political Economy*, vol. 86, no. 1, February, pp. 139–45.

"Money and the Great Depression: A Critique of Professor Temin's Thesis" (1978) *Explorations in Economic History*, vol. 15, no. 2, April, pp. 127–45.

"Monetarism: Economic Analysis or Weltanschauung?" (1978) *Banca Nazionale del Lavoro – Quarterly Review*, no. 126, September, pp. 233–50. Italian translation in *Moneta e 'Credito* (1978) September.

"A Comparison of Unemployment Rates and Income Fluctuations Prior to the Great Depression and in the Postwar Period" (1979) *Review of Economics and Statistics,* vol. 61, no. 1, February, pp. 142–6.

"Monetary Policy: Assessing the Burns Years: Discussion" (1979) *Journal of Finance,* vol. 34, no. 2, May, pp. 501–4.

"Competitive Equality as a Criterion for Financial Reform" (1980) *Journal of Banking and Finance*, vol. 4, no. 1, March, pp. 7–15.

"Economics as a Hard Science: Realistic Goal or Wishful Thinking?" (1980) *Economic Inquiry,* vol. 18, no. 2, April, pp. 165–78. Reprinted in Marr, W. and Raj, B. (eds), *How Economists Explain: A Reader in Methodology* (1983) University Press of America, Lanham, MD.

"David Hume and Monetarism" *Quarterly Journal of Economics* (1980) vol. 95, no. 1, August, pp. 89–101. Reprinted in Blaug, M. (ed.), *The History of Economic Thought* (1990) Edward Elgar, Aldershot, Hants, England; Brookfield, Vermont, USA. Also reprinted in Mayer, T., *Monetarism and Macroeconomic Policy* (1990) (Series: Economists of the Twentieth Century), Edward Elgar, Aldershot, Hants, England; Brookfield, Vermont, USA.

"A Case Study of Federal Reserve Policymaking: Regulation Q in 1966" (1982) *Journal of Monetary Economics*, vol. 10, no. 2, September, pp. 259–71. Reprinted in Mayer, T., *Monetarism and Macroeconomic Policy* (1990) (Series: Economists of the Twentieth Century), Edward Elgar, Aldershot, Hants, England; Brookfield, Vermont, USA.

"Financial Innovation – The Conflict Between Micro and Macro Optimality" (1982) *American Economic Review,* vol. 72, no. 2, May, pp. 29–34.

"Der Einfluss der modernen Geldtheorie auf die americanische Geldpolitik (On the Influence of Modern Monetary Theory on American Monetary Policy, with English Summary)" (1982) *Kredit und Kapital,* vol. 15, no. 3, pp. 366–86.

"Money Stock vs. Interest Rates as an Intermediate Target: An Institutional Approach" (1982) *Kredit und Kapital: Supplement,* vol. 15, no. 3, pp. 366–86.

"Monetary Trends in the United States and the United Kingdom: A Review Article" (1982) *Journal of Economic Literature,* vol. 20, no. 4, December, pp. 1528–39.

"Mortgage Rates and Regulation Q" (1983) *Journal of Money, Credit and Banking,* vol. 15, no. 1, February, pp. 107–15 (with H. Nathan).

"The Government Budget Constraint and Standard Macrotheory" (1984) *Journal of Monetary Economics,* vol. 13, no. 3, May, pp. 371–9.

Reprinted in Mayer, T., *Monetarism and Macroeconomic Policy* (1990) (Series: Economists of the Twentieth Century), pp. 184–95, Edward Elgar, Aldershot, Hants, England; Brookfield, Vermont, USA.

"Political Shocks and Investment: Some Evidence From the 1930s" (1985) *Journal of Economic History,* vol. 45, no. 4, December, pp. 913–24 (with M. Chatterji).

"Regulating Banks: Comment on Karaken" (1986) *Journal of Business,* vol. 59, no. 1, January, pp. 87–96.

"Replacing the FOMC with a PC" (1987) *Contemporary Policy Issues,* vol. 5, no. 2, April, pp. 31–43.

"The Debate About Monetarist Policy Recommendations" (1987) *Kredit und Kapital,* vol. 20, pp. 282–302.

"Absolute Liquidity Preference and the Pigou Effect: Comment" (1988) *Journal of Post Keynesian Economics,* vol. 10, no. 4, Summer, pp. 653–4.

"Modigliani on Monetarism: A Response" (1988) *Contemporary Policy Issues,* vol. 6, no. 4, October, pp. 19–24.

"Interpreting Federal Reserve Behavior" (1988) *Journal of Behavioral Economics,* vol. 17, no. 4, Winter, pp. 263–77.

"Were Businessmen Afraid of FDR? – A Comment on Mayer and Chatterji – Reply" (1990) *Journal of Economic History,* vol. 50, no. 4, December, pp. 942–4 (with M. Chatterji).

"U.S. Deposit Insurance Reform" (1992) *Contemporary Policy Issues,* vol. 10, no. 3, July , pp. 95–103 (with T. Cargill).

"Friedman's Methodology of Positive Economics: A Soft Reading" (1993) *Economic Inquiry,* vol. 31, no. 2, April, pp. 213–23.

"Open Peer Commentary on the Scientific Status of Econometrics: Comment" (1993) *Social Epistemology,* vol. 7, no. 3, pp. 269–73.

"Why Do Economists Disagree About So Much?" (1994) *Journal of Economic Methodology,* vol. 1, no. 1, June, pp. 1–13.

CHAPTERS IN BOOKS

"Portfolio Regulations and Practices of Financial Intermediaries" in Commission on Money and Credit, *Private Financial Institutions* (1963), Prentice-Hall, Englewood Cliffs, NJ (with T. Gies and E. Ettin).

"Comments" (on Strotz, R. "Empirical Evidence on the Impact of Monetary Variables on Aggregate Expenditure," this volume, pp. 295–315), in Horwich, G. (ed.), *Monetary Process and Policy: A Symposium* (1967) R.D. Irwin, Homewood, IL.

"Regulatory Goals for Financial Intermediaries" in Gies, T. and Apilado, V. (eds), *Banking Markets and Financial Institutions* (1971) (The Irwin Series in Finance), R.D. Irwin, Homewood, IL (with T. Gies and E. Ettin).

"Credit Allocation – A Critical View" in Brunner, K. (ed.), *Government Credit Allocation: Where Do We Go From Here?* (1975) Institute of Contemporary Studies, San Francisco, CA.

"The Structure and Operation of the Federal Reserve System: Some Needed Reforms" in US Congress, House Committee on Banking, Currency and Housing, Subcommittee on Financial Institutions Supervision, Regulation and Financial Institutions and the Nation's Economy, *Compendium of Papers Presented for the FINE Study* (1976), book 2, 94th Congress, 2nd session, US Government Printing Office, Washington, DC.

"Comments on Brunner and Meltzer" in Stein, J. (ed.), *Monetarism* (1976) North Holland Publishing Company, Amsterdam; American Elsevier Publishing Company, New York, NY.

"A Neoclassical Model of Wage and Price Dynamics: A Comment" in Federal Reserve Bank of San Francisco, *West Coast Academic/Federal Reserve Economic Research Seminar* (1978) Federal Reserve Bank of San Francisco, San Francisco, CA.

"Innovative Incomes Policies: A Skeptic's View" in Claudon, M. and Cornwall, R. (eds), *An Incomes Policy for the United States: New Approaches* (1981) Martinus Nijhoff, Boston; The Hague; London.

"Comments" (on "Monopoly Explanations of the Great Depression and Public Policies Toward Business") in Brunner, K. (ed.), *The Great Depression Revisited* (1981), Martinus Nijhoff, Boston, MA.

"Federal Reserve Policy in the 1973–75 Recession: A Case Study of Fed Behavior in a Quandary" in Wachtel, P. (ed.), *Crises in the Economic and Financial Structure* (1982) Lexington Books, Lexington, MA and Toronto.

"Comments on William Dewald's 'How Fast Does Inflation Adjust to its Underlying Determinants'" in Federal Reserve Bank of San Francisco, *West Coast Academic/Federal Reserve Economic Research Seminar* (1982).

"Discussion" (on Kaminow, I. "Politics, Economics, and Procedures of U.S. Monetary Growth Dynamics") in Lombra, R. and Whitte, W. (eds), *The Political Economy of International and Domestic Monetary Relations* (1982) Iowa State University Press, Ames, IA.

"Comments" (on Davis, R. "Monetary Targeting in a Zero-Balance World" and on Judd, J. and Scadding, J. "Financial Change and Monetary Targeting in the United States") in Federal Reserve Bank of San Francisco, *Interest Rate Deregulation and Monetary Policy* (1983) Federal Reserve Bank of San Francisco, San Francisco, CA.

"Discussion" in Federal Reserve Bank of San Francisco, *Monetary Targeting and Velocity: The Proceedings of the Conference on Monetary Targeting and Velocity* (1983) Federal Reserve Bank of San Francisco, San Francisco, CA.

"The Status of the Monetarist Debate in the United States" in Cansier, D. and Kath, D. (eds), *Öffentliche Finanzen, Kredit und Kapital* (1985) Dunker and Humblot, Berlin.

"The Keynesian Legacy: Does Countercyclical Policy Pay its Way?" in Willett, T. (ed.), *Political Business Cycles: The Political Economy of Money, Inflation, and Unemployment* (1988) Duke University Press, Durham, NC and London.

"Evaluating Proposals for Fundamental Monetary Reform" in Willett, T. (ed.), *Political Business Cycles: The Political Economy of Money, Inflation, and Unemployment* (1988) Duke University Press, Durham, NC and London (with T. Willett).

"Minimizing Regret: Cognitive Dissonance as an Explanation of FOMC Behavior" in Mayer, T. (ed.), *The Political Economy of American Monetary Policy* (1990, 1993) Cambridge University Press, New York, NY.

"Federal Reserve Policy Since October 1979: A Justified Response to Financial Innovations?" in Frowen, S. and Kath, D. (eds), *Monetary Policy and Financial Innovations in Five Industrial Countries: the U.K., the U.S.A., West Germany, France, and Japan* (1992) Macmillan Academic and Professional, London.

"Monetarism in a World Without 'Money'" in Frownen, S. (ed.), *Monetary Theory and Monetary Policy: New Tracks for the 1990s* (1993) St Martin's Press, New York, NY.

"The Monetarist Debate and the New Methodology" in Mayer, T. and Spinelli, F. (eds), *Macroeconomics and Macroeconomic Policy Issues* (1991) Avebury Academic Publishing Group, Aldershot, Hants, England; Gower Publishing Company, Brookfield, VT, USA.

"Monetarism and its Rhetoric" (in press) in Klein, P. (ed.), *The Role of Economic Theory*.

MISCELLANEOUS PUBLICATIONS

Consumer Loans of West Virginia Banks (1957) Bureau of Business Research, College of Commerce, West Virginia University, Morgantown.

"Statement" in US Congress, Joint Economic Committee, Subcommittee on Economic Progress, *Federal Reserve Portfolio, Statements by Individual Economists,* 89th Congress, second session (1966) US Government Printing Office, Washington, DC.

"Statement" in US Congress, House Committee on Banking and Currency, Subcommittee on Domestic Finance, *Compendium on Monetary Policy Guidelines and the Federal Reserve Structure, Pursuant to H.R. 11,* 90th Congress, second session (1968) US Government Printing Office, Washington, DC, December.

"Statement" in *Academic Views on Improving the Discount Mechanism* (1970) Board of Governors, Federal Reserve System.

"Statement" in US Congress, Senate Committee on Banking, Housing and Urban Affairs, *Monetary Policy Oversight: Hearing on Senate Concurrent Resolution 18 Referring to the Conduct of Monetary Policy,* 94th Congress, first session (1975) US Government Printing Office, Washington, DC, February, pp. 179–87. Reprinted in Havrilesky, T. and Boorman, J. (eds), *Current Issues in Monetary Theory and Policy* (1976), 1st edn, AHM Publishing Corporation, Arlington Heights, IL.

"Preventing the Failures of Large Banks" in US Congress, Senate Committee on Banking, Housing and Urban Affairs, *Compendium on Major Issues on Bank Regulation* (1975) US Government Printing Office, Washington, DC. Reprinted in Havrilesky, T. and Boorman, J. (eds), *Current Perspectives in Banking* (1976, 1980) AHM Publishing Corporation, Arlington Heights, IL. Revised version published in *Journal of Financial and Quantitative Analysis* (1975), vol. 10, no. 4, November.

"Testimony" in US Congress, House Committee on Banking, Currency and Housing, Subcommittee on Financial Institutions Supervision Regulations and Insurance, *Hearings: Financial Institutions and the Nation's Economy, Discussion Principles*, 94th Congress, first and second sessions (1975–76) US Government Printing Office, Washington, DC.

"Testimony" in US Congress, House Committee on Banking, Finance and Urban Affairs, *Hearings on H.R. 12706, 13476, 13477, 14072* (1978).

"The Measurement and Role of Monetary Aggregates" in US Congress, House Committee on Banking, Finance and Urban Affairs, Subcommittee on Domestic Monetary Policy, *Measuring the Money*

Aggregates, 96th Congress, second session (1980) US Government Printing Office, Washington, DC, February.

"Money," "Monetary Theory" and "Banking Systems" in *Academic American Encyclopedia* (1982) Grolier, Danbury, CT.

"Reply to Question" in US Congress Joint Economic Committee, Subcommittee on Monetary and Fiscal Policy, *Monetarism and the Federal Reserve's Conduct of Monetary Policy: Compendium of Views*, 97th Congress, second session (1982) US Government Printing Office, Washington, DC, October.

"Statement" in US Congress, House Committee on the Budget, *Impact of Budget Proposals on Income Maintenance Programs; Trade and Economic Policy; State and Local Issues*, 99th Congress, first session (1985) US Government Printing Office, Washington, DC, February.

"Foreword" in Toma, Eugenia and Toma, Mark (eds), *Central Bankers, Bureaucratic Incentives and Monetary Policy* (1986) Kluwer Academic Publishers, Dordrecht; Boston, MA.

"Simulations with Econometric Models" (1989) *Methodus*, vol. 1, no. 2, December.

"Inside and Outside Money" in Newman, P., Milgate, M. and Eatwell, J. (eds), *The New Palgrave Dictionary of Money and Finance* (1992) Stockton Press, New York, NY; Macmillan Press, London.

ARTICLES IN MAGAZINES AND NEWSPAPERS

"In Defense of Academic Research" (1974) *Yale Review,* vol. 63, no. 2, Winter, pp. 175–92. Reprinted in *Educational Yearbook* (1974) and in *Learning and the Law* (1976).

"The Case Against Credit Allocation" (1975) *National Review,* vol. 27, no. 49, 19 December, pp. 1472, 1491.

"The Case for a Good Recession" (1979) *New York Times,* vol. 127(44,447), Business and Finance Section: "Points of View," December 30, p. 12-F.

"Using the Constitution to Fight Inflation" (1979) *American Banker*, November 29.

"IBFs Are Not a Good Idea" (1981) *American Banker*, July 7, pp. 4, 6.

"The Need for Federal Reserve Commitment" (1981) *American Banker*, July 7, pp. 4, 15.

"Fervent Hopes vs. Dismal Reality" (1984) *Challenge,* vol. 27:1 (Symposium on Incomes Policy), March/April, pp. 49–52.

Index

Index